**AA**

# LONDON

*Where to go*
*What to do*

# ABOUT THIS BOOK

If you want to find out about most aspects of travelling to and in London, turn to the part of this book called *Finding Your Feet*, where there are details of tourist and travel information, and much practical advice about travel by public and private transport. This part of the book also has information on telephones, emergency services, lost property, etc. To find out where to go and what do do, the gazetteer part of the book includes hundreds of places and things arranged under easy-to-find headings, such as art galleries, parks, churches, etc. Entries are referenced to the maps: the number (*eg* 15) refers to the map page number, the letter (*eg* B) refers to the grid square in which the place is located. Entries outside the Inner London map area are referenced to the district map. Opening details are believed to be correct at the time of printing, but it is always advisable to check before making a visit to avoid disappointment.

Editors: *Michael Cady, Sally Knowles*
Art Editor: *Bob Johnson*
Ceremonies feature by *Shirley Hewson*
Original Photography: *Richard Surman*
Advertisement Sales: Tel. 0256 20123
Filmsetting by: Vantage Photosetting Co. Ltd., Eastleigh and London
Printed and bound by: Kingsdale Press, Reading

Maps and plans produced by the Cartographic Department of the Automobile Association. Atlas based on the Ordnance Survey maps, reproduced with the permission of the Controller of Her Majesty's Stationery Office. Crown Copyright reserved. Tube Map © London Transport.

ISBN 0 86145 480 4
AA Reference 54441

Published by the Automobile Association, Fanum House, Basingstoke, Hampshire RG21 2EA

Produced by the Publishing Division of the Automobile Association

# CONTENTS

# CEREMONIAL LONDON

*Bandsmen of the Scots Guards in The Mall*

## ROYAL EVENTS

London's ceremonies go back hundreds of years and range from grand royal occasions to small and sometimes bizarre gatherings in back streets or obscure churches.

### Royal Epiphany Gifts Service

On *6 January* the Sovereign (or a representative), accompanied by the Yeomen of the Guard, attends the Royal Epiphany Service at the Chapel Royal, St James's Palace. The contents of three purses, which symbolise the gifts of the three Wise Men, are distributed to the poor of the parish.

### Maundy Money

On the *Thursday before Easter*, Maundy Money – specially minted for the occasion – is distributed by the Sovereign. Formerly this always took place in Westminster Abbey, but in recent years different churches throughout the country have been chosen.

### Trooping the Colour

On the *second Saturday in June*, the Sovereign's official birthday is celebrated by the Trooping the Colour. The Colours (flags) of one of the five Foot Guards' Regiments are trooped before the Sovereign. Years ago this was necessary so that the regiments could recognise their own colours in battle. At the end of the ceremony, the Sovereign rides to Buckingham Palace ahead of her Guards.

The Royal Tournament is held in *July* at Earls Court Stadium. First held in 1880, it is a unique display by representatives of all Britain's armed forces and visiting armed services from abroad. The spectacular show includes feats of daring and training, simulated live battles and musical numbers. The Tournament is always visited by members of the Royal Family.

After a general election, and before each new session of Parliament in *mid-November*, the Sovereign attends the State Opening of Parliament, a ceremony dating from the mid-16th century. The Royal procession moves from Buckingham Palace to the Palace of Westminster, where the ceremony takes place in the House of Lords. Before the arrival of the procession, the Yeomen of the Guard search the cellars of the Houses of Parliament – a precaution that dates from the Gunpowder Plot of 1605.

In addition to these major ceremonies, on special occasions (like certain royal birthdays) 41-gun salutes are fired in Hyde Park by the King's Troop of the Royal Horse Artillery, and at the Tower of London by the Honourable Artillery Company.

From early times, the duty of guarding the Sovereign has been the responsibility of the bodyguard of the Yeomen of the Guard. During the Civil War, Charles I was guarded by troops loyal to his cause. At the Restoration, the responsibility of protecting the Sovereign became the daily task of the Life Guards and the three regiments of foot guards known as the Household Division.

This tradition continues today, for the Queen and her many homes are guarded by the Household Division. The most popular mounting of the Guard is the one that takes place *daily (during the summer)* at Buckingham Palace. Do arrive early if you want to see this ceremony.

Starting at 11am at St James's Palace, the detachment of the Old Guard forms up in Friary Court. After an inspection, the Drummers beat the call 'The Point of War' while the colour is brought on. The Old Guard marches up the Mall to Buckingham Palace, led by their Corps of Drums, while the Buckingham Palace detachment of the Old Guard falls-in and is inspected in the Palace forecourt by the subaltern. They await the arrival of the rest of the Old Guard, who then form up on the right of the Buckingham Palace Guard. The actual 'Changing' begins on the stroke of 11.30. The New Guard, headed by their regimental band, marches into the Palace via the North Centre Gate, to a central position facing the Old Guard. Accompanied by the band, the New Guard marches in slow time towards the Old Guard. Having paid each other military compliments, the Captains of the Guards march towards each other to carry out the symbolic ceremony of handing over the Palace keys.

## The Royal Tournament

## State Opening of Parliament

## DAILY CEREMONIAL EVENTS

## The Changing of the Guard

*Mounting the Guard; Household Cavalry at Horseguards*

*Men of the King's Troop, Royal Horse Artillery*

## Mounting Guard at Whitehall

## Ceremony of the Keys

*Ceremony of the Keys, Tower of London*

After saluting the Senior Captain on parade, the officers of both Guards go to the Guardroom to hand over their responsibilities. For about half an hour the band plays on. When each new sentry is posted, complete orders are read to him by the corporal, and when the new sentries take over at St James's, the sentries who have been relieved march into Buckingham Palace to complete the Old Guard. At 12.05 the Guards are brought to attention. The Old Guard departs from the central gate to return to their barracks after exchanging compliments with the New Guard. Now the detachment of the New Guard marches off to start their guard duties.

A detachment of the Household Cavalry guards the old entrance to the demolished Whitehall Palace – an area partly occupied by Horse Guards, a handsome 18th-century building whose east front faces onto Whitehall. Mounting Guard at Whitehall is a colourful spectacle, which takes place at *11am every weekday and 10am on Sundays*.

At the Tower of London, the Ceremony of the Keys has taken place every night for the last 700 years. The Tower is still officially owned by the Queen as a palace and fortress and is therefore closely guarded and securely locked at night. The Ceremony of the Keys occurs *a few minutes before 10pm nightly*, when the Chief Yeoman Warder of the Tower joins up with his escort of Guards (those performing public duties at the Tower on that particular day) under the archway of the Bloody Tower, facing Traitor's Gate. He carries the keys of the Tower, and his passage is lit with an ornate brass candle-lantern. He firmly turns the key in the West Gate, then moves to the Middle Tower and finally the Byward Tower, before marching back with his escort to the Bloody Tower archway. The sentry challenges him:
'Halt!'
The sergeant orders, 'Escort to the Keys, halt!'
'Who comes there?'
The Chief Yeoman Warder answers, 'The Keys.'
'Whose Keys?'
'Queen Elizabeth's Keys.'
'Pass, Queen Elizabeth's Keys. All's well.'
    The Escort and Chief Yeoman Warder can now pass up the steps into the inner ward of the Tower, where the officer of the main guard orders, 'Guard and escort, present arms.' The Chief Yeoman Warder exclaims 'God preserve Queen Elizabeth,' and the full guard and escort reply 'Amen.' A bugler sounds the Last Post and the Chief Warder marches to the Queen's House where he safely deposits the keys for the night. Meanwhile the escort rejoins the Main Guard.
    Applications for a pass to attend this ceremony, which lasts for about 20 minutes from start to finish, should be made in writing to the Resident Governor.

Not all London's pageants are associated with royalty. The ancient heart of London, the City, or more familiarly, the 'Square Mile', boasts some of the most colourful events.

The most famous City pageant is the Lord Mayor's Show, which takes place on the *second Saturday of November*. The Lord Mayor, elected annually, is head of the Corporation of London, the City's administrative body, and is host to visiting Heads of State and celebrities. This important office makes him or her the first citizen of the City, taking precedence over everyone except the Sovereign. The procession dates from the 14th century and the Lord Mayor rides in the state coach in order to be 'shown' to the citizens and to make the final declaration of office at the Law Courts. The coach is accompanied by floats and military bands.

The opening session of the Central Criminal Court, Old Bailey, is attended on *6 January* by the Lord Mayor of London, who leads a procession from the Mansion House, attended by the sheriffs, the swordbearer, the common crier and the City marshal.

Every *January* the first sitting of the newly-elected Court of Common Council, which governs the City of London, is heralded by the Lord Mayor and the Lord Mayor's officers, walking in procession from the Guildhall to attend a service at the Church of St Lawrence Jewry, Gresham Street.

Each year on *3 February*, St Blaise's day, sufferers of bad throats congregate for the Blessing of the Throats at the Church of St Ethelreda, Ely Place. The service commemorates St Blaise, Bishop of Dalmatia, who saved the life of a child with a fishbone in the throat, while on his way to a martyr's death during the third century.

The bells of St Clements, in the well known nursery rhyme, say 'oranges and lemons'. Every *March*, in the Oranges and Lemons Children's Service, children of the St Clement Dane's Primary School receive an orange and a lemon each.

Shrove Tuesday, the *last day before Lent*, is Pancake Day, and at Westminster School Pancake Greaze is celebrated. A pancake is tossed over a bar, and boys scramble for a piece; the one who obtains the largest piece gets a reward.

On *Ash Wednesday* Members of the Stationers Company walk from Stationers Hall to St Paul's Cathedral, where their chaplain preaches the Cakes and Ale Sermon in deference to the wishes of John Norton, a member of the Worshipful Company of Stationers who died during the reign of James I. Cakes and ale are distributed before or after the service.

**COMMON OBSERVANCE**

*Lord Mayor's Show*

*Old Bailey in Session*

*Court of Common Council Service*

*Blessing of the Throats*

*Oranges and Lemons Children's Service*

*Pancake Greaze*

*Cakes and Ale Sermon*

7

### Hot Cross Bun Service

At the Hot Cross Bun Service on *Good Friday*, in the Church of St Bartholomew the Great, Smithfield, 21 widows of the parish collect a bun and 'sixpence' from the top of the tomb in the churchyard.

### Spital Sermon

On the *second Wednesday after Easter* the Lord Mayor of London walks in procession with aldermen and other City dignitaries, from the Guildhall to the Church of St Lawrence Jewry, where a bishop nominated by the Archbishop of Canterbury preaches the Spital Sermon. Before the Great Fire of London, the sermon was preached at St Paul's Cross in the Cathedral churchyard. The sermon's peculiar name comes from an early variation of hospital.

### John Stow's Quill Pen Ceremony

Held *on or near 5 April* at the Church of St Andrew Undershaft, Leadenhall Street, it commemorates the writer of *A Survey of London* (1598). The Lord Mayor and other dignitaries attend, and during the service the Lord Mayor places a fresh quill in the hand of Stow's statue, which depicts him at work on his *Survey*.

### Oak Apple Day

Oak Apple Day is celebrated with Founders Day at the Chelsea Royal Hospital on *29 May*. Charles II founded the Hospital for non-commissioned army officers, and their colourful uniforms are a familiar part of Chelsea life. On Oak Apple Day the pensioners parade for inspection and all wear a sprig of oak. They give three cheers for their founder, Charles II, whose statue is decorated with oak boughs.

### Knollys Red Rose Rent

The Rent is an annual fine, imposed on Sir Robert Knollys in 1346 when he built a small bridge over Seething Lane, to connect two of his properties, without planning permission. He was ordered to present a red rose personally to the Lord Mayor on *Midsummer Day* each year. In 1924 this payment was revived and the churchwardens of All Hallows by the Tower still present a red rose to the Lord Mayor every year.

### THE LONDON SEASON

In addition to London's ceremonies and pageants, a series of (chiefly sporting) events marks the London Season. Traditionally this was the period when the gentry were in town before they disappeared to the country to visit Cowes, Goodwood and the grouse moors.

### Chelsea Flower Show

The first event in the Season is the Chelsea Flower Show, held at Chelsea Royal Hospital in the *third week in May*. The private view for members of the Royal Horticultural Society starts on the Tuesday, and public days are Wednesday, Thursday and Friday. Flowers of almost every season can be seen, together with gardens, furnishings, gardening aids, flower arrangements and advisory bureaux.

Royal Ascot Races take place in the *third week of June*. They are attended by the Queen and members of the Royal Family. Thursday is Ladies Day – famed for the stylish hats worn by the ladies. A great racing, fashion and social event.

One of the most prestigious tennis events in the world. There are five championships, for both men and women, four junior events and two over-35 events for men. The Championships last two weeks starting in *the third week in June* and continuing through to the first week in July.

The *first week in July* heralds Henley Royal Regatta at Henley-on-Thames. Though outside London, this annual international rowing regatta can be considered part of the Season.

The City's livery companies have always exercised great power. Being connected with a particular trade and craft they maintain even today strict control over standards of work. With power comes privilege and many of these privileges provide London with interesting ceremonies.

The Dyers and the Vintners have the right to own swans on the Thames. At the Swan Upping, in the *third week of July*, families of swans on the Thames are rounded up by the Companies' swanherds who travel up-river in skiffs (small boats) decorated with banners, together with the Queen's

*Wimbledon – highpoint of the tennis calendar*

*Royal Ascot*

*Wimbledon Lawn Tennis Championships*

*Henley Royal Regatta*

**CITY LIVERY COMPANIES**

*Swan Upping*

Keeper of Swans. Participants are dressed in garments of red, blue, green, white and gold. They mark the beaks of the new cygnets with one nick for the Dyers and two nicks for the Vintners. The Queen's birds remain unmarked. The event closes with a traditional banquet at a riverside inn, which includes a dish of swan meat.

### Doggett's Coat and Badge Race

Another summer pageant associated with the City, the Doggett's Coat and Badge Race, attracts people to the banks of the Thames *towards the end of July*. The oldest annually contested event in the British sporting calendar, it celebrates the accession of George I to the English throne. In 1715 Thomas Doggett, comedian and manager of London's oldest theatre, the *Drury Lane*, bequeathed a badge of silver and money to pay for a livery coat for the winner of a race for single sculls, starting at London Bridge and ending at Cadogan Pier in Chelsea – a total of $4\frac{1}{2}$ miles.

### Admission of Sheriffs

The election of two sheriffs and other officials of the City takes place at the Guildhall with much pageantry. The Lord Mayor and other city officials attend a church service before proceeding to the Guildhall, where members of the livery companies are assembled for the presenting of the chains of office to the sheriffs. The ceremony ocurs on *28 September or the preceding Friday*.

### Election of the Lord Mayor

On *29 September*, Michaelmas Day, the election of the new Lord Mayor takes place. There is a service at St Lawrence Jewry after which the current Lord Mayor goes in procession to the Guildhall, and, with the aldermen, makes the final selection from the candidates nominated by the livery companies. When the selection is made, the Lord Mayor and the Lord Mayor elect ride in the state coach to the Mansion House, to the accompaniment of the City bells.

### Quit-Rents Ceremony

The oldest public ceremony carried out in London is the Quit-Rents Ceremony. It is held every *October* at the Royal Courts of Justice, and involves the City Solicitor making token payment for two properties. The rents are two faggots of wood, a billhook and a hatchet for land in Shropshire, and six horseshoes and 61 nails, for a forge which once stood in the Strand. The Queen's Rembrancer receives these rents, the origins of which are so old that they are obscure.

### Installation of the Lord Mayor

On *8 November* the current Lord Mayor and the Lord Mayor elect both attend a luncheon at the Mansion House, attended by liverymen of each of their companies. Afterwards they go in procession to the Guildhall where they officially change places and transfer the insignia of office, and the City starts another year.

**S**TREET ATLAS AND KEY MAP

| ST JOHN'S WOOD | | REGENT'S PARK | | ST PANCRAS | FINSBURY | | SHOREDITCH |
|---|---|---|---|---|---|---|---|
| *12* | *13* ST MARYLEBONE | *14* | *15* | *16* | *17* | | *18* |
| MAIDA VALE | | BLOOMSBURY | | | HOLBORN | ST LUKE'S | |

| BAYSWATER | | | SOHO STRAND | CITY | WHITECHAPEL |
|---|---|---|---|---|---|
| *19* | *20* MAYFAIR | *21* | *22* ST JAMES'S | *23* | *24* | *25* BERMONDSEY |

| BROMPTON | | LAMBETH SOUTHWARK | | | |
|---|---|---|---|---|---|
| SOUTH KENSINGTON *26* | *27* | BELGRAVIA *28* WESTMINSTER *29* | *30* | *31* | *32* WALWORTH |
| CHELSEA | | KENNINGTON | | | |

| | | | |
|---|---|---|---|
| One- way street . . | ← | Official car park . . . . . . . | Ⓟ |
| Pedestrians only . . . . . | | Police . . . . . . . . | ⒫⒪⒧ |
| Banned turn . . . . | ⌐ | Hospital . . . . . . . | Ⓗ |
| Compulsory turn . . . . . | | Post Office . . . . . . . | ⒫⒪ |
| Restricted roads . . . . | - - - - | Church . . . . . . . . . | ✝ |
| No vehicular access . . . | | Place of Interest . . . . . . | Museum |
| British Rail station . . . . . . | ▭ | Park/Open space . . . . . | ◯ |
| London Transport station . . . . . | ⊖ | AA Centre . . . . . . . | **AA** |
| Multi-level car park . . . . . . . | Ⓖ | Page continuation number . . . . | ▲24 |

Scale: Seven inches to one mile

PRINCE ALBERT RD

Winfield House

Nuffield Foundation

London Central Mosque

**REGENT'S PARK**
**Closed between midnight & 0700**

Regent's College

Boat House

Boat House

Open Air Theatre

**REGENT'S PA**

**G**

**K**

INNER CIRCLE

CHE

PARK

HANOVER GATE

HANOVER TERRACE

KENT TERR

PAVLEY

CRESCENT

CIRCLE

ROAD

SUSSEX PLACE

Boating Lake

Queen Mary's Gardens

**14**

INNER CIRCLE

CIRC

RYLEBONE

Royal College of Obstetricians & Gynaecologists

YORK BRIDGE

YORK GATE

TERRACE

Royal Acad. of Music

ROSSMORE

BROADLEY ST

HAREWOOD

GROVE

MARYLEBONE STATION

TAUNTON PLACE

BALCOMBE ST

LINHOPE

BELL ST

DORSET SQUARE

MELCOMBE

GLOUCESTER PLACE

BAKER ST

GLENTWORTH

SIDDONS LANE

Rudolf Steiner Hall

CLARENCE GATE

ALLSOP PLACE

L.T. Lost Property Office

YORK

Madame Tussaud's

Planetarium

Cannon (Baker St)

Baker St

MARYLEBONE

**M  A  R  Y  L  E  B  O  N  E**

NOTTINGHAM

Princess Grace Hospital

DEVONSHIRE ST

MARYLEBONE

DORSET

BROADLEY

HARCOURT STREET

HATS PL

CUTTON STREET

COSWAY STREET

LISSON STREET

LISSON

Harewood Hotel

Marylebone

AVENUE

CRAWFORD STREET

Western Ophthalmic Hospital

Samaritan Hospital

Town Hall

BICKENHALL STREET

Polytechnic of Central London

CHILTERN

Screen on Baker Street

MANCHESTER

NOTTINGHAM ST

MARYLEBONE HIGH

PADDINGTON

STREET

**14**

MOXON ST

CRAMER STREET

P

PO

WEY

Edgware Road

EDGWARE

CHAPEL ST

HOMER STREET

SEYMOUR

CENTRAL

YORK STREET

WYNDHAM PLACE

UPPER MONTAGU STREET

GLOUCESTER PLACE

BAKER

STREET

DORSET

PO

DUMARTON

PAGE ST

KENDAL

BLANDFORD

THAYER STREET

MAY

PL

MANCHESTER

Clifton Ford Hotel

Seymour Hall

MOLYNEUX

BRENDON STREET

CRAWFORD PLACE

BRYANSTON PLACE

MONTAGU SQUARE

Fitzroy Nuffield Hospital

BRYANSTON

MONTAGU

SQUARE

BLANDFORD

STREET

**G  E  O  R  G  E**

ROBERT ADAM ST

MANCHESTER

Wallace Collection

HINDE

DUKE

Cine

HARROWBY

STREET

BROWN PLACE

SQUARE

SEYMOUR PL

GREAT

MONTAGU ST

MONTAGU

Portman Intercontinental Hotel

PORTMAN CL

Home House

FITZHARDINGE ST

MANDEVILLE PLACE

New Mand St

MARY

Holiday Inn

**20**

Bryanston Court Hotel

Churchill Hotel

**PORTMAN**

SQUARE

PO

**WIGMORE**

Selfridge

NUTFORD

FORSET

NORFOLK

PARK WEST PL

Arabic Centre (Cinema)

Montcalm Hotel

BERKELEY

OXFORD

PORCHESTER

SQUARE

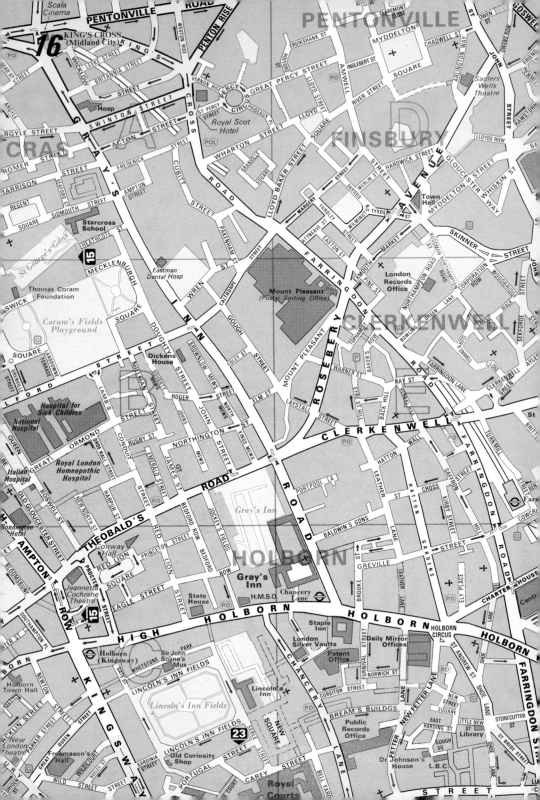

Scala Cinema

PENTONVILLE ROAD
PENTON RISE

PENTONVILLE

KING'S CROSS
(Midland City)

FINSBURY

CRAS

MYDDELTON SQUARE

Sadlers Wells Theatre

GRAY'S

Hosp

Royal Scot Hotel

GREAT PERCY STREET

GT PERCY CIRCUS

Town Hall

AVENUE

Starcross School

St George's Gdns

15

Eastman Dental Hosp

Mount Pleasant (Postal Sorting Office)

London Records Office

CLERKENWELL

Thomas Coram Foundation

Coram's Fields Playground

SQUARE

Dickens House

ROSEBERY

Warner St

CLERKENWELL

Hospital for Sick Children

National Hospital

NORTHINGTON STREET

CLERKENWELL ROAD

FARRINGDON

Italian Hospital

Royal London Homeopathic Hospital

Gray's Inn

Hatton Garden

Bonnington Hotel

THEOBALD'S ROAD

Conway Hall

Red Lion SQUARE

Gray's Inn

H.M.S.O.

HOLBORN

Jeannetta Cochrane Theatre

15

EAGLE STREET

State House

Chancery Lane

Staple Inn

Daily Mirror Offices

HOLBORN CIRCUS

HOLBORN

Holborn (Kingsway)

Sir John Soane's Mus

London Silver Vaults

Patent Office

Holborn Town Hall

HIGH HOLBORN

LINCOLN'S INN FIELDS

Lincoln's Inn

Public Records Office

KINGSWAY

Lincoln's Inn Fields

NEW SQUARE

Library

New London Theatre

Freemason's Hall

Old Curiosity Shop

23

PORTUGAL STREET

CAREY STREET

Dr. Johnson's House

L.B.C.

Royal Courts

FARRINGDON STREET

STREET

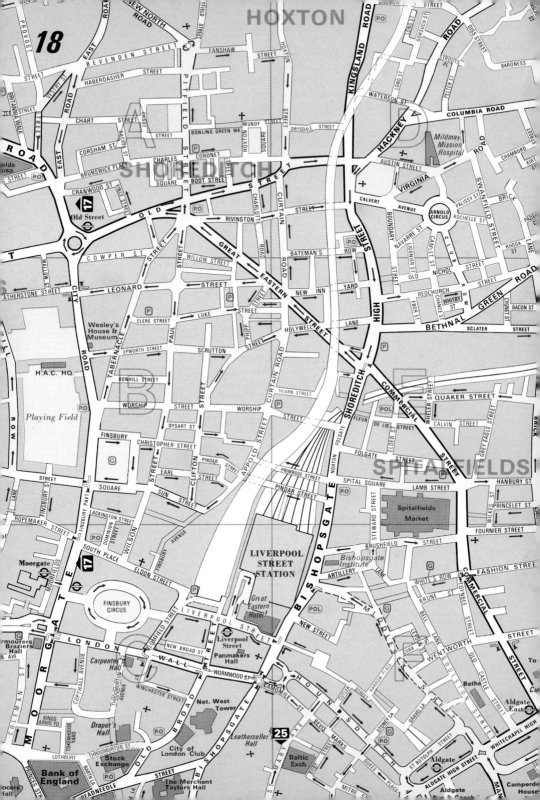

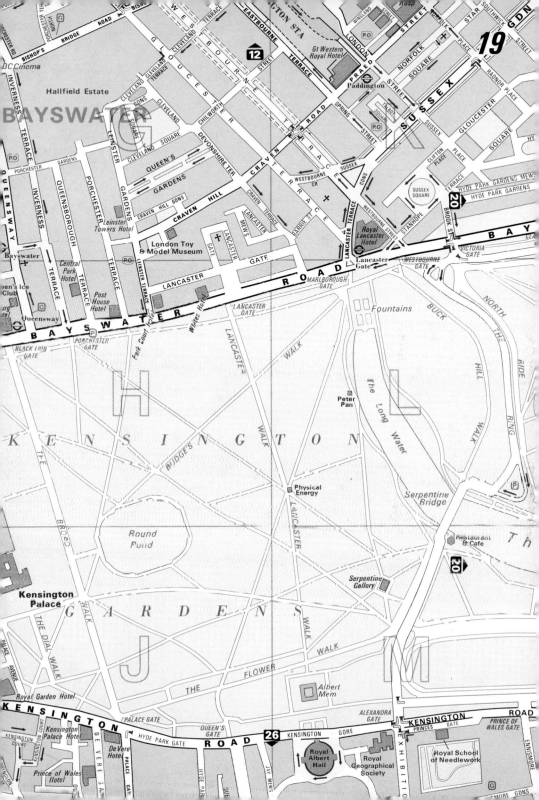

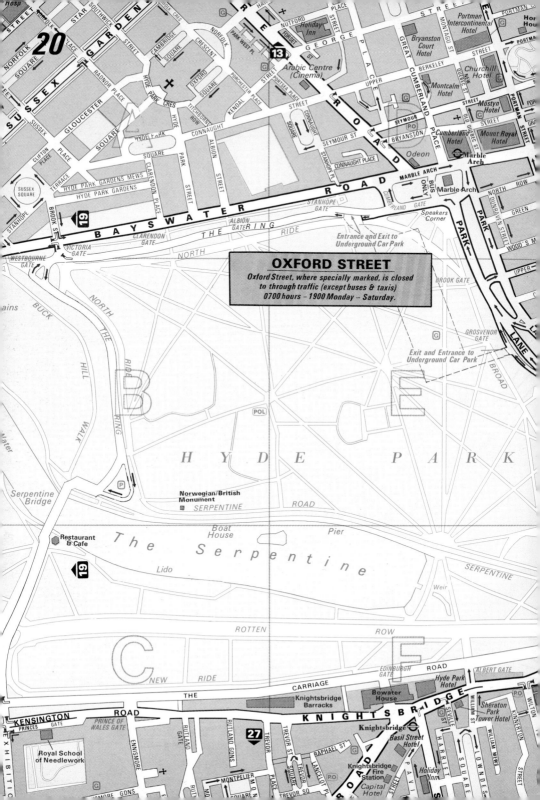

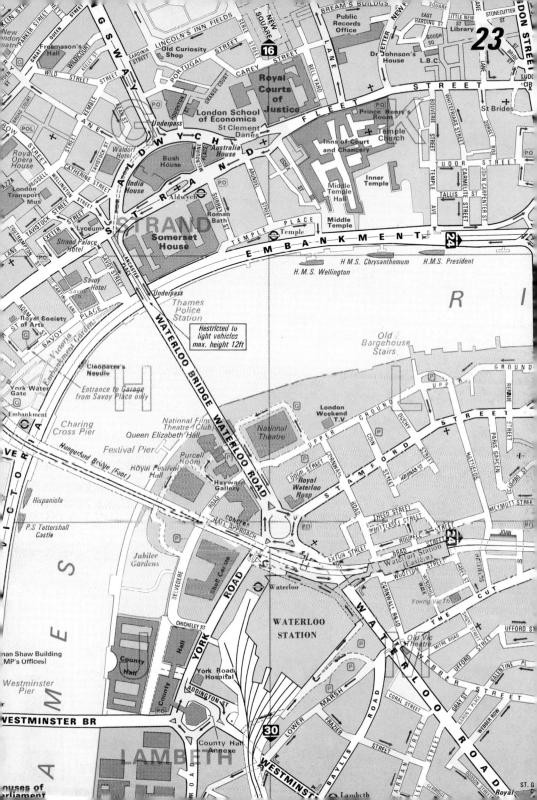

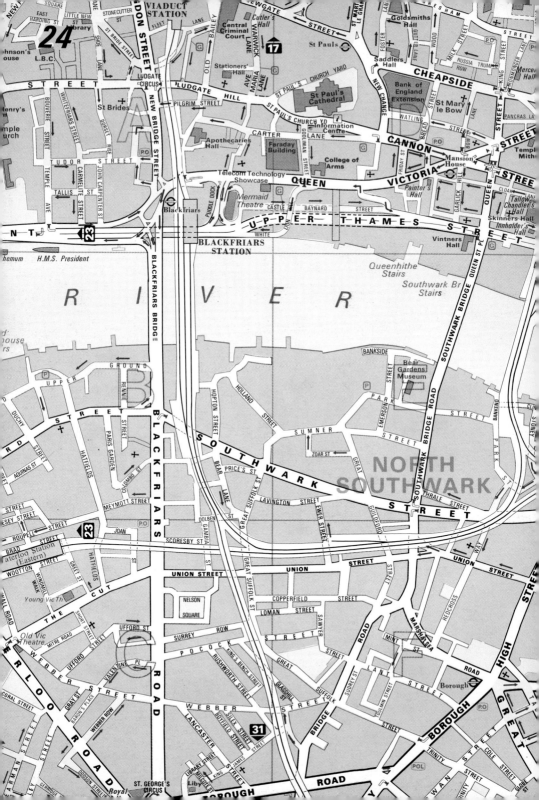

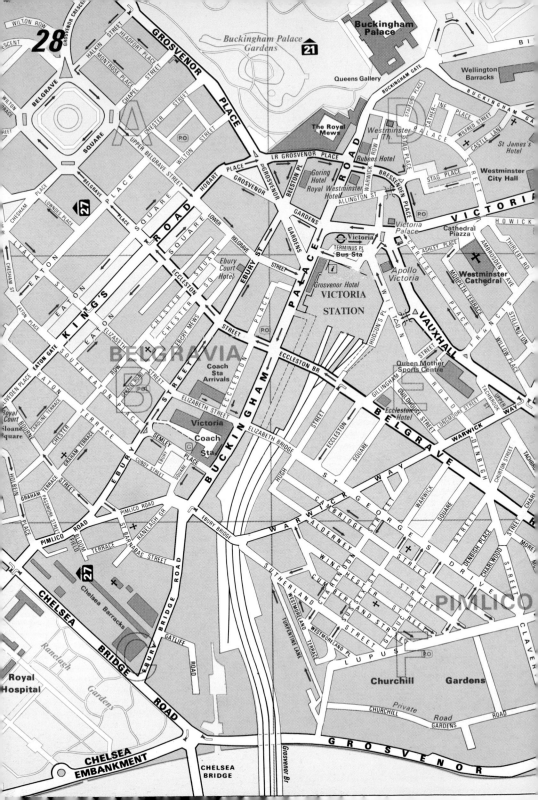

Buckingham Palace

Buckingham Palace Gardens

21

Queens Gallery

Wellington Barracks

WILTON ROW

GROSVENOR CRESCENT

Halkin Street

Headfort Place

Montrose Place

Chapel Street

GROSVENOR PLACE

Stafford Place

Buckingham Palace

Catherine Place

Wilfred Street

Castle Lane

St James's Hotel

WILTON CRESCENT

BELGRAVE

SQUARE

Chester Street

Upper Belgrave Street

Wilton Street

Grosvenor Street

P.O.

The Royal Mews

Westminster Th

Stag Place

Westminster City Hall

WILTON TERRACE

LR GROSVENOR PLACE

Rubens Hotel

HOWICK

CHESHAM

Lowndes Place

27

BELGRAVE PLACE

EATON SQUARE

Lower Belgrave Street

HOBART PLACE

GROSVENOR GARDENS

GROSVENOR GARDENS

Goring Hotel

Royal Westminster Hotel

ALLINGTON ST

WARWICK

BRESSENDEN PLACE

P.O.

Victoria Palace

Cathedral Piazza

THURLEBY RD

AMBROSDEN AVE

LYALL STREET

CHESHAM ST

EATON PLACE

KINGS ROAD

EATON SQUARE

EBURY ST

BELGRAVE

ROAD

Victoria

TERMINUS PL

Bus Sta

Apollo Victoria

CARLISLE PLACE

ASHLEY PLACE

Westminster Cathedral

MORPETH TERRACE

FRANCIS

STILLINGTON

CHESTER

EATON

ELIZABETH

CHESTER STREET

ECCLESTON STREET

Ebury Court Hotel

P.O.

Grosvenor Hotel

VICTORIA STATION

WILTON ROAD

HUDSON'S PL

GILLINGHAM

WILLOW PLACE

BELGRAVIA

SOUTH EATON PLACE

EATON ROW

ELIZABETH

EBURY MEWS

BUCKINGHAM PALACE ROAD

ECCLESTON BR

Queen Mother Sports Centre

VAUXHALL

Cliveden Place

Royal Court

Sloane Square

GRAHAM TERRACE

CAROLINE TERRACE

CHESTER

Coach Sta Arrivals

ECCLESTON

Elizabeth Street

Victoria Coach Sta

SEMLEY PLACE

CUNDY STREET

ELIZABETH BRIDGE

ELIZABETH BRIDGE

HIGH

STURGEON

ECCLESTON

SQUARE

GILLINGHAM STREET

LONGMORE STREET

GUILDHOUSE STREET

Ecclestone Hotel

BELGRAVE

WARWICK

TACHBROOK

DENBIGH

UPPER TACHBROOK ST

HOLBEIN PLACE

GRAHAM TERRACE

PASSMORE STREET

EBURY

EBURY

SQUARE

BUCKINGHAM PALACE ROAD

WAY

ST GEORGE'S

CAMBRIDGE

ALDERNEY

WARWICK

WAY

DENBIGH PLACE

CHURTON STREET

CHARLWOOD

PIMLICO ROAD

St BARNABAS STREET

RANELAGH GR

EBURY BRIDGE

SUTHERLAND STREET

WINCHESTER

CAMBRIDGE

DRIVE

MORETON

PIMLICO ROAD

BLOOMFIELD TERRACE

EBURY BRIDGE ROAD

GATLIFF ROAD

WESTMORELAND TERRACE

TURPENTINE LANE

WESTMORELAND PL

LUPUS STREET

CUMBERLAND STREET

SUTHERLAND STREET

GLOUCESTER STREET

CLAVERTON

PIMLICO

27

Chelsea Barracks

CHELSEA

BRIDGE

ROAD

Royal Hospital

Ranelagh Gardens

CHELSEA EMBANKMENT

CHELSEA BRIDGE

Grosvenor Br

Churchill Gardens

Private Road Gardens

CHURCHILL

GROSVENOR ROAD

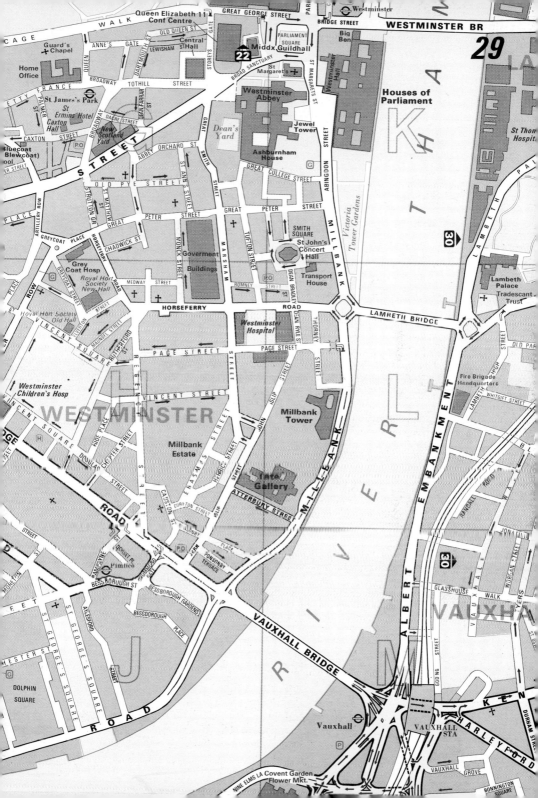

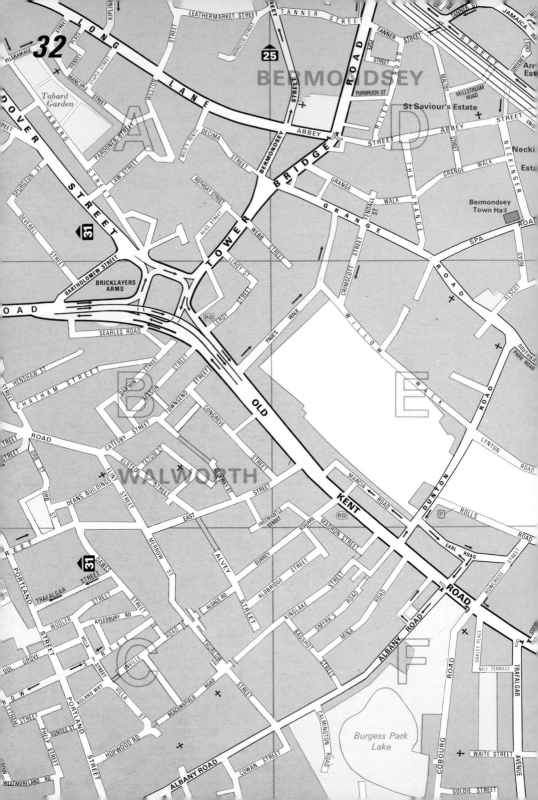

PILGRAMAGE
STREET
LONG LANE
KIPLIN
LEATHERMARKET STREET
STREET
TANNER STREET
JAMAICA
WA
STREET
MOROCCO STREET
TANNER STREET
ST
STREET
ARN
Est
25
BERMONDSEY
ROAD
TANNER STREET
RILEY ROAD
MALTBY STREET
SWEENEY CRES
FRANKS
MANCIPLE STREET
MAPLE STREET
WESTON STREET
PURBROOK ST
MILLSTREAM ROAD
Tabard
Garden
TABARD STREET
A
ABBEY STREET
St Saviour's Estate
ENID
PARDONER STREET
DECIMA STREET
D
WILD'S RENTS
BERMONDSEY
ABBEY STREET
STREET
NECKINGER
Est
DOVER STREET
LAW STREET
STREET
ROTHSAY STREET
BRIDGE
GRANGE
GRANGE WALK
Neckinger
Estate
ROAD
SPURGEON ST
ALICE STREET
FENDALL ST
WALK
Bermondsey
Town Hall
ALSCOT
STREET
31
WEBB STREET
GRANGE
THE GRANGE
SPA ROAD
SOUTHWARK PARK ROAD
DEVERELL STREET
LEROY ST
CRIMSCOTT STREET
ROAD
TOWER
LEROY
STREET
Bricklayers
Arms
ROAD
BARTHOLOMEW STREET
BRICKLAYERS ARMS
P.O
WILLOW
PAGE'S WALK
WALK
SEARLES ROAD
OLD
HENSHAW ST
CHATHAM STREET
ROAD
DARWIN
MASON STREET
STREET
TOWNSEND STREET
CONGREVE
STREET
LYNTON ROAD
B
WALWORTH
E
DUNTON ROAD
STREET
ORB ST
CATESBY STREET
TATUM'S
BLENDON'S
STREET
MARCIA ROAD
ROAD
DEANS BUILDINGS
ELSTED STREET
FLINT STREET
FREEMANTLE STREET
KENT
ROLLS
P
ROAD
STREET
EAST
SQUARE
MADRON STREET
P.O
EARL ROAD
31
OAKS STREET
ALVEY
SURREY
ALDBRIDGE STREET
STREET
MINA
ROAD
ROMCROSS
PORTLAND STREET
STREET
MARROW ST
STREET
KINGLAKE STREET
ALBANY
ROAD
C
WOOLER STREET
AYLESBURY RD
ALSAGE RD
STREET
SMYRK'S
BAGSHOT STREET
ROAD
OAKLEY PLACE
VILLA
HILLBECK RD
F
NILE TERRACE
TRAFALGAR
GROVE
INVILLE ROAD
COBOURG
AVENUE
OOL
ROW
STREET
ROLAND WAY
VILLA STREET
BEACONSFIELD ROAD
CALMINGTON ROAD
Burgess Park
Lake
WAITE STREET
YTHAM
PHELP STREET
SONDES ST
PORTLAND STREET
HOPWOOD ROAD
ALBANY ROAD
COWAN STREET
COBOURG ROAD
GOLDIE STREET
WESTMORELAND RD

## TOURIST INFORMATION

The London Visitor and Convention Bureau is London's official tourist board; all approved members – shops, hotels, tour agencies and operators – display its sign. Whatever information you need about London – what to do, where to go, how to get there, including instant hotel bookings, theatre and tour reservations – can be obtained at the LVCB's five central locations:

*Victoria Station* forecourt, SW1 open daily 9am – 8.30pm (8am – 10pm July & August)

*Selfridges Store*, Oxford Street, W1 (ground floor) open store hours

*Harrods Store*, Knightsbridge, SW1 (4th floor) open store hours

*Heathrow Airport*, Heathrow Central Station open daily 9am – 6pm

*Tower of London*, EC3 (West Gate) open daily April – October, 10am – 6pm

and telephone enquiries can be made on 730 3488, Mon – Fri, 9am – 5.30pm.

In addition, there are several Local Authority Tourist Information Centres around the capital.

## ACCOMMODATION

London is renowned for some of the best and most famous hotels in the world. There are also lots of smaller establishments with lower prices, and an enormous number of privately-run bed-and-breakfast guest houses. See page 123 for a list of AA-recommended places to stay.

It can all be very confusing, but help is on hand to assist you sort things out. If you wish to make advance reservations before leaving home, your local travel agent will know about special 'package' arrangements. For advance bookings of two nights or more, you can write to the London Visitor and **36** ▶

# *FINDING YOUR FEET*

The LVCB Tourist Information Centre at Victoria

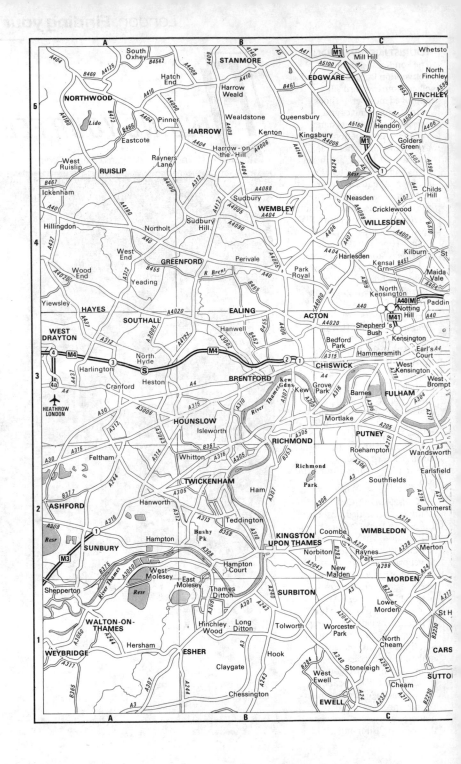

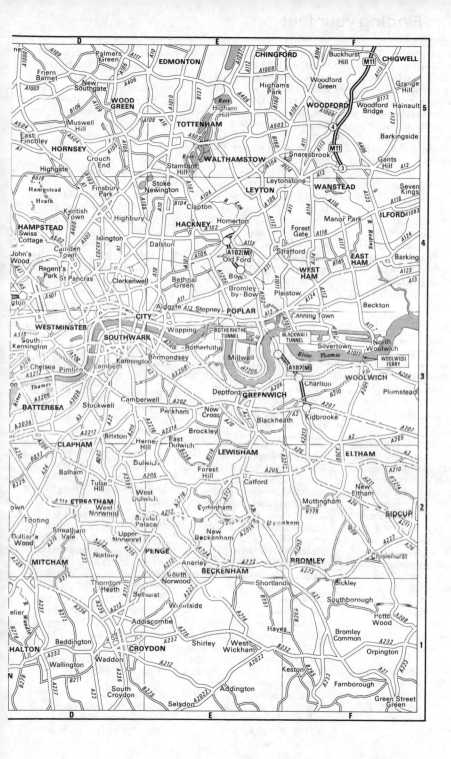

Convention Bureau at 26 Grosvenor Gardens, London SW1W 0DU *at least four weeks* before you intend to travel. They will act as an agency and make provisional reservations for you. For reservations on your arrival in London, you should go in person to one of the LVCB's five central Information Centres – at Victoria and Heathrow Stations, Harrods, Selfridges, and The Tower – or to the British Travel Centre in Regent Street (see page 37); you will find all the help you need at these centres. A returnable deposit must be paid when making a reservation there, and this is deducted from your final bill; in addition, a small non-returnable booking fee is charged.

If you think you will be arriving late at your hotel, you should mention this at the time of booking; similarly, if you are delayed for any reason, it is advisable to telephone the management to warn them of your late arrival.

### Charges

It is usual for breakfast to be included in the cost of a night's accommodation. Many hotels and guest houses offer special all-in prices for full-board (bed, breakfast, lunch and dinner) and half-board stays (bed, breakfast, and lunch or dinner).

All establishments with four or more bedrooms are required by law to display in their entrance halls notices showing the minimum and maximum overnight charges. All these displayed prices must include service charges (if any), and it must be clear whether they include meals and Value Added Tax (currently 15%).

You may find the following hotel booking agencies of help: Concordia, 52 Grosvenor Gardens, SW1 (tel: 730 3467) kiosk Victoria Station (tel: 828 3467)

Gatwick Airport (tel: 0293 34851)
GB Hotel Reserves, Sydney Hall, Pond Place, SW3 (tel: 581 0161/2)
HBI/HOTAC, Kingsgate House, Kingsgate Place, NW6 (tel: 625 8631)
Hotel Booking Service, 13 – 14 Golden Square, W1 (tel: 437 5052)
Hotel Finders, 20 Bell Lane, NW4 (tel: 202 7000)
Hotelguide, Faraday House, 8/10 Charing Cross Road, WC2 (tel: 836 5561/7677)
Hotel & Personal Accommodation Ltd., 10 Lower Belgrave Street, SW1 (tel: 730 6181)
British Hotel Reservation Centre personal callers: Victoria Station, outside Platform 8 (tel: 828 1027/1849) Liverpool Street Station, outside Platform 9 (tel: 621 1842)

## AIRPORTS

London is well served by its airports, to which it is connected by excellent road and rail links. The main London airports are Heathrow and Gatwick.

### Heathrow Airport

Travellers arriving at Heathrow pass through one of the busiest airports in the world. London's main airport, handling millions of passengers a year, it is situated some 15 miles to the west of central London, to which it is directly connected by the M4 motorway. The following public transport also serves Heathrow.

### *Underground*

The extension of the Piccadilly line tube, opened in 1977, provides a direct link from all Heathrow terminals to the West End of London. Departures from the airport start at about 5am on Monday to Saturday and at about 7am on Sunday; the last train leaves at just before midnight, Monday – Saturday, and just before 11pm on

Sunday. The first train to Heathrow leaves King's Cross station at about 6am on Monday to Saturday and at about 7.30am on Sunday; the last train leaves just after midnight, Monday – Saturday and at about 11.30pm on Sunday.

### *Airbus*

This bus service of London Regional Transport runs from 6.30am to 9.30pm, and takes about 50 minutes. Buses leave from Victoria Station (Grosvenor Gardens) and Euston Station, and serve major hotels en route.

Although airbuses and tubes do not operate during the night, there is an all-night bus service – No 97 – which runs at regular intervals from midnight to 5am between central London and Heathrow.

Heathrow Central Information Centre – tel: 730 3488.

### Gatwick Airport

Twenty-eight miles south of London, Gatwick is the second most important airport in Britain. One of the most convenient ways of travelling to Gatwick is by rail, as the station forms an integral part of the airport terminal building. Trains leave from Victoria Station in London every 15 minutes between 5.30am and 10pm, and every hour throughout the night; the journey takes about 40 minutes. Driving to Gatwick takes about an hour, depending on traffic conditions, via the A23 and the M23 motorway. Although there are no tubes or special airbuses, there is a good coach service to Gatwick from Victoria Coach Station.

Gatwick Information Desk – tel: 0293 31299.

### BRITISH RAIL

Britain's extensive rail network links all major cities in the country with London. British

Rail offer a full range of travel facilities at **The British Travel Centre**, 12 Regent Street, SW1 (tel: 730 3400). Here you can buy rail tickets and make reservations, book tickets for theatres and sightseeing tours, arrange accommodation, and change foreign money. The Centre is open from 9am to 6.30pm, Monday to Saturday, and on Sundays from 10am to 4pm. In addition, BR Travel Centres can be found at:

14 Kingsgate Parade, Victoria Street, SW1
87 King William Street, EC4
407 Oxford Street, W1
170b Strand, WC2
(Open 9am – 5pm, Mon – Fri)
and at these main London terminals:
Cannon Street, Charing Cross, Euston, King's Cross, London Bridge, Liverpool Street, Paddington, St Pancras, Victoria, and Waterloo.

Almost all the main-line London stations are worth a visit in themselves, if only for their architectural grandeur or Victorian pretensions. Each one serves a particular region of the country. The main ones are:

*King's Cross Station*
(tel: 278 2477)
The main London terminal of the Eastern Region, serving east and north-east England, and Scotland via the east coast. It is connected to the Northern, Piccadilly, Circle, Metropolitan, and Victoria lines of the Underground.

*Liverpool Street Station*
(tel: 283 7171)
The terminus for East Anglia, it is connected to the Central, Circle, and Metropolitan lines of the Underground.

*Euston Station* (tel: 387 7070)
Serves east and west Midlands, north-west England, Scotland via the west coast, and north Wales. A modern station of concrete and glass with direct escalators to the Northern and Victoria lines of the Underground.

*St Pancras Station*
(tel: 387 7070)
This famous Gothic-style station serving the east Midlands, is close to King's Cross and Waterloo – the passenger information available at this busy station is comprehensive

connects with the same tube lines.

*Victoria Station* (tel: 928 5100)
The main Southern Region terminus serving the south coast and connected to the Circle, District, and Victoria lines of the Underground. For a hundred years, Victoria has been the rail gateway to the Continent, and the Orient Express – though now privately-run – still starts from Platform 8.

*Waterloo Station*
(tel: 928 5100)
This Southern Region terminus is the biggest and busiest station in London, thanks to the enormous amount of commuter trains which pour in each day. It connects to the Underground's Bakerloo and Northern lines.

*Charing Cross Station*
(tel: 928 5100)
Designed by the great railway engineer, Brunel, Charing Cross serves the Southern Region and connects with the Jubilee,

The tube remains the favoured way of travelling in the capital

Bakerloo, and Northern lines of the Underground.

***Paddington Station***
(tel:262 6767)
Another Brunel station, this terminus of the Western Region serves the west Midlands, the west of England, and South Wales with 125mph high-speed trains, the fastest scheduled diesels in the world. The station is connected to the Bakerloo, District, Circle, and Metropolitan lines of the Underground.

Full details of scheduled rail services are shown in local timetables. Free copies are available from British Rail stations and Travel Centres.

British Rail fares are calculated on the distance travelled. It is generally cheaper to travel after the morning rush hour (9.30 Monday to Friday), and at any time over the weekend. Buy a Cheap Day Return or, for longer journeys, a Saver Return ticket. You must buy a ticket before travelling, and surrender it either to the guard on the train or to the ticket-collector on the platform at your destination. Children under five travel free; under 16, half-price.

## LONDON'S TRANSPORT
The visitor arriving in London will need to know first of all how to get about the capital. Fortunately, though Greater London is over 610 square miles in size, twice as large as New York or Paris, it is served by one of the finest transport systems in the world.

You have a choice of three means of public transport: the familiar red London bus, the Underground railway – or 'tube' – network, and the London taxi.

The buses and Underground are controlled by London Regional Transport whose headquarters is at 55 Broadway, Westminster, SW1. This authority maintains Travel Information Centres at the following Underground stations in Central London: Victoria and Piccadilly Circus (open 8.15am – 9.30pm), Charing Cross, King's Cross and Oxford Circus (open 8.15am – 6pm), Euston (open 7.15am – 6pm), St James's Park (open 8.15am – 5pm) and Heathrow (open 7.15am – 9.30pm). They answer all queries about travel in London, as well as issue tickets, book tours, and sell publications. Or you can

telephone 222 1234 anytime, day or night.

## THE UNDERGROUND
Please refer to the map of the London Underground at the back of this book.

As with many capital cities, the quickest and most efficient means of public transport in London is the Underground railway – known as 'the tube'. With more than 275 stations, the Underground covers a wide area reaching out from central London to the suburbs where it rises above ground as an ordinary surface railway. There is almost always a tube station close at hand throughout London, and trains run frequently between 5.30am and 0.15am (until 11.30pm on Sundays). There are no all-night services, however, and it is important to note that certain stations are closed at weekends.

There are large Underground maps posted at all stations, in the booking halls and on all platforms, and each car displays a map of that train's route. Each line has a name and is clearly indicated in a separate colour; it is usually easier to follow the colours than go by the names of the lines.

| | |
|---|---|
| Bakerloo line | – brown |
| Central line | – red |
| District line | – green |
| Circle line | – yellow |
| Jubilee line | – grey |
| Metropolitan line | – purple |
| Northern line | – black |
| Piccadilly line | – dark blue |
| Victoria line | – light blue |

Signs throughout the tube stations show the way to the line required, but make sure you wait on the correct platform and board the right train by checking the direction indicators both on the platform itself and on the front of the train.

A list of fares is displayed in ticket halls; you must buy a ticket before you begin your journey, either from the booking office or from automatic machines (these will save you queuing and some of them give change), and keep it safe to either show or surrender at your destination.

Under-14s travel at a reduced fare, as do 14- and 15-year-olds with a Child Rate Photocard – these are available free from Post Offices in the London area. Under-fives travel free.

### BUSES

One of the best ways of seeing London is to take a seat on the top deck of one of its famous double-decker buses. The fact that the traffic may be slow on occasions is no great handicap, but offers a wonderful opportunity for leisurely sightseeing. Buses operate from about 6am to midnight on most routes, including those connecting the main-line railway stations, and offer a comprehensive service in central London and the suburbs. A network of special All Night buses runs through central London serving Piccadilly Circus, Leicester Square, Victoria, Trafalgar Square, Hyde Park Corner, Marble Arch, and many other parts convenient for theatres, cinemas, and restaurants. However, do check times before using these buses; their stops have distinctive blue and yellow route numbers.

You should pick up a free, detailed bus map from any Travel Enquiry Office or Underground station. Each bus route is identified by a number which appears on the front, sides, and back of each bus. The final destination also appears on the front and back, and a short list of major ports of call on the sides. Bus-stop signs, which generally list the numbers of the buses which stop there, are displayed on a red or white background. Red backgrounds

Victoria, one of London's major bus termini

denote 'Request Stops', where the bus will only stop if hailed in good time; the white background signs are compulsory stops. You should always take your turn in the queue at a bus-stop – if there is one.

On double-decker buses, there are usually conductors who control the number of passengers allowed on and collect fares; on single-decker buses you give your fare to the driver as you get on. Always try and have a lot of change with you when you use buses, so that you can tender the right money. Smoking is not allowed on the ground floor of double-decker buses.

Under-14s pay a reduced flat fare until 10pm, as do 14- and 15-year-olds with a Child Rate Photocard, and up to two under-fives per person travel free. Remember to keep your ticket until you leave the bus.

### CONCESSIONARY FARES

If you intend using public transport in London extensively, there are a number of special tickets and passes available which will save you money and waste a good deal less of your precious time. With most of them you can travel when you like, as often as you like; there's no need to queue for separate tickets in the normal way or search for change on buses.

They can be bought from any London Transport or LVCB Information Centre, or any Underground station.

With the **London Explorer Pass** you get unlimited travel on all London's red buses (except the Official Sightseeing Tours) and almost all the Underground – even to and from Heathrow by Airbus or tube for 1, 3, 4, or 7 days, with special low prices for the under-16s.

**Red Bus Rover** tickets allow unlimited travel for one day on any of London's normal bus services.

The newest faresaver – and timesaver – in London is the **Capitalcard**. The combined British Rail, Underground, and bus network in Greater London is divided into five concentric zones. You just choose which zones you most wish to travel in, and buy the appropriate Capitalcard. You can then travel on any combination of train, tube, and bus within your selected zones, any number of times, for the duration of the ticket's validity (seven days or a month). There is also a **One Day Capitalcard** which gives you unlimited off-peak travel for the day throughout the whole of Greater London, by train, tube and bus: the only restriction is you have to travel after 9.30am, Monday to Friday (no restrictions at weekends). You can also buy combined British Rail tickets and seven-day or monthly Capitalcards, and One Day Capitalcards, from most stations outside Greater London, which is a great saving if you are not actually staying in the capital.

Within London, Capitalcards can be bought from any British Rail or Underground station. Before buying one, you will need a Photocard: just take a passport-size photograph of yourself with you when you buy your first ticket and you will be issued with one free. (There are instant-photo booths at the major railway and tube stations.)

## RUSH HOUR

From Monday to Friday the buses and trains of London Regional Transport carry a daily average of over 6,000,000 passengers. In Central London all forms of public transport become extremely crowded between 8am – 9.30am and 4pm – 6.30pm when most of London is travelling to and from work. London's rush hour is really most uncomfortable, and if travel can be arranged outside these times, the visit will be considerably more enjoyable. Buses and tubes also get quite

busy at lunch-time, but not as bad as during the rush hour.

## TAXIS

The London taxi is one of the friendliest sights a visitor will see. The traditional colour is still black, though in recent years red, blue and yellow vehicles have added a splash of colour to London's fleet. But the distinctive shape remains. Taxis are a salvation for those who get lost; after midnight they are a godsend and the only way to get about. Taxi drivers are also a useful source of information as they know London inside-out – they have to, in order to get their licence.

London taxis can be hailed in the street if the yellow 'For Hire' or 'Taxi' sign above the windscreen is lit, hired from taxi-ranks, or called by telephone: for numbers, see 'Taxi' in the S-Z section of the London Telephone Directory. Charges vary according to the distance covered and are recorded on the meter; additional charges are made for extra people, luggage, and night journeys. It is customary to tip about 10-15% of the fare, or perhaps a little more if the driver has been particularly helpful. For journeys over six miles – for example, from Heathrow

Airport to Central London – you should negotiate a fare in advance.

## SIGHTSEEING TOURS

An excellent way to get to know London – particularly if this is your first visit – is to join one of the many sightseeing bus or coach tours.

London Transport's **Official Sightseeing Tours** on double-decker red buses start from Piccadilly Circus (Haymarket), Marble Arch (Speakers Corner), Baker Street Station, and Victoria Station. The 18-mile route (lasting about 1½ hours) passes most of London's landmarks including St Paul's, Westminster Abbey, and The Tower. These guided tours leave every half-hour from each point from 10am to 5pm daily (except Christmas Day). Buy your tickets in advance from any London Transport or LVCB Information Centre at a special low rate; or just pay as you board the bus. A special tour includes direct entrance (no boring queuing) to Madame Tussaud's Waxworks. The buses are open-top in summer. Details from London Transport, 55 The Broadway, SW1 (tel: 222 1234).

**Culture Bus** (tel: 629 4999). Daily (except 24 & 25 December), every 20 minutes from 9am to 6.30pm. The distinctive yellow Culture buses follow a circular route in Central London passing many places of interest, with over 20 carefully-chosen stops. Once you've paid, you can hop on and off all day. Tickets bought in advance for the Culture bus can be used instead on one of **London Pride's** Grand Guided Tours (tel: 437 9580), which start from the Trocadero, Piccadilly Circus, W1: a 90-minute guided tour of the capital, with full commentary.

Other sightseeing bus/coach tours are run by:

The traditional London taxi can be a welcome sight

Evans Evans Tours Ltd.
(930 2377); Frames Rickards
(837 3111); Golden Tours
(937 8863); London Tour
Company (734 3502); London
Cityrama (720 5971);
Travellers Check-In (580 8284);
Harrods Sightseeing
(581 3603); London Crusader
(437 0124); and Thomas Cook
Ltd. (499 4000).

### WATER TRANSPORT

A holiday in London cannot be
complete without the unique
views offered by a boat trip on
the Thames. Passenger boat
services operate a full
programme during the summer
months and a restricted one in
the winter. From Westminster
Pier (930 4097), Charing Cross
Pier (839 3312), and Tower
Pier (488 0344), services
operate downstream to
Greenwich, and from
Westminster and Charing Cross
Piers downstream to the Tower.
Upstream services operate from
Westminster Pier to Kew,
Richmond, and Hampton Court,
and from Tower Pier to
Westminster. Check departure
times with the enquiry numbers
given with each Pier, or
telephone the River Boat
Information Service on
730 4012 (weekdays,
9am – 5.30pm).

London also has two canals –
the Grand Union and the
Regent's Canal. Boat trips
operate mainly on the Regent's
Canal; the Regent's Canal
Waterbus goes from Camden
Lock to Little Venice, via London
Zoo (200 0200); Jason's Canal
Cruises (286 3428) run
luncheon and evening trips
along the picturesque part of
Regent's Canal using a pair of
traditional narrow-boats; there
are cruises on the *Jenny Wren*
through the Zoo and Regent's
Park, and on the *My Fair Lady*, a
luxury cruising restaurant
(485 4433); the *Port A Bella
Packet* narrow-boat cruises on

Charing Cross Pier – departure point for river trips

the Grand Union and Regent's
Canals (960 5456). Telephone
for full details and itineraries.

### SEEING LONDON BY BICYCLE

A different way to get about
London is to use a bicycle.
Traffic, especially in Central
London, is often congested and
the cyclist has a freedom denied
the motorist. There are many
firms in London who offer a
cycle hire service and who are
able to meet the needs of both
the casual and experienced
cyclist, whether it be for a three-
speed or a ten-speed bike. Most
firms can also supply items of
cycling equipment and can
provide information on sights to
see. Rent-a-Bike, Kensington
Student Centre, Kensington
Church Street, W8 (937 6089),
the largest cycle hire company
in Britain, is open seven days a
week and offers daily, weekly,
and monthly (or longer) periods
of rental. The old-established
firm of *Savile's Cycle Stores Ltd*,
97 - 99 Battersea Rise, SW11
(228 4279), is open from
Monday to Saturday, excluding
Wednesdays and public
holidays. It offers an initial
weekly period of rental followed
by a daily rate thereafter.

### LONDON ON FOOT

If you want to discover London
by foot – one of the best ways to
get to know any city – several
firms organise guided walking
tours. Information from:
City Walks  937 4281
Cockney Walks  504 9159
Footloose in London  435 0259
London Walks  882 2763
Regent Canal Walks  586 2510
Royal London Walking
Tours  740 7100
Streets of London  882 3414
London Pub Walks  883 2656
Exciting Walks  624 9981
Discovering London
0277 213704
Citisights  241 0323
(archaeological walks)

If you want to explore London
on your own, the Silver Jubilee
Walkway covers ten miles of
historic London. This walkway
was created in 1977 to
commemorate the 25th
anniversary of the Queen's
accession to the throne. The
entire route is signposted by
silver plaques in the shape of a
crown set into the pavement.
Parliament Square is a good
place to start.

### PEDESTRIANS

At a Zebra street-crossing (one
with flashing orange beacons

Creditcall, Phonecard and
coin-operated telephones

and black-and-white stripes on
the road) you have absolute
right-of-way when you have
stepped off the kerb – but do use
this sensibly and make sure
drivers have seen you before you
cross.

At Pelican crossings (two
lines of studs with traffic lights to
halt the traffic), you have to
push a button to make the
signals stop the traffic for you.
When the signal shows a green
man, cross. If this signal starts to
flash while you are crossing,
carry on, you will have plenty of
time to reach the other side; do
not start to cross when this is
flashing nor, of course, when the
red man is showing.

Be aware of the bus lanes
where buses may travel in the
opposite direction to the main
flow of traffic.

## POST OFFICES
In the UK, the only place you
can buy stamps, post parcels,
and send telegrams is at a Post
Office. (Letters, cards, and small
packages can also be posted in
the hundreds of distinctive red
pillar-boxes dotted around the
capital.) Each district in London
has its own chief Post Office, and
there are also many smaller sub
offices. The London Chief Office
is in King Edward Street, EC1; it
is open for all kinds of postal
business on Monday to Friday
from 8am to 7pm, except on
public holidays, and on
Saturdays from 9am to
12.30pm. The Trafalgar Square
Post Office, 22 – 28 William IV
Street, WC2 (tel: 930 9580) is
open for all kinds of business,
Monday – Saturday 8am – 8pm,
and 10am – 5pm on Sundays
and public holidays (except
Christmas Day). It has the
longest post office counter in
Britain (56 metres long, with 33
positions), but it is also always
full of queues. So try to find one
of the smaller offices in which to
transact your business; these are
often combined with a general
shop or newsagent, and are
normally open from 9am to
5.30pm, Monday to Friday, and
on Saturday mornings.

## TELEPHONES
There are hundreds of public
payphones throughout the
capital, most still found in the
distinctive and easily
recognisable red phone boxes.
Additionally, many pubs,
restaurants, hotels, post offices,
and other places open to the
public have payphones which
you may use. There are four
types of payphones:
**Pay-on-answer** phones are the
older type. They take 10p coins
only, and are more suitable for
inland calls.
**Coin-operated payphones**: dial
direct to anywhere in the UK
and to all countries to which
International Direct Dialling is
available. They take 2p, 5p, 10p,
20p, 50p, and £1 coins.
**Phonecard phones** are quickly
becoming more widely
available. To use these phones
you must first buy one of the
special cards which are

available from post offices and shops displaying the 'Phonecard' sign. You may then make any number of calls up to the value of the card, whenever you wish, without the need for cash but only from the special Phonecard phones.

**Creditcall Payphones.** Phones that accept Visa, Mastercard, Diners Club, and American Express credit cards are now being installed in the London area and at airports.

In all cases, instructions for use will be clearly displayed.

British Telecom provides certain recorded information services which are of help to visitors and can be heard by telephoning at any time – e.g. Leisureline: in English, 246 8041; in French, 246 8043; in German, 246 8045. Weather forecast: 246 8091. Motoring conditions within 50 miles of London: 246 8021. Children's London: 246 8007.

Remember when dialling a London number from within the London area, you do not need to use the prefix 01. Just dial the last seven numbers.

### EMERGENCY SERVICES

If you are involved in any serious accident or if you need the police in an emergency, you should always dial 999 in any telephone box (these calls are free), and ask for Fire, Police, or Ambulance.

London Transport Police (for reporting thefts and other crimes which take place on London Transport): telephone 222 5600.

If you are injured and require medical attention in Central London, University College Hospital (Gower Street, WC1), the Middlesex Hospital (Mortimer Street, W1), St Thomas's Hospital (Lambeth Palace Road, SE1), and the Westminster Hospital (Horseferry Road, SW1), all

New-style public telephone boxes

have 24-hour casualty departments. Several chemists have extended opening hours; these include Boots, Piccadilly Circus, W1 (Monday–Friday 8.30am–8pm, Saturday 9am–8pm), H D Bliss, 5 Marble Arch, W1 (9am–midnight daily), Underwoods, 75 Queensway, W2 (9am–10pm daily), and the Churchill Pharmacy, 268 Oxford Street, W1 (8.30am–midnight daily). All foreign visitors to Britain can take advantage of the accident and emergency services of the National Health Service without charge.

Emergency dental treatment can be obtained, at a charge, from the Emergency Dental Service: telephone 677 6363.

### LOST PROPERTY

(a) if you lose anything while travelling on buses or the underground, you should write or go to the London Transport Lost Property Office at 200 Baker Street, NW1, adjoining Baker Street underground station. This office is open Monday to Friday, 9.30am–2pm (closed Saturdays and Sundays). (b) for property lost in London taxis or in the street, report any loss to the nearest police station. (c) taxis only: write to the Metropolitan Police Lost Property Office, 15 Penton Street, N1. It would be

helpful to quote the plate number of the taxi in which you travelled.
(d) if you lose anything in a store, hotel, airport, etc., contact the premises in question. Should property be lost on a train or at a railway station, contact the arrival/departure station of your journey.

### BANKS

All banks are open between 9.30am and 3.30pm Monday to Friday (3pm in the City), and some now open on Saturday mornings. They are closed on Sundays and Public Holidays. There are 24 hour banks at Heathrow and Gatwick airports. Most banks now operate a queuing system. When changing foreign currency, banks usually give the best rates at the lowest commission charges – look out for their special foreign exchange counters. Bureaux de Change are located throughout the capital and are usually open longer hours than banks, in the evenings and at weekends, but do check the rates of commission they charge – they can be very high, cancelling out the advantage of a seemingly generous exchange rate. Wherever you change money or cash cheques, exchange rates and charges should be clearly displayed.

A London office of one of the major car hire firms

should avoid the rush-hour traffic, which is at its height around 8 – 9.30am and 4 – 6.30pm. Particular areas to avoid are Buckingham Palace and The Mall between 11am and noon when the Changing of the Guard at the Palace causes traffic delays. Also, no cars are allowed to use Oxford Street between 7am and 7pm, Monday to Saturday.

### Car hire
Most of the major car hire firms in London are represented at Car Hire Centre International, 93 Regent Street, W1 (tel: 734 7661).

### Parking
Street parking in central London is controlled by a parking policy of meter zones known as the Inner London Parking Area. There are also parking zones in outer London, most of which include meters. The controlled zones are indicated by signs at their boundary points, giving the hours of operation. Special regulations may also apply in areas near to the wholesale markets and where Sunday street markets are held. Street parking other than at officially designated places is prohibited during the specified hours. In many zones, some parking places may be reserved exclusively for residents or other classes of users specified on nearby plates. Temporary restrictions may be found locally, especially for special events. The usual system of yellow lines indicates waiting restrictions.

Parking meters take 5p, 10p, 20p, and 50p coins but there are differences in charges and variations in the length of time for which parking is allowed. The car must be parked within the limits of the parking bay, indicated by the white lines on the roads. It must also face in the same direction as the traffic

### BLUE PLAQUES
Scattered throughout London are the homes of the famous and houses where history was made. Such buildings are marked with a blue plaque recording the event. This scheme was started in 1866 and there are now around 500 plaques commemorating important events and lives of soldiers, scientists, architects, artists, writers, composers, and politicians. You will see them as you stroll around London's streets.

### TIPPING
It is customary to tip for the following services: taxi-drivers; porters, doormen, bell-boys, and room-service waiters; tour guides; barbers and hairdressers; cloakroom attendants; and in restaurants, except where the menu specifically says that service is included.

NEVER tip bartenders in pubs.

### PUBLIC CONVENIENCES
London has a large range of well-signposted public loos, but unfortunately their opening times are sometimes erratic. New individual coin-in-the-slot, French-style conveniences are

being erected in Central London – for example, in Leicester Square, Soho, and Victoria Street, SW1; these cost 10p. There are conveniences in hotels, large stores, pubs, and at stations – but be sure you have plenty of change in advance; charges vary.

### DRIVING A CAR IN LONDON
The best advice for the visitor wanting a worry-free and enjoyable time in the capital, must be – don't take your car into central London. Traffic congestion is a problem and parking can be difficult. Many one-way street systems have been introduced which do create difficulties for the visitor. Those unfamiliar with the complexities of London traffic can take advantage of the services offered by the following two agencies which will provide a driver to meet the client and drive or guide him in his own car into or across central London: European Chauffeurs Ltd, 40 – 42 Oxford Street, W1 (tel: 580 7183/7193), and Universal Aunts Ltd, 250 Kings Road, SW3 (tel: 351 5761). Those who still wish to drive themselves and are unfamiliar with conditions in the capital

flow, unless angle parking is indicated by road marking. Payment must be made on arrival, although unexpired meter time paid for by a previous occupant of the space may be used. After the initial payment has been made, additional parking time may not be bought by making any further payments. Infringement of these rules results in penalties in the form of expensive 'parking tickets', which you will find stuck to the windscreen of the car, and – in extreme cases of misdemeanour – 'clamps' affixed to the front wheel which render the car completely immobile.

Cars may usually be parked at night without lights.

There is some free parking available on the roads in Hyde Park and Regent's Park. The times may be unusual, but are shown by the normal yellow lines and nearby plates.

**Public Car Parks**

There are many public car parks in Inner London, which include the multi storey blocks and underground car parks constructed in recent years to ease traffic congestion. Most are operated by National Car Parks Ltd. (tel: 499 7050) and are easily spotted by their large yellow NCP signs. Most of these car parks are open during normal business hours, or for a slightly longer period at each end of the working day, depending on local arrangements. It is advisable to ascertain closing arrangements from the car park at the time of entering. In most cases it is not possible to make advance reservations. Charges vary a good deal, but as a general guide, the rates in the West End or the City of London usually start at around £1.80 for the first two hours, rising to approximately £13 for a 24-hour period. Cheaper night rates are available between 6pm and 9am. In outer areas the charges are usually considerably lower.

When parking your car, always remember to secure it against theft and not to leave any valuable property inside.

Information about traffic conditions, parking, and motoring in general can always be obtained from the many AA Centres in London or phone their central number (01) 954 7373.

A good compromise is to park your car at a railway or underground station on the outskirts of London and continue your journey by train or tube to the centre. On, or near, the main approach routes into London, it is always possible to leave a car close to public transport facilities which provide a frequent service into the capital.

The opening hours of British Rail station car parks vary according to the opening and closing hours of the station, which are subject to the current time-table. Underground (tube) car parks are open from the time of the first to the time of the last train. Some run by other bodies may be open 24 hours.

You will find charges displayed at all train and underground car parks. Some operated by the London Borough in which they come are free of charge, but this policy could be varied at short notice. There is no standard rate of charges; some are raised during the morning peak hours to discourage commuter parking. On Saturdays some car parks double the weekday charges.

# AR PARKS

For people who have to bring their cars into the capital, the following selection of London's major public car parks may help you to ease the strain of searching for those elusive unoccupied parking meters, particularly in the West End.

Abbreviations used in text/type of car park

|  |  |
| --- | --- |
| C.Ch & L | Cars, coaches & lorries |
| M/S | Multi-storey |
| S | Surface |
| U/C | Under cover |
| U/G | Underground |
| P | Petrol facilities |
| * | Open 24 hours |
| Mdnt | Open until Midnight |

| | Type | Capacity |
| --- | --- | --- |
| **E1 Stepney, Whitechapel** | | |
| Shoreditch High Street (one-way, north/south direction), near junction Commercial Street | S*, C & L | 300 |
| Rodwell House, Middlesex Street | U/G* | 180 |

| | | |
|---|---|---|
| Spitalfields, Whites Row | M/S* | 450 |
| Steward Street | S Sun only | 100 |
| Fieldgate St (off Whitechapel Rd; south side) (entrance in Fieldgate St via Plumber's Row) | S | 120 |

**ECI Finsbury**

| | | |
|---|---|---|
| Aldersgate Street | M/S* | 850 |
| Bowling Green Lane | S | 150 |
| Charterhouse Square | S | 100 |
| Cowcross Street, Caxton House | U/G | 65 |
| Great Sutton Street | U/C | 40 |
| Gloucester Way, Rosebery Ave | S | 140 |
| Sans Walk/St James's Row | S | 62 |
| Saffron Hill, St Cross St | M/S | 400 |
| Skinner Street | U/G | 250 |
| Smithfield Central Market | U/G C, L | 450 |
| Smithfield Surface, Hosier Lane | S | 50 |
| Smithfield Street | S | 100 |
| Snowhill (off Farringdon Street) | U/C | 128 |
| Warner Street (off Farringdon Road) | S | 250 |

**EC2 Moorgate, Liverpool St**

| | | |
|---|---|---|
| Barbican Centre | U/G | 500 |
| Clere Street | S | 60 |
| Curtain Rd (entrance in Worship St) | S Mon–Fri 07.30–18.30 Sun 08.00–1400 | 100 |
| Finsbury Square | U/G, P (07.00––18.00) | 285 |
| London Wall | U/G | 250 |
| Rivington Street | S | 60 |

**EC3 Aldgate, Tower Hill**

| | | |
|---|---|---|
| Tower Hill, Lower Thames Street | U/G C & Ch | 210 |

**EC4 St Paul's, Cannon Street, Ludgate Circus**

| | | |
|---|---|---|
| Baynard House, Queen Victoria Street | U/G* | 300 |
| Distaff Lane (off Cannon Street) | U/C | 100 |
| Paternoster Row, Ave Maria Lane | U/G* | 265 |
| Seacoal Lane, Hillgate House | U/G* | 180 |
| Shoe Lane, | U/G | 80 |

**International Press Centre**

| | | |
|---|---|---|
| Swan Lane | M/S | 450 |
| Upper Thames Street, Vintry | M/S | 485 |
| Walbrook, Bucklersbury House | U/G | 40 |

**N1 Islington**

| | | |
|---|---|---|
| Britannia Walk (off City Road) | S | 100 |
| Pitfield St (off Old Street) | S | 100 |

**NW1 Camden Town, Euston, Marylebone**

| | | |
|---|---|---|
| Arlington Road | S | 60 |
| Euston Station | U/G* | 235 |
| Marylebone Road, Dorset House | U/G* | 180 |
| Park Road, Regent's Park | U/G | 97 |
| St Pancras Station | S | 50 |

**NW6 Kilburn**

| | | |
|---|---|---|
| Kilburn Square (off Kilburn High Road) | U/G | 120 |

**NW8 St John's Wood**

| | | |
|---|---|---|
| Acacia Garage, Kingsmill Terrace | M/S* | 250 |
| Church Street, Penfold Street | U/G | 150 |

**SE1 Elephant and Castle**

| | | |
|---|---|---|
| Elephant and Castle | U/G | 150 |
| Skipton Street | S | 110 |

**SE1 Waterloo—Royal Festival Hall—National Theatre Complex**

| | | |
|---|---|---|
| Doon Street (entrance in Upper Ground) | S, C & Ch 08.00–Mdnt | 50 |
| Royal Festival Hall, Belvedere Road | S 08.00–Mdnt | 140 |
| Jubilee Gardens (overflow) | S 08.00–Mdnt | 100 |
| National Theatre, South Bank | U/G 08.00–02.00 | 410 |
| Waterloo Station Approach (British Rail SR) | S* | 117 |

**SE1 Southwark, Bermondsey**

| | | |
|---|---|---|
| Barge House Street (off Upper Ground) | S | 52 |
| Snowsfields | M/S* | 500 |

**SW1 Westminster, Victoria**

| | | |
|---|---|---|
| Abingdon St (entrance: Gt College St) | U/G* | 250 |

| Location | Type | No. |
|---|---|---|
| Arlington Street, Arlington House | U/G* | 108 |
| Bury Street | S | 45 |
| Cadogan Place (off Sloane Street) | U/G* | 349 |
| Dolphin Square Garage, Grosvenor Road | U/G* P. Servicing | 250 |
| Knightsbridge, Park Tower Hotel | U/G* | 90 |
| Knightsbridge Green, Raphael Street | U/G | 65 |
| Pavilion Road | M/S* | 311 |
| Rochester Row | M/S* | 299 |
| Semley Place, Ebury Street | M/S* | 422 |
| Trafalgar Square, Spring Gardens | U/G* | 340 |
| Wilton Place, Berkeley Hotel | U/G 06.30–23.00 | 80 |

### SW3 Chelsea

| Location | Type | No. |
|---|---|---|
| Cale St, St Lukes | S, C | 150 |
| King's Road (near Smith Street) | S & U/C | 120 |

### SW5 Earls Court

| Location | Type | No. |
|---|---|---|
| Cromwell Road, London International Hotel | S U/C | 40 |
| Earls Court Exhibition | S & U/C | 1,300 |

### SW6 Fulham

| Location | Type | No. |
|---|---|---|
| 47/67 Lillie Road, West Centre Hotel | U/G* | 140 |

### SW7 South Kensington

| Location | Type | No. |
|---|---|---|
| 70/71 Ennismore Gardens | U/G Mon–Fri (07.30–23.00) Sat & Sun 08.00–23.00) | 60 |
| Cromwell Road, The Forum Hotel | U/G* | 95 |

### SW8 South Lambeth

| Location | Type | No. |
|---|---|---|
| Vauxhall Bridge Foot, Vauxhall Station | S C, Ch & L* | 100 |
| Wandsworth (Arndale Centre), Buckhold Road | M/S | 1,060 |

### SW17 Tooting

| Location | Type | No. |
|---|---|---|
| Upper Tooting Road, Castle Hotel | S | 75 |

### W1 West End

| Location | Type | No. |
|---|---|---|
| Adams Row, Britannia Hotel | U/G* | 175 |
| Audley Square, South Audley Street | M/S* | 310 |
| Brewer Street, Piccadilly Circus | M/S* | 450 |
| Carburton Street, Regent Crest Hotel | U/G* | 65 |
| Carrington Street, Shepherd Market | M/S | 310 |
| Cavendish Square | U/G Mon –Sat 07.00–23.00 | 545 |
| Chandos Street, Queen Anne Mews | U/G* | 390 |
| Chesterfield House, Chesterfield Gdns | U/G | 50 |
| Chiltern Street, Paddington Street | M/S* | 395 |
| Cleveland Street | U/G | 84 |
| Clipstone Street | U/G* | 347 |
| Cramer Street | S | 200 |
| Crawford Street | S & U/C | 60 |
| Dean Street (off Shaftesbury Avenue) | S | 70 |
| Denman Street | U/G* | 143 |
| Dufours Place, Broadwick Garage | U/C | 75 |
| Gloucester Place, Portman Square Garage | M/S* | 113 |
| Gt Cumberland Place, Bilton Towers | U/G* | 160 |
| Grosvenor Hill | M/S | 216 |
| Kingly Street (enter from Beak Street) | S | 35 |
| Bryanston Street, Cumberland Garage | M/S* | 310 |
| Marriot Hotel (off Duke Street) | U/G | 85 |
| Old Burlington Street, Burlington Garage | M/S | 477 |
| Old Park Lane, Brick Street | U/G | 83 |
| Orchard Street (enter from Duke Street) | M/S*P | 700 |
| Park Lane | U/G* | 1,000 |
| Park Lane, Hilton Hotel | U/G* | 235 |
| Poland Street | M/S Mon–Sat 06.00–Mdnt Sun & Bank Hols closed | 150 |
| Portland Place, Weymouth Mews | U/G | 35 |
| Portman Square, Churchill Hotel | U/G | 51 |
| Wardour Street | M/S* | 160 |
| Welbeck Street | M/S | 392 |

**W2 Paddington, Bayswater**

| | | |
|---|---|---|
| Bayswater Road, Kensington Gardens | S C & Ch | 240 |
| Bishop's Bridge Road, Colonnades, Porchester Terrace North | U/G* | 152 |
| Edgware Road, Burwood Place (Water Gardens, Flats) | U/G | 300 |
| Harrow Road, London Metropole Hotel | M/S* | 80 |
| Kendal Street | U/G* | 45 |
| Queensway | U/G* | 300 |
| Queensway, Arthur Court (north end of Queensway) | U/C* | 85 |

**W6 Hammersmith**

| | | |
|---|---|---|
| Hammersmith Broadway (Queen Caroline St) | S Mon– Sat 08.00– 22.00 | 300 |
| King's Mall, Glenthorne Road (eastern end) | M/S Mon– –Sat 08.00– 18.30 | 960 |

**W8 Kensington**

| | | |
|---|---|---|
| Hornton Street, Kensington Town Hall | U/G* | 410 |
| Royal Garden Hotel | U/G* | 160 |
| Young Street | M/S* | 250 |

**W12 Shepherds Bush**

| | | |
|---|---|---|
| Shepherds Bush Centre, Charecroft Way | Roof top part U/C | 300 |

**W14 West Kensington**

| | | |
|---|---|---|
| Holland Road Royal Kensington Hotel | U/G | 70 |
| Maclise Road (Olympia) | M/S* | 750 |
| Olympia Way | S | 300 |
| Warwick Road, (west side) | S* C Ch & L | 350 |

| | | |
|---|---|---|
| Warwick Road, Fenelon Place | S 08.00– 18.00 | 170 |
| Warwick Road, Radnor Terrace (TA Centre) | S | 200 |

Note: *All Warwick Road car parks are on the west side, and north of junction West Cromwell Road, and are listed in sequence of approach.*

**WC1 Bloomsbury, Holborn**

| | | |
|---|---|---|
| Bloomsbury Square | U/G* | 450 |
| Brunswick Square | U/G* | 443 |
| Coptic Street | S P Mon– Fri 08.00– 18.30 | 40 |
| Museum Street | M/S* | 250 |
| Ridgmount Place | S | 35 |
| Russell Court, Woburn Place | U/G | 110 |
| Russell Square, Imperial Hotel | U/G | 140 |
| Tottenham Court Road, Adeline Place YMCA | M/S* | 450 |
| Woburn Place, Royal National Hotel | U/G 07.00– 20.00 | 150 |

**WC2 Leicester Square, Strand**

| | | |
|---|---|---|
| Bedfordbury | U/G | 62 |
| Drury Lane, Parker Street | U/G 06.00– 24.00 | 450 |
| Savoy Place, Victoria Embankment | U/C* | 70 |
| Swiss Centre, Leicester Square | U/G | 90 |
| Trafalgar Square, St Martin's Street | S | 180 |
| Upper St Martin's Lane | M/S | 220 |
| Villiers Street | U/C Mon– Sat 07.30– Midnt P | 110 |
| Whitcomb Street | M/S* | 300 |

London is one of the best cities in the world for shopping, and whatever your tastes or requirements, you will find what you want somewhere in the capital.

Selfridges, Oxford Street, one of London's biggest department stores

On the following pages are introductions to London's main shopping areas, its specialist shops, and its street and trade markets, all of which make it a uniquely exciting place to shop.

Opening times vary a good deal, especially among the smaller shops, but in general the majority of establishments – including the large stores – open from 9am to 5.30pm Monday to Saturday, and close on Sundays. The Oxford Street and Kensington High Street shops remain open every Thursday until 8pm for late-night shopping; those in Knightsbridge every Wednesday until 8pm. Many of the shops in the fashionable Bond Street area close on Saturday afternoons, as do the department stores John Lewis in Oxford Street and Peter Jones in Sloane Square.

# SHOPS AND MARKETS

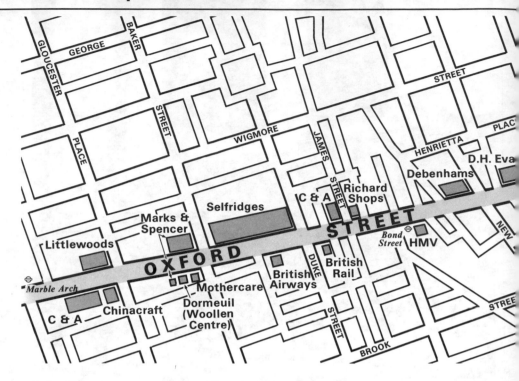

## Oxford Street

MAP REF 21 G/K

Justifiably famous, Oxford Street is the backbone of London's shopping areas. There are no particular specialities, but it is the home of many of London's big department stores and nearly every fashion and shoe shop chain has at least one branch in the street.

The busiest stretch is between Marble Arch and Oxford Circus. Here you will find branches of *Dolcis*, *Russell & Bromley*, *Bally*, and *Saxone* (shoes); *Dorothy Perkins* and *Etam* (ladies' fashions); *Lord John*, *Harry Fenton*, and *Hepworth* (gents' fashions); and *Littlewoods* and *C&A*, both large chain stores selling good value clothing for all the family. Also near the Marble Arch end is the largest branch of *Marks & Spencer*, a favourite with shoppers from all over the world. This open-plan store specialises in reasonably-priced, well-made clothes plus high-quality food and household goods. Almost opposite you'll find everything for the pregnant mother, baby, and young child at a large branch of *Mothercare*.

Nearby is *Selfridges*, London's second-largest department store, which is especially popular for its large food hall, restaurants, kitchenware, and cosmetic departments. Other department stores along Oxford Street are *Debenhams*, *D H Evans*, and *John Lewis*, which is excellent for household equipment and fabrics. It has a slogan 'never knowingly undersold': if you buy something here and subsequently find it cheaper elsewhere, the store will refund the difference.

Next to the entrance to Bond Street station is the *HMV* shop; with its four floors of records and tapes, it is the largest of its kind in Europe. Just past John Lewis towards Oxford Circus is a large branch of *British Home Stores*, another chain specialising in inexpensive clothing for men, women, and children, plus food and household requirements, particularly lighting. Beside the entrance to Oxford Circus station is the *Wedgwood Shop*, displaying fine pottery, porcelain, glass, and gifts; and opposite is the store *Peter Robinson*, with its wide range of fashions, particularly for the young.

Oxford Street continues past Oxford Street station towards Tottenham Court Road, and along this stretch are yet further branches of most of the shops already mentioned, including *Marks & Spencer* and a new, huge HMV shop. There are also branches of the chemist chains, *Boots* and *Underwoods*.

Marks & Spencer, Oxford Street

51

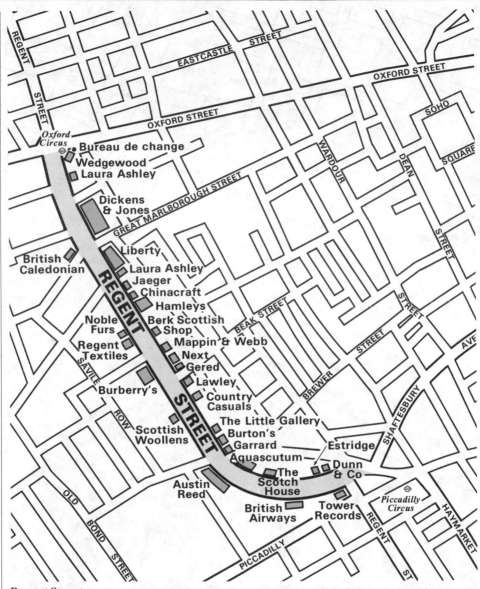

Map labels:
REGENT STREET · EASTCASTLE STREET · OXFORD STREET · WARDOUR STREET · DEAN STREET · SOHO SQUARE · OXFORD STREET · Oxford Circus · Bureau de change · Wedgewood · Laura Ashley · Dickens & Jones · GREAT MARLBOROUGH STREET · Liberty · British Caledonian · Laura Ashley · Jaeger · Chinacraft · Hamleys · BEAK STREET · Noble Furs · Berk Scottish Shop · Regent Textiles · Mappin & Webb · Next · Gered · SAVILE ROW · Burberry's · Lawley · Country Casuals · BREWER STREET · SHAFTESBURY · The Little Gallery · Scottish Woollens · Burton's · Garrard · Estridge · Aquascutum · Dunn & Co · The Scotch House · Austin Reed · OLD BOND STREET · British Airways · Tower Records · Piccadilly Circus · HAYMARKET · PICCADILLY · REGENT ST

## Regent Street

**MAP REF 21K/L**

Laid out in 1813–20 by John Nash, Regent Street crosses Oxford Street at Oxford Circus. The total rebuilding of the street that began in 1900 has made it one of the finest shopping streets in the world, renowned for its high-class fashion shops, including some of the best-known in British fashion.

Starting at Oxford Circus and heading towards Piccadilly Circus, you soon come to Regent Street's two department stores – *Dickens & Jones*, which concentrates on fashions and jewellery, and *Liberty & Co*, the landmark of the street and a most unusual building. Its neo-classical frontage is linked to a reproduction Tudor building at the rear; the half-timbering is structural, not decorative, the timbers coming from genuine men-of-war. Liberty's is world-famous for its fine fabrics, silks, antiques, and fashion.

There is a branch of *Laura Ashley*, whose fabrics and fashions are now instantly recognisable the world over. *Hamleys*, the largest toy shop in the world, has several floors packed with models, toys, dolls, and games of every description. Classic British-style clothes will be found in such shops as *Jaeger*; *Austin Reed*, purveyor of high-quality men's clothing; *Aquascutum*; the *Scotch House*, notable for woollens, cashmere, and tartans; and *Burberrys*, particularly famous for its raincoats. Among the top-quality jewellers are *Mappin & Webb*, and *Garrard*, the Queen's jeweller, which is responsible for the upkeep of the Crown Jewels.

On the other side of Piccadilly Circus, in Lower Regent Streeet, is *Lillywhites*, an enormous sports shop, where you can find everything from wet suits to golf balls.

## Bond Street

MAP REF 21K/L

New Bond Street runs down from Oxford Street to Burlington Gardens, where it becomes Old Bond Street, and continues to Piccadilly. This is one of London's most expensive streets, where leading names in fashion, jewellery, and beauty salons alternate with the premises of famous art dealers.

At the Oxford Street end there are branches of all the top-quality shoe shops. The street's one department store is *Fenwick's*, which sells mainly women's fashions. Fashion shops such as *Yves Saint Laurent*, *Ted Lapidus*, *Gucci* – the outstanding place in London to buy handbags and beautifully-designed leather goods – *Kurt Geiger*, and *Magli* are sprinkled along Bond Street and are the sort of establishments where anyone who has to ask the price

can't afford it. You must stop at the breathtaking window displays of *Asprey & Co*, a treasure-house of all that is fine and rare in leather, gold, silver, jewellery, and antiques. Farther along, more beautiful goods are to be found in *Cartier* and, opposite, *Georg Jensen*, noted for its silver and porcelain. There are a number of photographic shops in New Bond Street, notably *Dixons* and *Wallace Heaton*.

If you have the time, a stop at *Sotheby's* (34 New Bond Street), the world-famous fine art auctioneers, is really worthwhile. Even if you don't want to buy anything or have

nothing you want valued by the experts, it is great fun to wander around the previews (usually 9am to 4.30pm).

Across Burlington Gardens, into Old Bond Street, there are more fine art dealers, jewellers, oriental rug shops, and the beauty salons of *Max Factor*, *Elizabeth Arden*, and *Yardley*. Close to the Piccadilly end is a completely different sort of shop: at *Argos* you choose what you want from a catalogue of over 2000 popular brand items, and by the time you have paid, your goods are packed and waiting.

*Hamleys, in Regent Street sells toys of every description*

Above: figurine on Fortnum & Mason's famous clock. Right: Burlington Arcade; lined with shops for the discerning, it is also a pleasant place to stroll in

## Piccadilly

**MAP REF 21L/M**

There seem to be more airlines and tourist boards represented in Piccadilly than shops, but those that are here are some of the most important names in London. Piccadilly itself was a fashionable area in the 19th century, and the shops here reflect it.

Starting from Piccadilly Circus, you come to *Simpson*, a first-class tailor and outfitter, *Hatchards*, an excellent general bookshop, and the famous name of *Fortnum & Mason*, particularly renowned for its food hall and the assistants wearing full morning dress. Try and be there when the figurines on the mechanical clock strike the hour. *Swaine, Adeney, Brigg & Sons* is the place to go for high-quality leather goods,

umbrellas, and riding equipment.

Off Piccadilly, beyond Fortnums and on the opposite side of the street, you can step back in time by entering *Burlington Arcade*. This delightful covered walk is lined with bow-fronted shops selling antiques, jewellery, and knitwear. The arcade is still patrolled by a beadle in traditional dress who also closes the gates at either end each night.

The well-heeled gentleman can buy his clothes in the streets off either side of Piccadilly. He can have his shirts hand-made in *Jermyn Street*, and his suits supplied from a *Savile Row* or *Sackville Street* tailor.

## Kensington High Street

**DISTRICT MAP**

At the western end of Hyde Park, the two roads of Kensington High Street and Kensington Church Street make up this lively and fashionable off-centre shopping area.

Kensington High Street tube station is at the heart of things and its entrance is now a new shopping arcade with a branch of *Marks & Spencer* outstanding. From the station and heading towards Kensington Gardens, you pass a branch of another clothing chain store, *British Home Stores*, before arriving at *John Barker*. This large department store offers a wide range of international goods from fashions to food, but

specialising in household ware. Nearby is *Kensington Market*, a massive covered labyrinth containing over 40 up-to-date fashion boutiques and 150 stalls selling mostly antiques. Opposite is one of the world's largest antique hypermarkets; make sure you have a full wallet when you visit it, as most of the goods are top collectors' items.

If you turn the other way out of the underground station, you will pass many shoe shops, more fashion chain stores, chemists, individual fashion shops such as *Crocodile* and *Friends*, branches of *Mothercare* and the big stationers and bookshop, *W H Smith*, all mingling with exotic restaurants to create a most individual atmosphere.

Kensington Church Street is a haven for antique collectors at its eastern end all the way to Notting Hill Gate, and at its western, Kensington High Street end for those looking out for the most up-to-date in clothing.

## The King's Road

**MAP REF 26F/27J**
It is hard to believe that this bustling thoroughfare was once a quiet country footpath. Mary Quant, the designer who revolutionised women's clothing, opened a boutique here in the 1950s, and the whole road promptly achieved a fashionable reputation which it has never lost. Today the road is lined with boutiques, antique shops, pubs, and bistros. The shops are friendly and music pounds from every doorway, particularly on Saturdays when the road is at its busiest.

## Covent Garden

**MAP REF 22D**
Since the old Flower Market closed in 1974, Covent Garden has blossomed in another way – as one of the most popular shopping areas and tourist attractions in London.

*Covent Garden scenes. Since the old fruit and vegetable market moved, the Piazza has been transformed into one of the best – and liveliest – shopping areas in London*

The Piazza now holds dozens of different stalls six days a week, mostly specialising in antiques, hand-made clothes, jewellery, pottery, and glass. There are shops selling an amazing array of speciality goods of individual and excellent quality – some most unusual and ultra-modern. The atmosphere of the place is enhanced by musicians and other street entertainers who seem to be performing all the time. The restored Market building is Central London's only permanent late-night shopping facility, open until 8pm six days a week. Dozens of restaurants and wine bars cater for every taste. Covent Garden is a definite must for every visitor to the capital.

### Knightsbridge

**MAP REF 27G**

Though the Knightsbridge, Brompton Road, and Sloane Street area has some of the most luxurious fashion boutiques, antique shops, and department stores in London, they all tend to be overshadowed by the magnificence of *Harrods*, the largest department store in Europe. The legend of Harrods is that it sells everything – from fresh octopus to travelling rowing machines, from alabaster bathtubs to gold-plated xylophones.

The stretch of the Brompton Road between Harrods and Sloane Street is choc-a-bloc with shoe shops – *St Laurent*, *Charles Jourdan*, *Rayne*, *Bally*, *Russell & Bromley* – and fashion shops, particularly *The Scotch House*, which specialises in woollens, knitwear, and woven tartans. On the corner of Knightsbridge and Sloane Street is *Harvey Nichols*, a luxurious department store particularly noted for women's and children's wear as well as all kinds of furniture and furnishings.

### Beauchamp Place

**MAP REF 27G**

Not far from Harrods, you can turn off the Brompton Road into the delightful Regency Beauchamp Place, a street full of highly-fashionable boutiques, top-class restaurants, and unusual antique shops, each with its own speciality.

### Sloane Street

**MAP REF 27K/L**

This fashionable, long, straight road runs from Sloane Street station to Sloane Square; here you can buy some of the finest antique and modern furniture, and gifts in the country. Definitely worth a visit at the Sloane Square end is the *General Trading Company* with its marvellous range of expensive

Foyles, in Charing Cross Road, is a labyrinth of books

furniture and household goods. In Sloane Square is the large department store, *Peter Jones*, a branch of the John Lewis Partnership.

**SPECIALITY STREETS**

### Charing Cross Road

**MAP REF 22D**

At the southern end of Tottenham Court Road, running down to Trafalgar Square, Charing Cross Road is a magnet for scholars and musicians. There is a great variety of new and second-hand bookshops, many of the latter specialising in antique and out-of-print volumes. *Foyles*, the largest bookshop in London, has a stock of over four million volumes; here you can find any new book you like, provided you are prepared to search for it. *Zwemmer's* carry the most extensive stock of English and foreign books on art and architecture in London. There are several narrow pedestrian precincts linking Charing Cross

Road with St Martin's Lane: *Cecil Court*, in particular, is lined with antiquarian and second-hand bookshops. Of the many shops selling music and musical instruments along and around the street, *Macari's* is particularly notable.

### Carnaby Street

**MAP REF 21K**

The Bard of Avon on the wall of the Shakespeare's Head pub has seen some changes in Carnaby Street. Built in the 18th century for 'poor and miserable objects of the neighbourhood', it was never fashionable. Then in the early 1960s a transformation took place, and the decrepit shops and houses were turned into 'boutiques'. By the mid 1960s it was a teenagers' paradise, but the craze lost momentum as it spread to the King's Road. Nevertheless Carnaby Street is still a must for many foreign tourists.

### Neal's Yard

**WC2**

**MAP REF 22D**

A most unusual, small area sandwiched between Neal Street

Gieves and Hawkes, leading Savile Row tailors

and Monmouth Street, where you will find a number of co-operatively run shops, stalls, and eating places specialising in wholefoods and organically-grown foods. There is even a wine shop. It is a particularly delicious place to visit at lunchtimes.

### Old Compton Street

MAP REF 22D

This street is famous for its exotic provision shops, the legacy of the 19th-century flood of immigrants – particularly French, Italians and Greeks – into the area.

### Tottenham Court Road

MAP REF 14E/15J

Running up from New Oxford Street to the Euston Road, Tottenham Court Road is now renowned for its shops selling hi-fi and electrical equipment. You can find everything from spare parts to the very latest systems. *Laskys* is the largest supplier with a number of branches along the road.

Tottenham Court Road was once regarded as the furniture centre of London, and there are still a number of high-quality stores specialising in this field: *Maples* and *Heal & Son* are the largest, where you will find everything you need for equipping the home. There is also a branch of the *Habitat* chain, whose modern furniture, fabrics, and accessories are internationally popular. Other interesting shops are *Paperchase*, a lovely place in which to wander among unique ranges of wrapping paper, cards, posters, and other paper items, and *The Reject Shop* which stocks a wide range of seconds in pottery and household goods.

### SPECIALIST SHOPS

Following is a selection of the establishments which specialise in a certain field. It excludes those shops already mentioned in previous pages.

### ANCIENT AND OLD-ESTABLISHED SHOPS

There are a number of small, old-fashioned shops dotted around London's streets which typify the Victorian 'gaslight' image of the capital. Those mentioned below have retained their essential character, and many still retain their original façades and fittings.

### R Allen and Co

117 Mount Street, W1

MAP REF 21H

This traditional English butcher's shop has a dark sculptured exterior and has served the residents of Mayfair for almost 200 years. It retains the mosaic wall tiles and threshold for which butchers' shops were once famous.

### Arthur Beale

194 Shaftesbury Avenue, WC2

MAP REF 22D

Rope has been made by this company for something approaching 400 years. The premises were originally located on the old Fleet River. Arthur Beale is now a general chandlers selling wire, rope, rigging and charts.

### J Floris

89 Jermyn Street, SW1

MAP REF 21L

Established in 1739, J Floris continues to sell perfume from its small but impressive premises, which are presided over by descendants of the original founder. It is considered by many to be London's leading perfumer.

### Gieves and Hawkes

1 Savile Row, W1

MAP REF 21K

A good English gentleman's suit is the best in the world, and Savile Row has long been the home of England's best tailors. Gieves and Hawkes was founded in 1771 and has been making fine clothes for discerning, and frequently very eminent, clients ever since.

### Fulham Pottery

184 New King's Road, SW6
DISTRICT MAP
Founded in 1671, this is said to be the oldest pottery in the country. Nowadays clay, tools and other equipment are on sale and complete beginners kits are also available.

### Inderwick's

45 Carnaby Street, W1
MAP REF 21K
Established in 1797, Inderwick's are the country's oldest pipe-makers. Their extensive stock includes briars, hookahs, and meerschaums.

### James Lock

6 St James's Street, SW1
MAP REF 21L
Established as hatters for over 200 years, Locks made the first bowler hat, known as the *Coke* after its inventor. At first glance, the shop seems little changed since Regency times.

### The Old Curiosity Shop

Portsmouth Street, WC2
MAP REF 23G
This venerable antique shop, which may date from the latter part of the 16th century, is said to have been the model for Charles Dickens' *Old Curiosity Shop*.

### Paxton and Whitfield

93 Jermyn Street, SW1
MAP REF 21L
An old-established cheese shop, crammed with cheeses of every variety and of the highest standard from all over the world. An unmistakable aroma guides patrons to its portals.

### Philip Poole

182 Drury Lane, WC2
MAP REF 23G
The age of pen and ink has almost gone, but at Philip Poole it is still possible to buy all kinds of pens, nibs, quills, and blotters.

### Purdey

57 South Audley Street, W1
MAP REF 21H
For more than 100 years, Purdey's have been the foremost makers of sporting guns. Each weapon is hand-made and today an order takes around four years to be completed.

### G Smith & Sons

74 Charing Cross Road, WC2
MAP REF 22D
An old-established tobacconists, specialising in snuff.

### James Smith

53 New Oxford Street, WC1
MAP REF 22D
Umbrellas and sticks of all kinds have been made and sold here since 1830. Smith's is notable for its old-fashioned signs and for the variety of its stock, which includes custom-made sword sticks and ceremonial maces for African chiefs. They also undertake repairs.

## ANTIQUE SHOPS

### Halcyon Days
15 Brook Street, W1
MAP REF 21G
Beautiful enamel boxes are one of the specialities of this shop.

### Spink
5 King Street, SW1
MAP REF 21L
Famous as coin and medal dealers since the mid-17th century, this shop has a wide selection of ancient and modern coins and decorations from all parts of the world.

### Strike One
51 Camden Passage, N1
DISTRICT MAP
These specialists in English 18th- and 19th-century clocks also repair and restore.

### Winifred Myers
91 St Martin's Lane, WC2
MAP REF 22E
A dealer in autographs. The stock includes the correspondence of famous men and women in the field of the arts, politics, etc, and covers a period of 500 years.

### Through the Looking Glass
563 King's Road, SW6
MAP REF 27J
Specialists in 19th-century mirrors which come in all imaginable sizes.

Purdey's, makers of sporting guns

## ART AND HANDICRAFT SHOPS

### British Crafts Centre
43 Earlham Street, WC2
MAP REF 22D
Exhibitions and retail displays of wallhangings, furniture, studio ceramics, pottery, wood, jewellery, etc.

### Candle Makers Supplies
28 Blythe Road, W14
DISTRICT MAP
Candle-making kits are sold here together with moulds and all necessary materials associated with the craft.

### Handweavers Studio and Gallery
29 Haroldstone Road, Walthamstow, E17
DISTRICT MAP
This shop sells and hires looms, spinning wheels, and weaving materials. Instruction for weavers is also available.

### London Diamond Centre
10 Hanover Street, W1
MAP REF 21K
Diamond cutters and polishers can be seen at work here; exhibitions and displays.

### Alec Tiranti

21 Goodge Place, W1
**MAP REF 14F**
All materials required for
sculpting and wood-carving
may be obtained here, including
casting equipment.

### Edgar Udny

83 – 85 Bondway, SW8
**MAP REF 29M**
Specialises in all kinds of mosaic
tiles, together with laying and
cutting tools.

**BUTTON AND BEAD SHOPS**

### The Button Queen

19 Marylebone Lane, W1
**MAP REF 21G**
Buttons of all kinds, both
modern and antique are the
speciality here.

### Eaton Bag Co

16 Manette Street, W1
**MAP REF 22D (Greek St)**
All kinds of sea shells are on sale
here, together with fossils,
polished and natural stones and
other objects.

### Ells and Farrier

5 Princes Street, W1
**MAP REF 21K**
Sells all kinds of beads and
sequins suitable for stringing or
decorating.

### A Taylor

1 Silver Place, W1
**MAP REF 22A (Ingestre Pl)**
Leather, horn, and plastic are
among the materials used to
make the buttons for sale here.
Buttons are also made and dyed
on the premises.

**BOOKS, MUSIC AND
RECORDS**

### Cinema Bookshop

13 Great Russell Street, WC1
**MAP REF 15J**
As the name implies, this shop is
filled with books and magazines
covering all aspects of the world
of cinema, including biographies
of stars and directors and
theoretical textbooks.

### Dillons

82 Gower Street, WC1
**MAP REF 15H (Goodge St)**
A huge new bookshop, with
more than 50 specialist
departments, on four floors.
The University of London's
bookshop.

### Dobell's Jazz and Folk Record Shop

21 Tower Street, WC2
**MAP REF 22D**
A treasure-house for all lovers of
jazz, folk, and the blues, Dobell's
has a huge collection of new and
secondhand records. Tapes are
also available. British musicians
are represented as strongly as
the American greats.

### Dress Circle

43 The Market, Covent Garden,
WC2
**MAP REF 23G**
This shop specialises in rare,
deleted and currently available
records of soundtracks, stage
musicals and recordings of
nostalgic interest as well as of
personalities. The catalogues
which the shop issues reveal the
astonishing amount and variety
of their stock.

### The Folk Shop

Cecil Sharp House, 2 Regents
Park Road, NW1
**DISTRICT MAP**
Folk music books and records
are available together with a
variety of traditional folk
instruments such as dulcimers,
tabors, and melodeons.

### A Moroni and Son

68 Old Compton Street, W1
**MAP REF 22D**
Newspapers and magazines
from all over the world are sold
here.

### Motor Books

33 St Martin's Court, WC2
**MAP REF 22E**
Literature on all aspects of the
motor car is available here,
together with volumes dealing
with motorcycles and aircraft.

### Stanford's

12 Long Acre, WC2
**MAP REF 22D**
Maps and guides are the
speciality here. The guide book
section is one of London's most
extensive, and there are not only
maps of Britain (including very
large scale Ordnance Survey
maps) but also of a wide range of
foreign cities and countries.
General books are also sold.

### Young World Children's Book Centre

229 Kensington High Street, W8
**DISTRICT MAP**
This shop is devoted to books for
children up to the age of
thirteen. Talks by authors and
artists are often given and a
quarterly newsletter dealing
with new children's books is also
available.

**CLOTHING SHOPS**

### Bedlam

114 Kensington Church Street,
W8
**DISTRICT MAP**
811 Fulham Road, SW6
**DISTRICT MAP**
Old-fashioned nightshirts and
caps are the speciality here.

### Berman and Nathan

18 Irving Street, WC2
**MAP REF 22E**
An old-established theatrical
costumiers, with hire service.

### John Lobb

9 St James's Street, SW1
**MAP REF 21L**
Craftsmen can be seen at work
in this old-established bespoke
shoemakers.

### Moss Bros

Bedford Street, WC2
MAP REF 22D
This is the most famous clothing hire firm in Britain. Clothes for all occasions are available and can be altered to suit individual requirements. They can also be purchased.

### Pineapple Dance Warehouse

7 Langley Street, WC2
MAP REF 22D
A combined studio and shop, where all kinds of dance wear and a large selection of leisure and activity wear, including shoes, can be bought.

### E H Rann

21 Sicilian Avenue, WC1
MAP REF 15M (Bloomsbury Way)
Specialists in school and regimental ties and badges.

### Patricia Roberts

31 James Street, WC2
MAP REF 22D
Highly individual designer knitwear is available here, along with exotic wools and Patricia Roberts' own knitting patterns.

### Theatre Zoo

8 New Row, WC2
MAP REF 22D
Animal costumes of all descriptions are available for hire here, plus stage jewellery, make-up and masks, etc.

#### FOOD SHOPS

### Bendicks Chocolates

53 Wigmore Street, W1
MAP REF 14C
Some 32 varieties of handmade chocolates are on sale here including bittermints and mint crisps.

### Justin de Blank (provisions)

42 Elizabeth Street, SW1
MAP REF 28B
High-quality take-away foods are presented here. All kinds of fresh quiches and pies, plus many kinds of preserved food are available.

### Camisa Fratelli

1a Berwick Street, W1
MAP REF 22A
A delicious, family-run Italian delicatessen, whose specialities are cheeses and home-made sausages.

### Ceres

269a Portobello Road, W11
DISTRICT MAP
A health food store with a wide selection of goods, including breads and cakes which are baked here.

### Cranks

Unit 11, Covent Garden Market, WC2
MAP REF 23G
A health and vegetarian shop, with its own wholegrain store.

### Curry Shop

37 The Market, Covent Garden, WC2
MAP REF 23G
All the items needed to make curry are available here, including cooking implements, serving dishes, tableware and a wide variety of herbs, spices, sauces, pulses, and the like.

### Markovitch

371–373 Edgware Road, W2
MAP REF 12E
Specialists in kosher food – meat, groceries, hot beef sandwiches, etc.

### Knightsbridge Coffee Centre

248 Fulham Road, SW10
MAP REF 26F
Retail coffee merchants selling freshly-ground coffee, together with coffee-making equipment.

An antique teapot at Twinings, long-established tea merchants

### Prestat

40 South Molton Street, W1
MAP REF 21G
A confectionery shop specialising in chocolates, some of which are made on the premises.

### Twinings

216 The Strand, WC2
MAP REF 23K
A famous tea merchant in a fascinating shop. Twinings have had premises here since 1716

#### MODEL, SPORT AND TOY SHOPS

### Barnums Carnival Novelties Ltd

67 Hammersmith Road, W14
DISTRICT MAP
Masks, false noses, and many varieties of false beards and moustaches are on sale here.

### Beatties

202 High Holborn, WC1
MAP REF 15M
Perhaps the largest model shop in the country. Model railways are a speciality here, with a secondhand department, but car, aeroplane and boat kits are also on sale.

61

### Davenport and Co

51 Great Russell Street, WC1
MAP REF 15M
The sign showing a rabbit
emerging from the traditional
top hat that proclaims an abundance
of conjurers' equipment
(professionals get their supplies
here).

### Kay Desmonde

17 Kensington Church Walk,
W8
DISTRICT MAP
A huge collection of English,
French, and German dolls,
mostly dating from the early
19th century.

### The Doll's House

Unit 29, The Market, Covent
Garden, WC2
MAP REF 23G
Reproduction and some antique
doll's houses are displayed here,
but it is very much a collectors'
shop. Miniature dolls and
furnishings are also available.

### Hardy Bros

61 Pall Mall, SW1
MAP REF 22B
This shop is world-famous for
fishing tackle and has sea, game
and coarse fishing equipment.

### Just Games

62 Brewer Street, W1
MAP REF 22A
Specialists in adult board games,
war games, card games, and
puzzles.

### The Kite Store

69 Neal Street, WC2
MAP REF 22D
Sells ready-made kites, materials
for making them and books on
the subject. Also available are
model hot air balloons.

### Steam Age, Mechanical Antiquities

19 Abingdon Road, W8
DISTRICT MAP
Engines, railways and

steamboats, mostly collectors'
items.

### Tradition

5A Shepherd Street, W1
MAP REF 21H
All kinds of lead soldiers are sold
here. The stock ranges from
Greek and Roman to modern
soldiers and includes painted
and unpainted items. Antique
uniforms and swords are also
available.

**MISCELLANEOUS SHOPS**

### Anything Left-Handed

65 Beak Street, W1
MAP REF 22A
Just what the name implies.
Scissors, tin-openers, pen nibs,
gardening, kitchen and
needlework aids are all
available, along with left-
handed playing cards (with the
symbols on all four corners).

### F H Brundle

75 Culford Road, N1
DISTRICT MAP
Specialists in nails. All kinds
available – wire nails, square
nails, lath nails, etc.

### L Cornelissen and Son

22 Great Queen Street, WC2
MAP REF 23G
Artist's materials are sold here
but an interesting speciality are
the quill pens and quills from
which pens can be made.

### The Glasshouse

65 Long Acre, WC2
MAP REF 22D
Glassblowers may be seen at
work on the premises. All kinds
of handblown articles are on
sale.

### Thomas Goode

19 South Audley Street, W1
MAP REF 21H
This company has produced top
quality china for around 150
years, with numerous crowned
heads, including Queen

Victoria, among its customers.
Personal crests or monograms
can be provided.

### Keith Harding

93 Hornsey Road, N7
DISTRICT MAP
Specialists in musical boxes of
which they hold an extensive
stock. Repairs and restoration
are also undertaken and books
on the subject are sold.

### Strangeways

Unit 19, Covent Garden Market,
WC2
MAP REF 23G
One of the best places to go for
the unusual and highly original:
including ceramics, prints and
objects with no immediate
practical function.

## STREET MARKETS

There is very little that cannot be bought in a London street market. Whether you want to pick up a bargain or buy an antique worth thousands, choose from the best meat and vegetable produce in the country, watch the traders at work, or just soak up the colourful atmosphere, there is a market to suit you.

### *Berwick Street Market*

W1
**MAP REF 22A**
This cheerful, cluttered market, with stalls on either side of the road, runs through the heart of Soho. The stallholders are noted for their generally good-humoured banter as they clamour to attract customers. Fruit and vegetable stalls predominate here, but shellfish, clothing, and household goods are also available, and some of the stalls are attached to neighbouring shops. The market is especially crowded at lunchtimes, as shoppers queue up at stalls which are reputed to sell some of the best quality fruit and vegetables in London.
*Monday – Saturday*

### *Brixton Market*

Electric Avenue, SW9
**DISTRICT MAP**
This market has a distinct Caribbean flavour, with much exotic food on display. There are also second-hand clothes and

*Street markets have a unique atmosphere; this is Berwick Street, in Soho*

household goods stalls, and the entire market is enlivened by the compulsive rhythms of West Indian music.
*Monday – Saturday
(Wednesday am only)*

### *Camden Lock*

NW1
**DISTRICT MAP**
Many of the stalls here are presided over by young and enthusiastic traders. You will find antiques, bric-à-brac, clothes, craft and food stalls in an attractive canalside setting.
*Saturday and Sunday*

63

Leadenhall Market: founded in the 14th century, the present buildings date from the 1880s

### Camden Passage

N1
**DISTRICT MAP**
A rich and varied mixture of antique shops and stalls. A holiday atmosphere pervades the market, largely because the majority of the traders give the impression of thoroughly enjoying their work. A few of the shopkeepers have been known to carry relaxation to the extreme by conducting their business from the Camden Head, the market's adopted pub, leaving a note on the shop door to direct prospective customers to their temporary premises. The arcades of the market become very crowded on Saturdays, and only those arriving early can hope to find a bargain. Camden Passage is as good a place as any for a wide variety of antiques, with dealers specialising in furniture, jewellery, prints, pottery, books, pub mirrors, period clothing, and silverware.
*Wednesday and Saturday*

### Chapel Market

White Conduit Street, N1
**DISTRICT MAP**
This rather congested market is very popular with the locals at weekends. Fruit and vegetables are always available, and there are usually stalls selling fish, groceries, and household goods.
*Tuesday – Sunday am*

### Church Street and Bell Street

Lisson Grove, NW8
**MAP REF 12E/F**
A mixture of stalls is to be found in these adjacent markets.

Antiques are well represented; there are also clothes, household and food stalls.
*Tuesday – Sunday*

### Columbia Road Market

Shoreditch, E2
**MAP REF 18D**
An enormous variety of flowers, plants, and shrubs make this market a Mecca for all gardening enthusiasts.
*Sunday am*

### East Street Market

Walworth, SE17
**MAP REF 31M**
This is an old-established general market with some bric-à-brac stalls. Plants and fruit are usually available on Sundays.
*Tuesday and Thursday – Sunday am (Saturday all day)*

### Jubilee Market

Covent Garden, WC2
**MAP REF 23G**
There are fruit, vegetable, and bric-à-brac stalls, and antiques (Mon), general goods (Tue – Fri), crafts (Sat & Sun).
*Monday – Sunday*

### Leadenhall Market

Gracechurch Street, EC3
**MAP REF 25G**
There has been a market in the general area of this site since the 14th century. Samuel Pepys recorded in his diary that he purchased a 'leg of beef, a good one, for sixpence' here. While still specialising in meat and poultry, Leadenhall also offers fish, vegetables, and plants. The Victorian arcade, containing cafes and pubs as well as rows of carcasses suspended on tiers of hooks outside the shops, is noted for its old-world market atmosphere, and is a favourite haunt for City office workers.
*Monday – Friday*

### Leather Lane

Holborn, EC1
**MAP REF 16F**

Fruit, groceries, vegetables, clothing, household goods of all descriptions – particularly crockery – are always on display here, and some of the most vociferous and quick-witted stallholders in the capital provide a feast of noisy entertainment for the vast crowds who throng the market during the lunch-hour. Bargains abound and the sight of an entire dinner service being expertly tossed in the air is a regular occurrence.

*Monday – Friday*

## Lower Marsh and The Cut

Lambeth, SE1
MAP REF 23M
This busy general market nestles in the shadow of Waterloo Station and becomes very popular during the lunch period.

*Monday – Saturday*

## New Caledonian Market

Bermondsey Square, SE1
MAP REF 32D (Bermondsey St)
The Old Caledonian Market moved to this site from Islington after the end of World War II, and its modern offspring is now primarily a dealers' antique market. An enormous selection of articles is on view, set out on closely-packed stalls, but you need to get there early to pick up a bargain; trading begins at 5am. Although something of a closed community, run principally by dealers for dealers, private collectors and casual visitors are made very welcome.

*Friday am*

## Northcote Road

Battersea, SW11
DISTRICT MAP
A fruit and vegetable market at its busiest on Saturdays.

*Monday – Saturday*

## North End Road

Fulham, SW6
DISTRICT MAP

This general market specialises in fruit and vegetables, and flowers and plants are on sale during the summer months.

*Monday – Saturday (Thursday am only)*

## Petticoat Lane

Middlesex Street, E1
MAP REF 18F
This most famous of all London markets got its name during the 17th century because of the number of old clothes dealers who congregated here. It opens around 9am, but the stallholders begin to set up their premises about 7.30am before an interested audience of sightseers. Despite its present-day cosmopolitan atmosphere, engendered by the Indian, West Indian, and Jewish communities which are prevalent in the area, Petticoat Lane still retains its essential Cockney character. The maze of stalls occupies every available corner, and there is very little in the way of household goods and clothes of every description that cannot be purchased.

*Sunday am*

## Portobello Road

Notting Hill, W11
DISTRICT MAP
A general market with fruit, vegetable and meat stalls operates all the week, but it is at its best on Saturdays. Then all the stalls and shops open – more than 2,000 of them – containing all kinds of furniture, clothes, jewellery, ancient gramophones and records, books, bottles, coins, medals, toys, a great deal of Victoriana, and an endless selection of junk. Buskers, street singers, photographers (some with monkeys), jostle with the crowds. It is rare to find a genuine bargain in the antique stalls at the lower end of the road these days, since all the traders are experts, but real finds can sometimes be made amongst the

piles of junk on the stalls beyond the Westway Flyover. A great cosmopolitan atmosphere.

*Monday – Saturday*

## Ridley Road

Hackney, E8
DISTRICT MAP
One of the better known of London's East End markets, the stalls here are patronised by the local Jewish and West Indian communities. It is a general market, with many fruit and vegetable stalls, and becomes very crowded on Saturdays.

*Monday – Saturday*

## Roman Road

Tower Hamlets, E3
DISTRICT MAP
A busy market with stalls on either side of the road offering a good variety of wares.

*Monday – Sunday (Monday, Wednesday, Friday and Sunday am only).*

## Shepherd's Bush

W12
DISTRICT MAP
A general market stretching alongside and under the railway viaduct between Shepherd's Bush and Goldhawk Road.

*Monday – Saturday (Thursday am only)*

## Walthamstow

The High Street, E17
DISTRICT MAP
This extensive general market straggles along either side of Walthamstow's main street. It is particularly busy towards the end of the week.

*Monday – Saturday (Wednesday am only)*

## Whitechapel Road

Tower Hamlets, E1
DISTRICT MAP
Stalls line the pavements of this famous East End thoroughfare, multiplying on Saturdays when the market really comes to life.

*Monday – Saturday*

### Whitecross Street

Islington, EC1
**MAP REF 17L**
A busy market which caters, to a large extent, for lunch-time shoppers. It is particularly crowded on Wednesdays and Fridays.
*Monday – Saturday*

### TRADE MARKETS

Noise, a rich variety of smells, and seeming confusion typify London's wholesale markets. In fact, all the business is carried out with breath-taking efficiency. Although the public is admitted, hordes of visitors are not encouraged; you have to be there early to see the markets in full swing.

### Billingsgate

North Quay, West India Docks, Isle of Dogs, E14
**DISTRICT MAP**
The first official mention of this historic wholesale fish market was made as long ago as the end of the 13th century, when a royal charter was granted to the Corporation of London for the sale of fish. A market is known to have been held on Billingsgate's old site in Lower Thames Street in the City of London at least 400 years earlier. From about 5am, Tuesday – Saturday, the market becomes a hive of activity and the air is pervaded by a pungent aroma of fish and the uninhibited language of the porters. By 8am most of the business is over and about 300 tons of fish will have changed hands.

### Borough Market

Stoney Street, SE3
**MAP REF 25H**
This fruit and vegetable market claims a direct descent from the market which was held on London Bridge in the 13th century; it was moved to the present site in 1757. It operates from Monday to Saturday, with traders commencing business as early as 3am. Activity builds up in a crescendo of noise and bustle between 6 and 7am, and most of the business has been completed by the middle of the morning.

### Covent Garden

Nine Elms, SW8
**DISTRICT MAP**
To the sorrow of many people – as the original Covent Garden had a unique and irreplaceable character – this famous fruit, vegetable, and flower market was moved in 1974 to its present purpose-built premises beside the river at Vauxhall. Trading begins about 4am; the flower market is on Saturdays during the summer.

### Smithfield

Charterhouse Street, EC1
**MAP REF 17J**
Smithfield is London's principal wholesale meat market, and its annual turnover of some 200,000 tons of produce makes it one of the largest meat, poultry, and provision markets in the world. The total area covered by all the market buildings is over eight acres. The site has great historical significance as the scene of tournaments and fairs, and has had livestock connections since the 12th century. Trading begins at 5am, Monday to Friday.

### Spitalfields

Commercial Street, E1
**MAP REF 18E**
Named after the priory of St Mary Spital which was founded here in 1197, Spitalfields refers both to the area and to the wholesale market, which trades in fruit, vegetables, and flowers. The market covers five acres to the east of Liverpool Street Station, on a site which was once a Roman burial ground. There are extensive underground chambers, used principally for ripening bananas, beneath the market. Trading begins at 4.30am every weekday and is generally completed by 9am.

*Smithfield meat market*

# CHURCHES AND CATHEDRALS

London's churches suffered great damage during the Fire of 1666 and, much later, the air raids of World War II. Of those which stand today, most date from the 17th and 18th centuries, but there are some earlier survivors, and a number of superb Victorian examples. A selection of the most interesting is given on the following pages.

### All Hallows

London Wall, EC2
**MAP REF 18C**
A stretch of the Roman wall which once surrounded the City of London can be seen in the churchyard. The church itself was designed by George Dance the Younger in the 18th century; its elegant and sumptuously decorated interior is by Sir John Soane. Exhibitions of church art are held here.

### All Souls'

Langham Place, W1
**MAP REF 14F**
John Nash designed and built this large church in 1822 to close the northward vista of Regent Street. It has a circular Classical portico surmounted by a slender needle spire.

### Brompton Oratory

Brompton Road, SW3
**MAP REF 26D**
An imposing Roman Catholic church built in Italian Renaissance style at the end of the 19th century. Its interior is rich in marble and mosaic decoration and the nave is a remarkable 51ft wide.

### Holy Trinity

Sloane Street, SW1
**MAP REF 26D**
Magnificent stained-glass windows designed by Edward Burne-Jones and made by William Morris light the interior of this splendid 19th-century church. It was designed by J D Sedding, one of the principal architects of the Arts and Crafts Movement.

The remarkable ceiling of Brompton Oratory

### St Alfege

Church Street, Greenwich, SE10
**DISTRICT MAP**
Built in 1718 to the designs of Nicholas Hawksmoor, this church houses the tombs of General Wolfe (d.1759) and the 'father of English church music', Thomas Tallis.

### St Anne Limehouse

Commercial Road, E14
**DISTRICT MAP**
One of Hawksmoor's spectacular Classical-style East End churches. It was built in 1712 and is especially notable for its imposing tower.

### St Bartholomew the Great

West Smithfield, EC1
**MAP REF 17J**
This is one of the few surviving examples of Norman architecture in London. It dates from the 12th century and is the chancel of a great Norman monastery church which once stood here. It contains a fine oriel window, the font where Hogarth was baptised in 1697, a 15th-century stone screen, and a half-timbered Elizabethan gatehouse above a 13th-century arch.

### St Ethelburga-the-Virgin

Bishopsgate, EC2
**MAP REF 18C**
Entered by a 14th-century doorway, this tiny medieval building is one of the best preserved of the City's pre-Fire churches.

### St Etheldreda, or Ely Chapel

Ely Place, EC1
**MAP REF 16F**
Originally built in the 13th century as the chapel of a palace of the Bishops of Ely, the structure is two-storeyed and has a massive vaulted undercroft dating from 1252. It is the oldest pre-Reformation Roman Catholic church in London.

### St George

Bloomsbury Way, WC1
**MAP REF 15M**
Noted for its striking façade, this 18th-century church was built by Nicholas Hawksmoor.

### St Giles-in-the-Field

St Giles High Street, WC2
**MAP REF 15J**
This church's fine 161ft Baroque steeple makes it a prominent landmark. A church was founded on this site by Matilda, the wife of Henry I, in the 12th century, but the present building dates from the 18th century. It was beautifully restored in 1952–53, and has superb interior decorations and fittings.

### St Helen Bishopsgate

Great St Helen's, EC3
**MAP REF 25G**
One of the largest churches in the City, this magnificent structure was built in the 13th century and was originally two churches joined by an arcade of pillars. The church is famous for its beautiful brasses, two fine sword-rests (one dating from 1665 and very rare), and a carved Jacobean pulpit.

### St James's

Piccadilly, W1
**MAP REF 22B**
A Wren church of 1676 with a magnificent galleried interior beneath a barrel-vaulted ceiling. The font, reredos, altarpiece, and organ case are all the work of the master-woodcarver, Grinling Gibbons.

St Martin-in-the-Fields was the first church to combine a classical portico with a steeple

between 1066 and 1290 when the neighbourhood had a large Jewish population. The church was rebuilt after bomb damage, and the present spire incorporates a replica of the incendiary bomb which gutted the interior. It is the guild church of the Corporation of London.

## St Martin-in-the Fields
Trafalgar Square, WC2
**MAP REF 22E**
The medieval church on this site was extensively rebuilt by James Gibbs in the early 18th century. It has an imposing temple-like portico, and a spacious galleried interior. Buckingham Palace is within the parish boundaries, and there are royal boxes at the east end of the church. The vaulted crypt contains a 16th-century chest and an 18th-century whipping post, but is better known for the fact that it is opened each evening as a shelter for the homeless.

## St Mary-le-Bow
Cheapside, EC2
**MAP REF 24D**
Restored by Wren after the Great Fire, this church was extensively fire-damaged during the Blitz. Wren's steeple survived, however, and still towers over Cheapside. The famous Bow Bells originally rang as a curfew. Those born within their sound are said to be true Cockneys.

## St Paul's
Covent Garden, WC2
**MAP REF 22D**
The first new Anglican church to be built in London after the Reformation, St Paul's was designed by Inigo Jones between 1631 and 1633, and is known as the Actors' Church.

## St James Garlickhythe
Upper Thames Street, EC4
**MAP REF 24D**
Founded as long ago as the 12th century, the present church on this site was built by Wren after the Great Fire, and is one of his more elaborate designs. Its most distinguishing exterior feature is the handsome spire. The interior, which was restored after bomb damage, has excellent woodwork, as well as ironwork hat racks and sword rests. The church reputedly owes its name to the fact that garlic was once sold nearby.

## St John
Smith Square, SW1
**MAP REF 29K**
This notable baroque-style church (1713–28) by Thomas Archer was gutted during World War II, and now serves as a musical and cultural centre.

## St Lawrence Jewry
Gresham Street, EC2
**MAP REF 17M**
Rebuilt by Wren on the site of a medieval church, this church stands in the forecourt of the Guildhall. The name Jewry has survived from the period

Inside St Paul's Cathedral – Sir
Christopher Wren's masterpiece

## *St Paul's Cathedral*

Ludgate Hill, EC4

**MAP REF 24D**

Wren's crowning masterpiece,
begun in 1675 after the Great
Fire. The beautiful central dome
rises to a height of 365ft and
around its interior is the famous
Whispering Gallery, where a
message whispered into the wall
on one side can clearly be heard
112ft away on the other side.
The Gallery is reached through a
doorway in the western corner
of the South Transept that leads
to the stairs, which also give
access to the library and the two
external galleries of the dome
with their panoramic views
across London. From the end of
the nave there is a superb view
along the whole length of the
cathedral through the Choir to
the High Altar and its ornate
canopy, the focal point of the
whole building. The altar is a

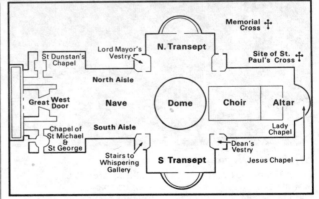

modern replacement of the one
which was damaged during
World War II, and is an exact
copy of Wren's original design.
The cathedral contains
numerous chapels, many of
which contain exquisite
furniture and decorations. Holy
Communion is celebrated on
most days in the Chapel of St
Dunstan at the western end of
the cathedral. The crypt
contains the tombs of Wren,

Nelson, Wellington, Reynolds,
and Turner, and among other
notable monuments is the 17th-
century effigy of John Donne,
poet and Dean of the Cathedral,
which survived the Great Fire.
The carved wooden choir stalls
are by Grinling Gibbons.

Their Royal Highnesses the
Prince and Princess of Wales
were married in St Paul's in
1981.

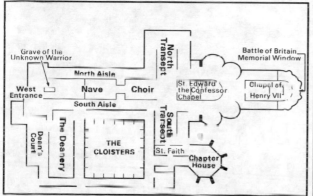

## Westminster Abbey

Parliament Square, SW1
**MAP REF 29G**
Edward the Confessor was determined to have the abbey at Westminster enlarged and made the crowning-place of English kings; his Norman church was consecrated on 28 December 1065, and every English sovereign since has been crowned here. All that remains of Edward the Confessor's building are the Chamber of Pyx (once the Royal Treasury) and the Norman Undercroft (which now houses a museum). The whole abbey was rebuilt from 1245 to 1269 in honour of Edward, and rebuilding continued throughout the 15th and early 16th centuries. The 225ft-high towers were added in the mid-18th century by Nicholas Hawksmoor. Much 19th-century renovation has

*The nave of Westminster Abbey is over 100ft tall*

marred the external detail, but the abbey's proportions still give a sense of continuity and permanence. The graceful flying buttresses and the delicately-shaped walls of the Henry VII Chapel make it one of the most impressive sights in the capital, particularly when viewed from Parliament Square or Dean's Yard to the south

The Abbey presents a stunning array of historical and commemorative monuments and memorials in a setting of outstanding architectural beauty. There are elaborately-carved royal tombs, including that of Elizabeth I; memorials to the nation's statesmen, politicians, scientists, servicemen; and the famous Poets' Corner. The Coronation Throne, with the historic Stone of Scone, and the tomb of the Unknown Warrior, brought from Flanders in 1920, attract particular attention.

### Southwark Cathedral

Borough High Street, SE1
**MAP REF 25H**
A church has stood on this site since the 7th century, but it was not until 1905 that the basically 16th-century parish church of St Saviour was elevated to cathedral status. Despite rebuilding, particularly during the 19th century, its medieval Gothic style has remained largely intact, and parts of the church date back to at least the 13th century. It is, after Westminster Abbey, the most important Gothic building in London.

Begun in 1895, Westminster Cathedral is an exuberant exercise in Italian-inspired architecture. It has the widest nave in England

### Westminster Cathedral

Ashley Place, Victoria Street, SW1
**MAP REF 28E**
The principal Roman Catholic cathedral in Britain was built between 1895 and 1903 in an Italian-Byzantine style by the distinguished architect J F Bentley. It is an imposing building, with a 273ft campanile and the widest nave in England. The most outstanding works of the interior are Eric Gill's early 20th-century Stations of the Cross.

Among the other outstanding Wren City Churches are: *St Andrew*, Holborn Circus, EC1, which contains the organ (given by Handel in 1750), font, and pulpit from the Foundling

Hospital; *St Anne and St Agnes*, Gresham Street, EC2, with its fine collection of ecclesiastical antiquities; *St Benet*, Paul's Wharf, off Queen Victoria Street, EC4, the Welsh Metropolitan Church; *St Bride*, Fleet Street, EC4; *St Clement Danes*, Strand, WC2, the memorial church of the RAF; *St Clement Eastcheap*, Clements Lane, EC4; *St Magnus the Martyr*, Lower Thames Street, EC3, containing outstanding woodwork; *St Margaret Pattens*, Rood Lane, Eastcheap, EC3, with two canopied pews, one marked C W; *St Martin-within-Ludgate*, Ludgate Hill, EC4; *St Mary Abchurch*, Abchurch Lane, EC4, containing Grinling Gibbons reredos of 1686 and a notable painted dome; and *Stephen Walbrook*, Walbrook, EC4.

# PALACES

### Buckingham Palace
The Mall, SW1
**MAP REF 21M**
This most famous of royal homes was built in 1703 by the Duke of Buckingham, and subsequently bought by George III in 1762. Nash altered and remodelled it for George IV in 1825, but it was not much used until Victoria came to the throne in 1837. It has been the London home of the monarch ever since, and the interior is not open to the public. When the sovereign is in residence, the Royal Standard is flown. The Changing of the Guard, a colourful and very popular ceremony, is carried out by the Brigade of Guards in the forecourt most mornings (see page 5).

### Royal Mews
Buckingham Palace, SW1
**MAP REF 28D**
Designed by John Nash, the Royal Mews contain the state coaches, including the Gold State Coach of 1762 which has been used for every coronation since. In the stables are the Windsor Greys and Cleveland Bay carriage horses.
*Open daily Spring & Summer 10.30 – 5 weekends only Autumn & Winter. Admission charge.*

### Greenwich
**DISTRICT MAP**
The best way to visit Greenwich, which has one of England's finest riverside vistas, and a superb group of royal buildings, is by one of the boats which leave from Charing Cross, Westminster, or Tower piers.

### Royal Naval College
Consists of buildings designed by Webb and Wren, with additions by Hawksmoor, Vanbrugh, and Ripley. Formerly the Naval Hospital, it became a College in

Buckingham Palace overlooks the green expanse of St James's Park

1873. Particularly splendid are the Chapel, rebuilt in the 18th century, and the Painted Hall with its ceiling by Sir James Thornhill.
*Painted Hall and Chapel only open daily (ex Thu) 2.30 – 5 (Closed 25 Dec). Admission free.*

### Queen's House

Built by Inigo Jones for Queen Henrietta Maria as part of the original Greenwich Palace (subsequently demolished by Charles II), it now houses part of the National Maritime Museum: a notable collection of paintings, maps, and models. The Nelson collection, Navigation Room, and the Barge House are of considerable interest.

*Open Mon–Fri, BHs 10–6; Sun 2.30–6. Admission free.*

### Old Royal Observatory

In Greenwich Park – which was laid out to plans by Le Nôtre, Famous French gardener of the time of Louis XIV – the Observatory is now part of the National Maritime Museum, exhibiting items of astronomical, horological, and navigational interest.

*Open Mon–Fri 10–5 (6 in summer); Sat 10–5.30 (6 in summer); Sun 2–5 (5.30 in summer) (Closed Good Fri, May Day, 24–26 Dec & 1 Jan). Admission charge.*

### Cutty Sark

Greenwich Pier

This famous tea clipper was the fastest to be built (in 1869). She once sailed 363 miles in a single day, and has been preserved here in dry dock since 1957.

*Open Mon–Fri 10.30–5; Sun 2.30–5 (6 in summer) (Closed 24–26 Dec & 1 Jan). Admission charge.*

### Gipsy Moth IV

Greenwich Pier

The yacht in which Sir Francis Chichester sailed single-handed round the world in 1966–67, starting the fashion for round-the-world sailing races.

*Open daily Apr–Oct 10.30–6. Admission charge.*

## Hampton Court Palace

DISTRICT MAP

Built by Cardinal Wolsey for Henry VIII, this magnificent group of buildings played an important part in the lives of the monarchy, and the influence of the individual kings and queens can still be seen: Henry VIII built the stunning hammer-beamed Great Hall; Elizabeth I added extensively to the gardens with plants brought from the New World; William and Mary commissioned Wren to remodel parts of the palace, and his Fountain Court is particularly fine; William also created the famous maze.

The last monarch to live in Hampton Court was George II, and today it can be seen as a grand palace, filled with paintings, tapestries, and furniture, resounding to the echoes of great moments of English history.

*Open: Gardens and grounds daily, summer 7–9 (or dusk) winter 9–dusk. Kitchens, cellars and Tudor tennis courts Apr–Sep, Mon–Sat 9.30–6; Sun 11–6. Admission free.*

*State apartments open Apr–Sep, Mon–Sat 9.30–6, Sun 11–6; Oct–Mar, Mon–Sat 9.30–5, Sun 2–5 (Closed Good Fri, 24–26 Dec & 1 Jan). Admission charge.*

## Houses of Parliament and Westminster Hall

SW1

MAP REF 29K

The Houses of Parliament are also known as the Palace of Westminster because from the time of Edward the Confessor to Henry VIII the site was the main London residence of the monarch.

Most of the original palace was destroyed by fire in 1834, and the present Gothic-style building was designed by Sir Charles Barry and Augustus Pugin. The two chambers of Parliament are set either side of a central hall and corridor – the House of Lords to the south and

One of the superb details which give the Houses of Parliament much of their character

the House of Commons to the north.

At the north end is the famous Clock Tower known to all as Big Ben. The name actually refers to the huge 13½-ton bell which strikes the hours. The minute hands on the clock's four 23ft-wide dials are each as tall as a double-decker bus. It is well known for keeping perfect time; tiny adjustments are made by adding or removing old pennies to or from the mechanism.

While Parliament is in session the Union Jack flies from the south tower, Victoria Tower, by day and by night a light shines from the Clock Tower.

The House of Commons suffered bomb damage in 1941 and a new chamber was constructed to the design of Sir Giles Gilbert Scott and opened in 1950.

*To gain admission to the Strangers' Galleries join the queue*

Westminster Hall, with the statue of Oliver Cromwell in the foreground

at St Stephens entrance from approx 4.30pm Mon–Thu, approx 9.30am Fri (House of Commons) or from approx 2.30pm Tue & Wed, from 3pm Thu & occasionally 11am Fri (House of Lords) or by arrangement with MP (House of Commons) or Peer (House of Lords). Free although guides require payment if employed.

Westminster Hall was originally constructed by William Rufus, son of William the Conqueror, as an addition to the Palace of Westminster. It was remodelled at the end of the 14th century: the lower parts of the Norman walls were retained and massive buttresses added to support the 600 tons of roof. An outstanding engineering feat in its day, it meant that supporting piers were no longer needed and it is the earliest surviving example of a hammer-beam roof. The Hall has miraculously survived almost intact.

*Open Mon–Thu am, by arrangement with an MP only. Free although guides require payment if employed.*

### Kensington Palace

W8

**MAP REF 19J**

Acquired by William III in 1689, remodelled and enlarged by Wren, the Palace is today still a Royal residence, that of Princess Margaret. The state apartments are open to the public and contain pictures and furniture from the royal collection.

The *Court Dress Collection* displays costumes worn at court from 1750 to the present day.

Westminster Hall, with the statue of Oliver Cromwell in the foreground

*Open Mon–Sat 9–5; Sun 1–5 (Closed Good Fri, 24–26 Dec & 1 Jan). Admission charge*

### Kew Palace

Kew

**DISTRICT MAP**

Standing in the Royal Botanical Gardens, this Dutch-gabled 17th- to 18th-century house contains souvenirs of George III. Queen Charlotte died here in 1818.

*Open daily Apr–Sep, 11–5.30.*

**Queen Charlotte's Cottage**

The interior remains as it was in the 18th century when royalty were in residence.

*Open Sat, Sun & BH, Apr–Sep 11–5.30. Admission charge.*

The most picturesque parts of St James's Palace date from Tudor times

## Lambeth Palace

Lambeth Palace Road, SE1
**MAP REF 30B**
Unlike other palaces, this one has no connection with royalty. It has been the London residence of the Archbishop of Canterbury for 700 years, but much of it was rebuilt during the 19th century. Of the old palace, the most interesting parts are the Lollards Tower and the Gatehouse, both of the 15th century, and the 13th-century Chapel Crypt. Parts of the palace, and its grounds, are open to the public.

## Lancaster House

Stable Yard, off The Mall, SW1
**MAP REF 22C**
This massive palace was originally built in the 19th century for the 'grand old' Duke of York. Chopin played here before Queen Victoria in 1848. It is now a government hospitality centre and is usually open to the public.

## Marlborough House

Pall Mall, SW1
**MAP REF 22C**
Built by Wren for the Duke of Marlborough. In 1850 it became the official residence of the Prince of Wales. George V was born here; later both Queen Alexandra and Queen Mary lived here. The house is now the Commonwealth Centre and is open by appointment.

## St James's Palace

St James's Street, SW1
**MAP REF 22C**
The original palace was started by Henry VIII in 1531, and, after the destruction of Whitehall Palace, was the sovereign's official London residence. Foreign ambassadors are still appointed to the Court of St James's. The Gatehouse facing St James's Street is the main remnant of the Tudor building, and has the initials of Henry VIII and Anne Boleyn carved over the doors. The Chapel Royal was originally built by Henry VIII but was much altered in 1837. However, the ceiling by Holbein is original.

St James's Palace is now occupied by servants of the Crown, and is not open to the public. However, services may be attended in the Chapel Royal between October and July.

## Tower of London

EC3
**MAP REF 25L**
Begun by William the Conqueror in about 1078 as a symbol of power over rebellious Londoners, the Tower stands today as perhaps the most important castle in England. As well as being used as a royal palace until the 17th century, it has also been a mint, observatory, arsenal, menagerie, public records office and, of course, state prison, mainly reserved for the high and mighty who incurred the displeasure of king or government.

The nucleus of the fortress, from which it gets the name 'Tower' rather than 'Castle', is the original White Tower, which now contains the Royal Armouries – including four of Henry VIII's personal armours. Also notable here is the Chapel of St John, probably London's most outstanding example of early Norman architecture, little changed since the 11th century.

Forming part of the Tower's inner defences is the Bell Tower, in which many famous prisoners were detained, among them Princess Elizabeth and the Duke of Monmouth.

Originally called the Garden Tower, the Bloody Tower is believed to have been the site of the murder of the little Princes by their uncle Richard III. However, the tower was not called 'Bloody' until 1597. Its most famous prisoner was

probably Sir Walter Raleigh, who spent 12 years here in a specially constructed top floor. The gateway under the Bloody Tower opens out on to Tower Green, where Royal prisoners were executed. The less exalted – though equally famous – ended their days on the more public scaffold on nearby Tower Hill. In the days when the Thames was one of London's principal highways, prisoners were brought by boat from Westminster to the Tower, arriving at the infamous Traitors' Gate.

Other royal deaths associated with the Tower include those of Henry VI, who may have been murdered in 1471 in the Wakefield Tower, and the Duke of Clarence, believed to have been drowned in a butt of malmsey wine in the Bowyer Tower in 1478.

The half-timbered Queen's House is the finest example of a Tudor domestic building in London. All state prisoners were taken here on arrival, where they were searched and registered.

The Yeoman Warders - universally known as 'beefeaters' - wear a ceremonial uniform unchanged in style since the reign of Henry VIII; their everyday uniform is similar but less colourful. In the inner ward of the Tower there are tame ravens which may originate from the former King's Menagerie at one time kept here. Tradition has it that if the ravens leave, the Tower will fall.

*Left: the White Tower, or keep, of the Tower of London. Above: a Yeoman Warder. Below: one of the exhibits in the Royal Armouries*

Although six is the minimum requirement, eight are kept for safety's sake.

The magnificent Crown Jewels are kept underground in a new Jewel House entered from the Waterloo barracks.

The Tower is locked up each night during the Ceremony of the Keys, which the public may view by appointment only. *Open Mar – Oct, Mon – Sat 9.30 – 5, Sun 2 – 5; Nov – Feb, Mon – Sat 9.30 – 4 (Closed 1 Jan, Good Fri & 24 – 26 Dec. Jewel House closed Feb). Admission charges.*

### Carlyle's House

24 Cheyne Row, Chelsea, SW3
**DISTRICT MAP**
Thomas Carlyle, one of the most distinguished essayists in the English language, moved from Scotland to London in 1834; he lived in this house in Chelsea for the rest of his life.

Here he wrote his major historical works, including *The French Revolution*, and he became known as the Sage of Chelsea. The house, now owned by the National Trust, contains much Carlyle memorabilia; his sound-proofed attic study, where he took refuge from 'dogs, cocks, pianofortes and insipid men', is faithfully preserved, as is the kitchen where he often entertained Tennyson.

*Open 29 Mar – Oct Wed – Sun & BH Mons, 11 – 5. Admission charge.*

### Dickens' House

48 Doughty Street, WC1
**MAP REF 16B**
Dickens and his family lived here from 1837 to 1839, during which period he completed *The Pickwick Papers*, wrote *Oliver Twist* and *Nicholas Nickleby*, and began *Barnaby Rudge*. There is a reconstruction of Dingly Dell Kitchen, as described in *The Pickwick Papers*, in the basement. The Dotheboys Hall display case proves that Dickens did not exaggerate the horrors of 19th-century school life: Smike was based on a boy called George Taylor whose 'Happy' letter to his mother was followed by the bill for his tombstone.

*Open Mon – Sat 10 – 5 (Closed Sun, BH, Good Fri & Xmas week). Admission charge.*

### Hogarth's House

Hogarth Lane, Great West Road, Chiswick, W4
**DISTRICT MAP**
In 1749 Hogarth moved to this 17th-century house in Chiswick which he called 'a little country

box by the Thames'. It was his home for 15 years, and now contains many paintings, prints, and personal mementoes.

*Open Mon, Wed – Sat 11 – 6; Sun 2 – 6 (4pm Oct – Mar) (Closed Tue, Good Fri, 1st 2 weeks Sep, last 3 weeks Dec & 1 Jan). Admission free.*

### Dr Johnson's House

17 Gough Square, EC4
**MAP REF 23K**
Samuel Johnson lived in this handsome 18th-century house between 1749 and 1759 and it

Below: the exterior of Dr Johnson's House, little changed since the 18th century. Right: the interior of the house, furnished in contemporary style

was here that he completed his *Dictionary*. The house is full of mementoes of the man who is the most frequently quoted Englishman after Shakespeare.

*Open Mon – Sat; May – Sep 11 – 5.30, Oct – Apr 11 – 5 (Closed Sun, BH, Good Fri & Xmas). Admission charge.*

### Keats's House

Wentworth Place, Keats Grove, Hampstead, NW3
**DISTRICT MAP**
From 1818 to 1820 John Keats lived at Wentworth Place with his friend Charles Brown, while next door lived his lover and nurse Fanny Brawne. It was here that Keats produced his greatest poetry, including the famous *Odes*. The two Regency houses occupied by Keats and Fanny have now been made into one. They are furnished in period style and contain manuscripts, letters, and relics. *Ode to a Nightingale* was written in the garden.

*Open Mon – Sat 10 – 1 & 2 – 6; Sun & BH 2 – 5 (Closed Good Fri, Etr Sat, May Day, Xmas & 1 Jan). Admission free.*

## Wellington Museum (Apsley House)

149 Piccadilly, W1
**MAP REF 21J**
This mansion was designed by Robert Adam in the late 18th century and was the London home of the 1st Duke of Wellington from 1829 until his death in 1852. Apsley House, known during the Iron Duke's time as 'Number One, London', now contains some outstanding paintings; these include Goya's *Wellington on Horseback*, Murillo's *Unknown Man*, Caravaggio's *Agony in the Garden*, and a number by Velazquez. There are busts and statues – including one of Napoleon by Canova which was presented to Wellington by George IV – fine porcelain, banners, uniforms, and a host of other memorabilia.
*Open Tue – Thu & Sat 10 –6; Sun 2.30 – 6. Admission charge.*

Some famous London homes you can only view from the outside:

### Wren's House

49 Bankside, SE1
**MAP REF 24E**
A plaque on the wall of this 17th-century house marks the building in which Wren lived while supervising the rebuilding of St Paul's.

### Pepys's House

12 Buckingham Street, WC2
**MAP REF 22E**
Samuel Pepys, most famous of all diarists for his descriptive account of life in Charles II's London, lived in this house from 1679 until 1688.

### Handel's House

25 Brook Street, W1
**MAP REF 21G**
George Frederick Handel lived in this house for 35 years, until his death in 1759. *The Messiah* was composed here.

### Karl Marx's House

Leoni's Quo Vadis, 26 Dean Street, W1
**MAP REF 22A**
Karl Marx lived in a room above this long-established Italian restaurant from 1851 to 1856.

### Oscar Wilde's House

34 Tite Street, SW3
**MAP REF 27M**
Oscar Wilde, famous dramatist and wit, lived here with his wife from 1884 until his trial in 1895.

## Wesley's House

47 City Road, EC1
**MAP REF 18B**
John Wesley, founder of Methodism, lived in this house from 1778 until his death in 1791. His study, bedroom, and prayer room are preserved, along with his furniture and many personal items.
*Open Mon – Sat 10 – 4, Admission charge.*

# BUILDINGS

## Bank of England
Threadneedle Street, EC2
**MAP REF 25G**
This is the bank of the Government, incorporated in 1694 by Royal Charter. The old 18th-century building was almost entirely rebuilt between 1925 and 1939 by Sir Herbert Baker, who retained only the massive outer walls and columns. In the vaults is stored Britain's gold reserve. Since the 'No Popery' riots of 1780, a nightly 'picket' from the Brigade of Guards keeps watch at the Bank.

*The Bank of England – storehouse of the nation's gold*

## British Telecom Tower
Maple Street, W1
**MAP REF 14E**
Completed in 1964, this 619ft-high needle of concrete and glass is one of the tallest buildings in London. It has a revolving restaurant and a viewing platform which are reached by high-speed lift now closed to the public.

## Caxton Hall
Caxton Street, SW1
**MAP REF 29G**
The name and look of this registry office were once familiar to all followers of high society doings, as until 1977 it was the most fashionable place for out-of-church weddings.

## Central Criminal Courts
Old Bailey, EC4
**MAP REF 17J**
The notorious Newgate Prison, which stood on this site, was the scene of public executions between 1783 and 1868. It was demolished in 1902 and replaced by the Central Criminal Court, which takes its popular name from the street in which it stands. Most of the major trials of this century have been heard here, including those of Crippen, Christie, Haig, and the Kray brothers. The public may view the proceedings in No 1 Court by queueing for a seat in the Visitors' Gallery (entrance in Newgate Street).
*Admission free.*

## Clarence House
Stable Yard, St James's Palace, SW1
**MAP REF 22C**
Designed by Nash for William IV when he was Duke of Clarence, this house was restored for Princess Elizabeth before her accession in 1952. Princess Anne was born here and it is now the home of Queen Elizabeth, the Queen Mother.

## The College of Arms
Queen Victoria Street, EC4
**MAP REF 24D**
Sometimes called the Heralds' Office, this is the official authority on all heraldic matters. Its officers, who have resounding titles such as Rouge Dragon Pursuivant, also assist the Earl Marshal, an office hereditary to the Duke of Norfolk since 1672, in arranging state ceremonies such as coronations. The imposing 17th-century building itself stands on a site that has been occupied by the College of Arms since 1555.

## Commonwealth Institute
Kensington High Street, W8
**DISTRICT MAP**

Contains over 40 exhibitions depicting life in the countries of the Commonwealth. There is also a library, art gallery, and arts centre.

*Open Mon–Sat 10–5.30; Sun 2–5 (Closed Good Fri, May Day, 24–26 Dec & 1 Jan). Admission free in daytime; admission charge in the evening.*

## The Guildhall

EC2

**MAP REF 17M**

The building dates from 1411, but only the walls of the medieval great hall, porch, and crypt survive. Restoration work after Blitz damage was completed in 1954 to the designs of Sir Giles Gilbert Scott. Here the Court of Common Council, which administers the

City, meets and entertains; the Lord Mayor's Banquet is held in the great hall, at the end of which stand huge wooden **figures** of Gog and Magog, legendary British giants who are said to have fought against Trojan invaders around 1000 BC.

*Open May–Sep, Mon–Sat 10–5; Sun & BH 2–5. Admission free.*

**The Guildhall Library**, founded in 1425, contains an unrivalled collection of books, manuscripts, and prints on all aspects of London.

*Open Mon–Fri 9.30–5 (Closed BH).*

**The Guildhall Clock Museum** contains 700 exhibits illustrating 500 years of time-keeping.

The Great Hall of the Guildhall has been the setting for City ceremonial since the 15th century

*Open Mon–Fri 9.30–5 (Closed BH).*

## The House of St Barnabas

Greek Street, W1

**MAP REF 22D**

One of the finest Georgian houses in London, with richly decorated ceilings, woodcarvings, and ironwork, the House of St Barnabas was founded as a charitable institution in 1846 to help the destitute in London.

*Open Wed 2.30–4.15; Thu 11–12.30 (guided tours). Admission free (donations).*

Richard Rogers' Lloyd's Building brings Post-modernism to the City

## The Inns of Court

There used to be 12 Inns of Court, but only three still exist in their traditional capacity for the education and lodging of lawyers – Gray's Inn, Lincoln's Inn, and Temple. The others survive only in the names of streets and buildings, or as premises whose function has changed.

### Gray's Inn

Gray's Inn Road, WC1
MAP REF 23K
The Hall dates back to 1560; the Library is 18th-century. Both were restored after being extensively damaged during World War II. The gardens are thought to have been laid out by Francis Bacon, the most notable member of the Inn, who lived here from 1576 to 1626.
*Open: gardens May – Sep, Mon – Fri 12 – 2.30. Buildings by prior arrangement. Admission free.*

### Lincoln's Inn

Chancery Lane, WC2
MAP REF 23K
Rightly recognised for its fine architecture (some, like the Gatehouse with its original oak doors, dating from the early 16th century) it is perhaps best known for its 12 acres of peaceful and beautifully-kept gardens – Lincoln's Inn Fields.
*Open: gardens and Chapel Mon – Fri 12 – 2.30 (Closed Easter, Christmas, 1 Jan); other buildings only by prior arrangement.*

### The Temple

Fleet Street, EC4
MAP REF 23K
The best way to enjoy this Inn of Court, named after the Knights Templar who occupied the riverside site from about 1160, is to walk through its lanes and alleys. The buildings are very fine and generally very old, and the sense of space is well married to that indefinable air of peace peculiar to all the Inns.

The Temple Church, whose nave and porch date from the 12th century, is one of only four round churches surviving in England.
*Temple Church: open daily 10 – 4 (except for services) Middle Temple Hall: open Mon – Fri 10 – 11.30, 3 – 4.00 (Closed Xmas, week after Etr, Aug – mid Sept) Inner Temple Hall: open Mon – Fri 10 – 11, 1.45 – 4. Admission free.*

## The Jewel Tower

Abingdon Street, SW1
MAP REF 29K
This inconspicuous moated tower is in fact a survival of the medieval Palace of Westminster. It was built in 1365 to house the monarch's personal treasure, and this remained its function until the death of Henry VIII. It now houses a collection of pottery and other items found during excavations in the area.
*Open Apr – Sep, Mon – Sat 9.30 – 1 & 2 – 6.30; Oct – Mar, Mon – Sat 9.30 – 1 & 2 – 4. Admission free.*

## Lloyd's of London

Lime Street, EC3
MAP REF 25G/K
The world's leading insurance market. It incorporates a purpose-built exhibition encompassing Lloyd's 300 years in the City. There is a visitors' viewing area.
*Open Mon – Fri 10 – 2 (Closed PH). Admission free.*

## The Royal Exchange

Cornhill, EC4
MAP REF 25G
Dating from 1568 as a meeting place for City merchants, Queen Victoria opened the present building in 1844. No business has been transacted here for over 40 years, but important announcements such as the

proclamation of new sovereigns and declarations of war are traditionally made from the broad flight of steps at its entrance.

## The Royal Hospital

Royal Hospital Road, Chelsea, SW3
**MAP REF 27M**
Built by Wren in 1682 as an asylum for aged and invalid soldiers, it is considered one of the finest examples of his work. Alterations and additions were made by Robert Adam and Sir John Soane. The Hospital now houses 500 army pensioners, unmistakable in their scarlet frock-coats. The famous Chelsea Flower Show is held annually in the grounds during the early summer.

*Open: grounds Mon – Sat 10 – dusk; Sun 2 – dusk (Ranelagh Gardens closed 12.45 – 2); buildings Mon – Sat 10 – 12 & 2 – 4; Sun 2 – 4. Admission free.*

## Stock Exchange

Throgmorton Street, EC2
**MAP REF 25G**
The centre of industrial finance, where stocks and shares in individual companies are bought and sold. The trading floor may be viewed (but not heard) from the gallery and guides are present to describe the scene.

*Open Mon – Fri 9.45 – 3.15, last guided tour 2.30 (Closed PH). Parties must book in advance. Admission free.*

## The Temple of Mithras

Temple Court, EC4
**MAP REF 25G**
The excavated foundations of a Mithraic Temple, dating from the Roman occupation of London, and reconstructed near to the site where they were discovered in 1954. Viewing platform. Finds from the site are displayed in the Museum of London (see page 105).

## Thames Barrier Centre

Unity Way, SE18
**DISTRICT MAP**
Justifiably described as the 'Eighth Wonder of the World', the ⅓-mile span barrier built to save London from disastrous flooding is the world's largest movable flood barrier.

The nearby exhibition building has displays explaining the construction of the £480 million project. Barrier gates raised for testing monthly.

*Open daily 10.30 – 5 (6pm Apr – Sep) (Closed 24 – 26 Dec & 1 Jan). Admission free.*

## US Embassy

Grosvenor Square, W1
**MAP REF 21H**
The design of this huge modern building, by Eero Saarinen, is one of the most controversial in London. An eagle with a wingspan of 35ft dominates the structure.

# STREETS AND AREAS

Old, new, practical and pretty are combined in the City's Barbican complex

## The Barbican

**MAP REF 17J/M**

This impressive new devopment, built around the remaining portion of the old Roman wall, is an ambitious scheme to promote the City as a residential area rather than a place to be visited only for the purpose of daily work. It contains high-rise blocks of flats, shops, offices, pubs, the new City of London School for Girls, the 16th-century church of St Giles Cripplegate, and the new Guildhall School of Music. The centrepiece of the scheme is the Barbican Arts Centre (see page 113), which contains the permanent London homes of the Royal Shakespeare Company (the Barbican Theatre) and the London Symphony Orchestra (the Barbican Hall). The Museum of London (see page 105) lies on the south-western extremity of the development.

*The Centre is open daily 10am – 10pm. Admission free.*

## Brook Street

**MAP REF 21G**

The 18th-century composer Handel lived at No 25 for over thirty years. Nearly all his works were written here, including the *Messiah* (1741).

## Bruton Place

**MAP REF 21L**

Emerging from the pavement here are several oddly-shaped bollards which were created by the simple expedient of placing redundant 19th-century cannons upright in the ground.

## Carlton House Terrace

**MAP REF 22E**

John Nash designed this dignified group of buildings as part of his architectural scheme for Regent Street. The terrace gets its name from Carlton House, which stood on the spot now occupied by the southern half of Waterloo Place. At No 6 is the Royal Society and No 12 is now the Institute of Contemporary Arts.

## Cheyne Walk

**DISTRICT MAP**

A beautiful, unspoilt row of 18th-century houses, some with plaques denoting famous past residents, fronting the river.

## Coram's Fields

MAP REF 15L

Coram's Fields are a playground laid out on the grounds of the Foundling Hospital, which was established in 1729 by Captain Thomas Coram. Among the governors of the school were the painters William Hogarth and Sir Joshua Reynolds, and the choir was trained by Handel.

## Flask Walk

DISTRICT MAP

Flask Walk runs out of Well Walk, which takes its name from the wells which made Hampstead a fashionable spa in the 18th century. In Flask Walk itself are the Victorian Flask Walk Baths (now closed). Next to them is an attractive group of restored Georgian artisans' cottages.

## Fleet Street

MAP REF 23K

It is one of the most ancient thoroughfares in London, and has had links with the printing trade since about 1500. The present buildings are mostly modern.

## Greek Street

MAP REF 21D

Many famous people are associated with this street: Dr Johnson and Sir Joshua Reynolds founded a Literary Club here; Sir Thomas Lawrence, the 18th-century portrait painter lived and worked here; Thomas de Quincey indulged his opium addiction here; and Josiah Wedgwood had his London showroom here to show off his famous china.

## Jermyn Street

MAP REF 22B

Jermyn Street is famous for its many old-established shops. One of the most interesting is the ancient premises of Paxton and

Whitfield, the cheese shop. Further along is the Cavendish Hotel with its wrought-iron lamps, which although it has been rebuilt still carries memories of the eccentric hotelier Rosa Lewis, the original 'Duchess of Duke Street'.

## Meard Street

MAP REF 22A/D

For those who like old houses this short 18th-century street, named after a carpenter, John Meard, is the most rewarding in all Soho. Nos 1–21 are exceptionally well preserved.

## Pall Mall

MAP REF 22B/E

Pall Mall takes its name from *paille maille*, a French ball game similar to croquet, introduced

New technology may be pushing the newspaper industry away from Fleet Street, but it will remain the 'street of ink' in the minds of many

into England in the reign of Charles I. Numerous famous, and usually exclusive, clubs are situated in Pall Mall. Outside the entrance to the Athenaeum Club, in Waterloo Place, are two slabs of stone, placed here as a mounting-block at the request of the Duke of Wellington.

## Queen Anne's Gate

MAP REF 29G

This quiet close, built in 1704, is undoubtedly one of the most charming streets in London. It has been the home of several distinguished figures in British

Historic ships help to keep memories of the Port of London alive at St Katherine's Dock

## Seething Lane

**MAP REF 25K/L**
This is the site of the Navy Office in which the diarist Samuel Pepys worked. Almost opposite is St Olave's, which Pepys calls 'myne owne Church', and where he and his wife are buried.

## Shaftesbury Avenue

**MAP REF 22D**
Laid out in 1877–86, the Avenue is now known chiefly for its theatres. At its southern end it runs into
*Piccadilly Circus*
Famous for its illuminations and its archer (Eros, see page 97), this is the very heart of London's West End and it is always packed with shoppers and sightseers.

## Shepherd Market

**MAP REF 21H**
Set in the heart of Mayfair, this is one of the most delightful areas in all London. Some of the original 18th-century buildings survive, but it is the unique 'village' atmosphere which gives this tiny oasis its special charm.

## The Strand

**MAP REF 23G/H**
In Elizabethan times and long afterwards, the Strand was bordered by noblemen's mansions with gardens running down to the riverside or 'strand'. It is still, as it always was, the principal route between the West End and the City, running for nearly a mile, from Charing Cross to the Temple Bar Memorial – where statues of Queen Victoria and Edward VII, and a griffin in the road mark the boundary of the City.

history. No 26 still has the snuffer for extinguishing the linkman's torch after he had lighted its owners home.

## St Katherine's Dock

**MAP REF 25L**
Designed by Thomas Telford, one of the greatest engineers of the 19th century, and forced to close after World War II, the recently restored dock basins now offer a lovely place to wander round. There is a path around the dock which will take you past the tastefully-modernised warehouses, and you can have a drink at the Dickens Inn while gazing at the yachts in the marina.
*Open at all times; admission free.*

## St Martin's Lane

**MAP REF 22D/E**
St Martin's Lane is easily recognised by the globe on top of the London Coliseum, now the home of the English National Opera. Thomas Chippendale, the greatest furniture maker in England's history, opened his workshop at No 62 in 1753.

## The Victoria Embankment

**MAP REF 23H/K**
Sir Joseph Bazalgette built this fine riverside parade in the latter half of the 19th century. All

along it there are fine iron lamp posts with dolphins twined round their bases, and seats supported by kneeling camels. The river wall is made of granite and is eight feet thick.

### Whitehall

MAP REF 23E/F
Most people to whom the name 'Whitehall' is synonymous with Government, will be surprised to learn that the road called Whitehall running from Parliament Square to Trafalgar Square only became the home of most government offices during the early 18th century. In Downing Street, No 10 has been the official residence of the Prime Minister since Robert Walpole first lived there in 1735. No 11 is the residence of the Chancellor of the Exchequeur, and the Government Whips' Office is at No 12. Among the other

government buildings still found in Whitehall are the Treasury and the Admiralty, and Horse Guards, behind which is Horse Guards Parade where Trooping the Colour takes place. The Ministry of Defence stands near the surviving relic of the former Palace of Whitehall, the Banqueting House. This was designed by Inigo Jones in a fine Palladian style and erected in 1625 *(Open Tue – Sat 10 – 5; Sun 2 – 5 (Closed Good Fri, 24 – 26 Dec and for Government functions). Admission charge).* Charles I was executed outside the Banqueting House in 1649.

In the middle of Whitehall stands the Cenotaph, a simple pillar of Portland stone designed by Sir Edwin Lutyens to commemorate those who fell during World War I. Now services for the dead of both world wars are held here annually on the second Sunday

in November.

At the north end of Whitehall, passing Great Scotland Yard, until 1891 headquarters of the Metropolitan Police, you come to Trafalgar Square. Inhabited by thousands of pigeons, and dominated by Nelson's Column with its four lions designed by the Victorian painter Landseer, the Square was laid out in memory of Nelson and completed in 1841; the fountains were added in 1948.

### Woburn Walk

MAP REF 15G
This genteel little thoroughfare has a double row of early 19th-century houses, all of which have picturesque shop fronts. The Irish poet W B Yeats (1865 – 1939) lived at No 5 for a while.

Woburn Walk

Green Park. In spring the grass beneath the stately trees is spangled with flowers

# PARKS AND GARDENS

London's ten Royal Parks are the survivors of areas enclosed by Henry VIII for hunting, and were first opened to the public by Charles I and Charles II. They are:

## Bushy Park

DISTRICT MAP

The famous ¾-mile Chestnut Avenue, laid out by Wren, runs from Hampton Court to the Teddington Gate. This superb double row of enormous trees is best seen in springtime.

## Green Park

MAP REF 21M

Once meadowland where duels were fought, this is the smallest of the parks in Central London, situated in the triangle between teeming Piccadilly, the processional Mall, and Constitutional Hill (which gets its name from where Charles II took his constitutional stroll). There are no flowerbeds, though in springtime the grass is sprinkled with daffodils and crocuses. Tyburn Stream flows just beneath the surface and is the reason for the park's greenness.

## Greenwich Park

DISTRICT MAP

Mostly laid out by Le Nôtre, whose love of symmetry is very noticeable, this park contains the Meridian, a stone-set strip of brass that marks zero degrees longitude, and the Wilderness, 13 acres of woodland and wild flowers inhabited by a herd of fallow deer. On the northern perimeter is the largest children's playground in any Royal park; in the centre is the historic 20ft stump of Queen Elizabeth's Oak.

## Hampton Court

DISTRICT MAP

An outstanding collection of formal gardens – particularly fine is the Privy Garden with its combination of flowers, statues, and fountains. There is the Orangery, the 200-year-old-vine, the modern reproduction Knot Garden, and the geometric perfection of the famous Maze.

## Hyde Park

MAP REF 20B/E

A Royal park since 1536, Hyde Park now consists of 340 acres of trees and grass intersected by paths. Main features include the Serpentine – the habitat of wild creatures that cannot find sanctuary elsewhere in the city centre – and Speakers' Corner near Marble Arch, where, every Sunday, anyone can stand up and say just what they please.

## Kensington Gardens

MAP REF 19H/J

The boundary between Kensington Gardens and Hyde Park, which were one and the same before William III enclosed his palace garden, runs north to south across the Serpentine Bridge. Noted for its tranquillity and formality, Kensington Gardens includes the Round Pond, Queen Anne's Orangery, and the Sunken Garden and Flower Walk.

And the band played on . . . in St James's Park

## Primrose Hill

DISTRICT MAP

Once part of the same hunting forest as Regent's Park, Primrose Hill retains in its name the rural character and charm that it undoubtedly had in the past. The view from the summit is panoramic and encompasses virtually the whole of central London. In 1842 its 62 acres gained gaslights, a gymnasium, and respectability as a Royal park.

## Regent's Park

MAP REF 13G/K

Laid out by John Nash, who also designed the imposing terraces which surround it. It contains the Zoo, a boating lake, the lovely Queen Mary's Rose Garden, and the Regent's Canal. The elegant charm of the park is enhanced by several Victorian garden ornaments; a group of fossil tree trunks are the only surviving reminders that the Royal Botanic Gardens were once situated here.

## Richmond Park

DISTRICT MAP

With its herds of deer, abundant wild life, and centuries-old oaks, Richmond is a favourite haunt for visitors and naturalists. A formal garden can be seen at Pembroke Lodge, and the various plantations show a wealth of exotic shrubs and wild flowers. Model sail boats are allowed on Adam's Pond, where the deer drink, and 18-acre Pen Ponds have been specially made for angling (a fishing permit is required).

## St James's Park

MAP REF 22C/F

This most delightful of the Royal parks contains walks and paths threading through a mixture of flower borders, shrubs, and trees. Weeping willows drape themselves into the Chinese-style lake, the nucleus of the park. Duck Island in the centre is a haven for water birds, the most famous being the pelicans.

Escape from the crowded streets and hectic bustle of London also lies elsewhere within the capital:

## Hampstead Heath

NW3 and NW11

DISTRICT MAP

The 790 acres of Hampstead Heath include some of the highest ground in the capital, and the views of London that can be enjoyed from the heath are famous. There are extensive tracts of open grassland dotted with majestic old trees, and carefully planned formalised areas that were originally set out during the Regency period. Part of society's interest in Hampstead was due to the springs which rise from its depths. These were claimed to have health-giving properties, and the 18th-century fad for 'taking the waters' ensured its popularity.

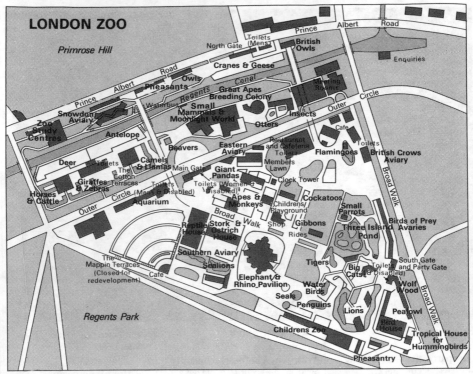

**LONDON ZOO**

Primrose Hill

Prince Albert Road

North Gate

Toilets (Mens)

British Owls

Enquiries

Cranes & Geese

Owls

Pheasants

Canal

Regents

Great Apes Breeding Colony

Feeding Rooms

Outer Circle

Albert Road

Prince

Waterbus

Small Mammals & Moonlight World

Insects

Snowdon Aviary

Zoo Study Centres

Antelope

Otters

Cafe

Toilets

Beavers

Eastern Aviary

Restaurant and Cafeteria

Flamingoes

Toilets

British Crows Aviary

Deer

Toilets

The Cotton Terraces

Camels & Llamas

Main Gate

Members Lawn

Clock Tower

Giant Pandas

Giraffes & Zebras

Toilets

Toilets (Women & Disabled)

Toilets (Disabled)

Cockatoos

Broad Walk

Horses & Cattle

Outer Circle (Main & Disabled)

Aquarium

Apes & Monkeys

Childrens/ Playground

Small Parrots

Reptile House

Stork & Ostrich House

Broad Walk

Shop

Gibbons

Rides

Three Island Pond

Birds of Prey Avaries

Southern Aviary

Sealions

Tigers

Big Cats

South Gate and Party Gate

Toilets (Disabled)

The Mappin Terraces (Closed for redevelopment)

Cafe

Elephant & Rhino Pavilion

Water Birds

Wolf Wood

Regents Park

Seals

Penguins

Lions

Peafowl

Childrens Zoo

Bird House

Broad Walk

Tropical House for Hummingbirds

Pheasantry

### Highgate Cemetery

Swains Lane, N6
**DISTRICT MAP**
One of the private cemeteries
which were created in the
1830s. The western part,
decaying and overgrown
through years of neglect,
provides a marvellous backdrop
for the many magnificent
Victorian tombs, vaults, and
monuments, including those of
George Eliot, Faraday, and
Charles Dickens's family. Most
famous, of course, for the
enormous grave of Karl Marx.

*Open: Eastern cemetery, daily,*
*Apr – Sep 10 – 5; Oct – Mar 10 – 4;*
*Western cemetery guided tours on*
*the hour daily, Apr – Sep 10 – 4,*
*Oct – Mar 10 – 3. Admission free*
*(donations).*

### Kew Gardens

**DISTRICT MAP**
The 300 acres of the legendary
Royal Botanic Gardens now
contain over 50,000 different
types of plants and flowers. The
largest living collection in the
gardens is the Arboretum,
where many species of trees and
shrubs grow harmoniously. The
Tropical and Palm Houses are
interesting too, while the
magnificent flower borders of
the Herbaceous Section are a
constant delight. Great cushions
of alpines grow amongst
sandstone outcrops and beside
the stream of the Rock Garden,
and the woodland garden
around The Mound exudes a
green coolness.

*Gardens open from 10 to*
*between 4 & 8pm (depending on*
*season); museums & glasshouses*
*from 10am, some buildings close*
*lunchtime (closed 25 Dec & 1 Jan).*
*Admission charge.*

### The Zoo

Regent's Park, NW1
**MAP REF 13G/K**
In 1828, the Zoological Society
founded a small collection of
animals on a five-acre site in
Regent's Park, from which
modest beginnings has grown
one of the world's foremost zoos
– a collection that still receives
no aid from the government,
and subsists entirely on the
proceeds of ticket sales. Today it
shows a staggering 6,000 living
species of animals, many in
environments that are hardly a
whisker away from their natural
habitats. Some of the creatures
are such as might be
encountered on a country walk
in southern England; others are
endangered species that would
be difficult to find anywhere.

Among the outstanding
buildings are the large Lion
Terraces; the walled-and-

ditched Mappin Terraces; the Freshwater, Seawater, and Tropical Halls of the Aquarium; the Reptile House; the Elephant and Rhino Pavilion; the amazing night-time world of the Charles Clore Pavilion for Small Mammals, where day and night are reversed; and Lord Snowdon's famous aviary. Nobody can deny that this is an ideal place to see birds. Inside the enclosure in a cantilevered bridge from which visitors can watch free-flying birds in a number of recreated habitats – nesting, fighting, and feeding as they would in the wild. Deer and antelope roam the Cotton Terraces above the Regent's Canal. The best views of them are obtained from the waterbuses which cruise along the canal between Little Venice and the zoo. Elsewhere are camels and llamas, giraffes, and a worldwide selection of cattle.

There is a lovely Children's Zoo, where the young are encouraged to mingle with the animals. Keep an eye open for notices of feeding times.

*Open Mon – Sat 9 – 6; Sun 9 – 7 (Closed 25 Dec). Admission charge.*

Among the public parks and other oases of greenery are: *Battersea Park*, SW11, with its sub-tropical and wildflower gardens, and masses of things for children to do; *Chelsea Physic Garden*, Royal Hospital Road, SW3, the second oldest botanic garden in England, set up in 1673; *Holland Park*, W8, a quiet haven in the heart of Kensington, which Macaulay called the 'favourite resort of wits and beauties, painters and poets, scholars, philosophers, and statesmen'; *Lincoln's Inn Fields*, WC2 (see page 82); *Syon Park*, Isleworth – beautifully laid

Leopards. The 'big cats' are among the prime attractions at the zoo

out in the 16th century by Capability Brown, this was the country's first national gardening centre; *Waterlow Park*, Highgate Hill, N6 – pretty terraces, flower gardens, lake, and ponds; *Wimbledon Common*, SW19, with attractive ponds and an ancient earthwork known as Caesar's Camp; *Victoria Embankment Gardens*, WC2, containing numerous statues and memorials; *Victoria Tower Gardens*, SW1, with the Buxton Drinking Fountain commemorating the emancipation of slaves in the British Empire in 1834; and *Vauxhall Bridge Gardens*, SW1, from where convicted prisoners began their journeys of transportation.

# RIDGES

## Albert Bridge

**DISTRICT MAP**

This combined cantilever and suspension structure resembles a gigantic iron cobweb and is one of the most distinctive of all London's bridges. It was designed by R M Ordish and opened in 1873.

## Blackfriars Bridge

**MAP REF 24B**

This bridge, designed by James Cubitt in 1899, replaced an 18th-century structure. Its name derives from the Dominican Priory which once stood nearby. Beneath the bridge the Fleet River, which runs below the streets of London, can be seen flowing into the Thames.

## Chelsea Bridge

**MAP REF 28C**

This handsome suspension bridge was opened in 1937 and replaced a similar structure of 1858. The river here is the widest reach west of London Bridge.

## Chiswick Bridge

**DISTRICT MAP**

This concrete bridge was built in 1933 to the designs of the architect Sir Herbert Baker. Just downstream from it, opposite the Ship Inn, is the finishing point of the Oxford and Cambridge Boat Race. Between the bridge and the inn is an attractive group of houses of varying dates, and beyond them, on the south bank, is the huge Mortlake Brewery.

## Hammersmith Bridge

**DISTRICT MAP**

Sir Joseph Bazalgette, the architect who did so much to change the appearance of the Thames in central London, designed this fanciful suspension bridge in 1887. Just downstream from the bridge, on the south bank, is Harrods Furniture Depository, an imposing building decorated in *art-nouveau* style.

## London Bridge

**MAP REF 25H**

London Bridge was first built in stone between 1176 and 1209. It became almost a town on its own, having houses, shops, a chapel, fortified gates, and even water mills built upon it. All the buildings were pulled down in 1760, and the bridge itself was replaced in 1832 as it was rapidly being eroded away. The present structure was opened in 1973, at which time its predecessor was reassembled stone by stone in the USA.

## Putney Bridge

**DISTRICT MAP**

Graceful Putney Bridge is a 19th-century replacement of an earlier wooden toll bridge. It marks the starting point of the Oxford and Cambridge Boat Race, and all along the riverside here there are well-kept boat- and clubhouses.

## Southwark Bridge

**MAP REF 24E**

Sir Ernest George designed this undistinguished bridge in 1919. Many archaeological finds have been made on the north bank of the river here.

## Tower Bridge

**MAP REF 25L**

This fairy-tale structure was built in 1894. Much of the original machinery for raising and lowering the bridge is still in place, though in 1975 electric

motors replaced the great steam hydraulic engines. These can still be seen in a museum in the main South Tower. Also recently open to the public is the main North Tower and the high level walkways, which provide unique views of the River.

*Towers & walkways open daily, Apr–Oct 10–6.30; Nov–Mar 10–4.45. Admission charge.*

### Waterloo Bridge

**MAP REF 23H**

John Rennie's beautiful Waterloo Bridge, which had been built in the early part of the 19th century, began to show signs of structural weakness in 1923. In 1934 demolition work began, and the old bridge was replaced by the present structure in 1939. It was designed by Sir Giles Scott and is considered to be the most graceful bridge in London.

### Westminster Bridge

**MAP REF 24J**

The present bridge was designed by Thomas Page and completed in 1862. It replaced a stone bridge of 1750 on which Wordsworth composed his famous sonnet in 1802. At the western end stands a statue of Queen Boudicea (see p.97). Westminster Pier is situated just north of the bridge and is one of the principal starting places for trips up and down the river.

One of the world's loveliest bridges, Tower Bridge is also a tribute to Victorian engineering

# QUARES

Soho has a sleazy reputation, but its square is as elegant as any in London

### Belgrave Square
SW1
**MAP REF 27K**
Sheer size robs Belgrave of its square-like characteristics, because it is not possible to see from one side to the other, but the carefully tended lawns and gardens have an air of exclusiveness undoubtedly lent by the elegant cream-coloured terraces that surround it.

### Berkeley Square
W1
**MAP REF 21H/L**
Famous for its huge, 200-year-old plane trees, and that nightingale.

### Bloomsbury Square
WC1
**MAP REF 15M**
The Square was laid out on its site in 1661, and was the first open space in London to be called a 'square'. The original mansions have all disappeared, but the houses on the north side date from 1800–14. The gardens were planted in about 1800 by the celebrated landscape gardener Humphrey Repton.

### Fitzroy Square
W1
**MAP REF 14E**
Designed by the famous Adam brothers in the 18th century, Fitzroy Square preserves well-built terraces typical of their designers' work, particularly on the eastern side.

### Golden Square
W1
**MAP REF 22A**
According to popular legend, this Soho square had its name changed from 'Gelding' to 'Golden' by some of its more society-conscious residents. It is now a centre for the woollen trade.

### Gordon Square
WC1
**MAP REF 15H**
Gordon Square is associated with the circle of 20th-century writers, critics, and intellectuals known as the Bloomsbury Group. Virginia Woolf lived at No 46 for a time before she married. The same house was later the home of the leading economist John Maynard Keynes. The critic and biographer Lytton Strachey lived at No 51.

### Grosvenor Square
W1
**MAP REF 21G/F**
Built and rebuilt on the site of a 17th-century citizens' blockade against Charles I, Grosvenor Square is now the home of the US Embassy.

The open garden around which the square is formed was designed by William Kent, a distinguished 18th-century architect and designer, and occupies some six acres.

### Leicester Square
WC2
**MAP REF 22E**
This large square gets its name from Leicester House, a mansion built here by the Earl of Leicester in the 17th century. The open space, then known as Leicester Fields, was ideal for fighting duels. The mansion has long since disappeared, and in Victorian times the fields were laid out as a garden, with a statue of Shakespeare in the centre and busts of famous local residents at the four corners.

## Manchester Square

W1

MAP REF 13M

The leafy centre of Manchester Square contrasts prettily with the dark brick of the Georgian architecture that surrounds it. It is a quiet place, situated just far enough away from Oxford Street to be unaffected by the noise, yet close enough to be a haven for those weary of shopping in the famous thoroughfare.

## Parliament Square

SW1

MAP REF 22F

The square was originally laid out by Sir Charles Barry in 1850, and redesigned in 1951 for the Festival of Britain. There are many statues of British politicians in and around the square.

## Portman Square

W1

MAP REF 13M

Once second only to Grosvenor Square in the eyes of high society, Portman Square took 20 years to build during the 18th century. The centre of the square is occupied by a garden in which grass, shrubs, and trees combine effectively.

## St James's Square

SW1

MAP REF 22B

At the centre of this orderly and elegant square, originally created by architect Henry Jermyn, is a garden which is particularly noted for its lovely trees. An equestrian statue of William III forms the central focal point for ranks of tall plane trees, the pastel softness of flowering almond and cherry blossom, the fragrant pyramids of lilac bloom, and golden crowns of laburnum.

## Soho Square

W1

MAP REF 22D

The name 'Soho' is said to come from the cry of huntsmen unleashing dogs to chase hares, *so* meaning 'see', and *ho* 'after him'. The Duke of Monmouth, Charles II's illegitimate son, had a mansion in Soho Square, and when he and his followers made a bid for the Crown at the Battle of Sedgemoor, 'Soho!' was their battlecry. On the east side of the square is the Roman Catholic Church of St Patrick, built in 1891–3. It has a fine Italianate interior. In the north-west corner is the French Protestant Church of London, founded in 1550 under a royal charter from Edward VI. The present building dates from 1893. Soho has been a foreign quarter since the reign of Charles II, when a great number of French Protestants fled here as the result of religious persecution. They were mostly silk-weavers, and in the back gardens around Soho Square there may still be some of the mulberry trees they planted for their silkworms.

Trafalgar Square, with Nelson's Column and St Martin-in-the-Fields

A detail of Rodin's Burghers of Calais in Victoria Tower Gardens

# STATUES AND MONUMENTS

### The Albert Memorial

Kensington Gore, SW7
MAP REF 19M
This enormous and imposing memorial was commissioned by Queen Victoria in memory of her husband, and was designed by Sir George Gilbert Scott in 1872. The Prince is depicted reading a catalogue of the Great Exhibition of 1851, for which he was largely responsible.

### Alfred the Great

Trinity Church Square, off Trinity Street, SE1
MAP REF 31K
Thought to date from 1395, this is the oldest statue in London.

### The Burghers of Calais

Victoria Tower Gardens, SW1
MAP REF 29K
Rodin's superb group of figures represents the citizens of Calais who surrendered to Edward III in 1340 to save their town from destruction.

### Charles I

Trafalgar Square, WC2
MAP REF 22E
Cast in bronze in 1633, this statue was to have been melted down during the Commonwealth, but was hidden and re-erected in 1660.

### Sir Winston Churchill

Parliament Square, SW1
MAP REF 22F
This statue of the great statesman and war leader was unveiled in 1973 and depicts Churchill in a typically pugnacious attitude.

### Cleopatra's Needle

Victoria Embankment, SW1
MAP REF 23H
Originally this famous landmark stood in Heliopolis, Egypt, where it was one of a pair erected 3,500 years ago. It was presented to Britain in 1819. Its twin now stands in Central Park, New York, and neither has any connection with Cleopatra.

### The 1st Duke of Wellington

Hyde Park Corner, W1
MAP REF 21J
The Duke can be seen on Copenhagen, the horse he rode throughout the Battle of Waterloo. Copenhagen was buried with full military honours at the Duke's country home, Stratfield Saye, Hampshire.

### The Duke of York Column

Waterloo Place, SW1
MAP REF 22E
This tall monument commemorates the second son of George III – the 'Grand Old Duke of York' – who marched ten thousand men up and down a hill in the nursery rhyme. The same men paid for the

Superb views can be obtained from the top of the Monument

memorial – most of its cost was met by stopping one day's pay for every soldier in the army. The column was designed by Benjamin Wyatt in 1833.

## Eros

Piccadilly Circus, W1
**MAP REF 22B**
One of London's most famous landmarks, this figure of an archer was erected as a memorial to the Victorian reformer and philanthropist, the Earl of Shaftesbury. The statue actually represents the Angel of Christian Charity, not Eros at all. It has recently been completely restored.

## The Fat Boy

Giltspur Street, EC1
**MAP REF 18J**
This peculiar gilded figure marks the spot, originally known as Pie Corner, where the Great Fire was halted in 1666.

## The Griffin

Strand, EC4
**MAP REF 23K**
The Griffin, the unofficial badge of the City of London, stands at the point where the Strand ends and Fleet Street begins. Originally this was the site of the Old Temple Bar gateway, and the spot traditionally marks the western limit of the City.

## Sir Henry Irving

St Martin's Place, WC2
**MAP REF 22E**
Erected in 1910, this is the only statue in London of an actor.

## James II

Trafalgar Square, WC2
**MAP REF 22E**
Usually regarded as the finest statue in London, this figure of the King was made by Grinling Gibbons.

## The London Stone

Cannon Street, EC4
(Oversea – Chinese Banking Corporation)
**MAP REF 25G**
This is said to be the milestone from which distances were measured on the great military roads radiating outwards from Roman London.

## Lord Nelson

Trafalgar Square, WC2
**MAP REF 22E**
This 17ft 4in statue by E H Bailey stands on the top of the famous column. Together they reach a combined height of almost 185ft. Four identical lions, cast from a single original by Sir Edwin Landseer, guard the base of the column.

## The Monument

Monument Street, EC3
**MAP REF 25H**
Designed by Wren and Hooke to commemorate the Great Fire of 1666, which is reputed to have started in nearby Pudding Lane. Be prepared for a climb of 311 steps to the summit from where there are splendid views over the City.
　　Open Apr – Sep, Mon – Fri 9 – 5.40, Sat & Sun 2 – 5.40; Oct – Mar, Mon – Sat 9 – 5.40. Admission charge.

## Peter Pan

Kensington Gardens, W2
**MAP REF 19L**
This statue of Sir James Barrie's immortal character has delighted several generations of children. It was made by Sir George Frampton in 1911.

## Queen Boadicea

Westminster Bridge, SW1
**MAP REF 23J**
Thomas Thornycroft made this statue of Queen Boadicea, or Boudicca, in 1902. She is depicted in her war chariot, accompanied by her daughters, and appears to be defiantly waving her spear at the Houses of Parliament.

## Queen Victoria

Queen Victoria Memorial, The Mall, SW1
**MAP REF 21M**
This elegant group of statuary stands in front of Buckingham Palace.

## The Whittington Stone

Highgate Hill, N19
**DISTRICT MAP**
Dick Whittington is supposed to have sat on this spot and heard the Bow Bells of St Mary-le-Bow chiming: 'Turn again Whittington, Thrice Mayor of London'. Whittington actually was mayor of London three times during the 14th century.

Ye Olde Cheshire Cheese is one of London's best known historic pubs

*UBS*

It can be great fun exploring that most typical of British institutions, the pub. There are thousands in London, each with its own atmosphere and character, some relying on special attractions like music (all sorts), drag shows, and plays. Here, as a starting point, is a list of those noted for their historical interest. Note: the British drink-and-drive laws are most strict, and we do recommend that you use public transport when going pub-hunting.

### The Anchor

1 Bankside, SE1
**MAP REF 24E**
An historic pub, the third to stand on this site, very close to where both Shakespeare's Globe Theatre and the Old Clink Prison once stood.

### The Antelope

22 Eaton Terrace, SW1
**MAP REF 27L**
Regency inn of character and charm.

### The Black Friar

174 Queen Victoria Street, EC4
**MAP REF 24A**
Gold leaf on the ceiling, gas lighting, open fireplaces, and some good art nouveau decorations.

### The Bunch of Grapes

207 Brompton Road, SW3
**MAP REF 28G**
Victorian gem, with perfectly preserved glass, decorated windows and doors.

### The City Barge

27 Strand-on-the-Green, W4
**DISTRICT MAP**
Old pub on the bank of the Thames.

### The George Inn

77 Borough High Street, SE1
**MAP REF 25J**
The last remaining galleried coaching inn in London. Actors play scenes from Shakespeare and Dickens in the inn's courtyard during the summer months.

### The Grenadier

18 Wilton Row, SW1
**MAP REF 21J**
Old-world mews pub, said to be haunted.

### Henekey's Long Bar

22 High Holborn, WC1
**MAP REF 16F**
A lofty, barn-like bar.

### Jack Straw's Castle

Hampstead Heath, NW3
DISTRICT MAP
This enormous old coaching inn
has Dick Turpin associations.

### King's Head

115 Upper Street, N1
DISTRICT MAP
Lovely pub, famous for its
theatrical evenings.

### Lamb and Flag

33 Rose Street, WC2
MAP REF 22D
400-year-old ale tavern in a
back alley, reputed to be the
scene of the attempted
assassination of Dryden in
1679.

### The Mayflower

117 Rotherhithe Street, SE16
DISTRICT MAP
Very old pub which changed its
name in the 17th century as a
tribute to the original *Mayflower*
which sailed for the New World
from nearby.

### Olde Bull and Bush

North End Way, NW3
DISTRICT MAP
'Come and have a drink or two
down at the Olde Bull and Bush'
sang Florrie Ford in her still-
popular Music Hall song, and
down the years people have
happily done just that.

### Old Wine Shades

6 Martin Lane, EC4
MAP REF 25G
This old tavern and wine shop,
built in 1663, was the only City
hostelry to survive the Great
Fire.

### Prospect of Whitby

57 Wapping Wall, E1
DISTRICT MAP
London's most famous pub, on
the river and near the docks.
Among past habitués were
Pepys, Whistler, Turner,
Dickens, and Judge Jeffreys.

The Bunch of Grapes, a Victorian pub in Chelsea

### St Stephen's Tavern

10 Bridge Street, SW1
MAP REF 22F
Frequented by MPs and
journalists. The House of
Commons division bell rings in
the bar.

### The Salisbury

90 St Martin's Lane, WC2
MAP 22D
Very large, plush Victorian pub
in the heart of theatreland.

### The Spaniards Inn

Hampstead Heath, NW3
DISTRICT MAP
Very famous 15th-century inn,
always crowded. A lovely
summer pub.

### The Swan

66 Bayswater Road, W2
MAP REF 19L
Old coaching-house; its terrace
is always very crowded on
summer evenings.

### The Swiss Cottage

98 Finchley Road, NW3
DISTRICT MAP
Very large, chalet-type pub.

### The Waterman's Arms

1 Glengarnock Avenue, Isle of
Dogs, E14
DISTRICT MAP
Victorian pub with an authentic
Cockney atmosphere.

### The Windsor Castle

114 Camden Hill Road, W8
DISTRICT MAP
Fashionable west London pub,
very popular in the summer
because of its walled beer
garden.

### Ye Olde Cheshire Cheese

145 Fleet Street, EC4
MAP REF 23K
17th-century tavern of
architectural, historical, and
literary interest, well-known
haunt of Dr Johnson.

World War II cruiser HMS *Belfast* was saved from the breaker's yard and is now a floating museum

# ART GALLERIES AND MUSEUMS

Of the many hundreds of museums and art galleries open to the public in the capital, a selection of the more notable ones is described on the following pages. Many, in addition to their permanent collections, mount special exhibitions from time to time, and details of these can be obtained from newspapers and periodicals.

### Bear Gardens Museum
Bear Gardens, SE1
**MAP REF 24E**
This museum stands on the site of the last bear-baiting ring on Bankside, close to the site of the Hope Theatre and Shakespeare's Globe. It occupies a 19th-century warehouse and consists of a permanent exhibition relating to Elizabethan theatre.
*Open Sat 10 – 5.30; Sun 2 – 6 (at other times by appointment). Admission charge.*

## HMS Belfast

Symons Wharf, Vine Lane,
Tooley Street, SE1
**MAP REF 25L**
At 11,000 tons, this is the
largest cruiser ever built for the
Royal Navy. She was saved from
the breaker's yard to be opened
to the public in 1971 as a
permanent floating naval
museum.

*Open 20 Mar–Oct, 11–5.50;
Nov–19 Mar, 11–4.30 (Closed
Good Fri, May Day, 24–26 Dec &
1 Jan). Admission charge.*

## Bethnal Green Museum of Childhood

Cambridge Heath Road, E2
**DISTRICT MAP**
A branch of the Victoria and
Albert Museum. Its chief
exhibits are toys, dolls and dolls-
houses, model soldiers, puppets,
games, model theatres, wedding
dresses, children's costumes, all
housed in an attractive
Victorian building.

*Open Mon–Thu & Sat 10–6;
Sun 2.30–6 (Closed Fri, Spring
BH Mon, 24–26 Dec & 1 Jan).
Admission free.*

## The British Museum

Great Russell Street, WC1
**MAP REF 15J**
One of the greatest museums of
the world, founded in 1753, the
British Museum shows the
works of man from all over the
world, from prehistoric times.

Amongst the vast array of
treasures not to be missed are
the *Elgin Marbles* in the Duveen
Gallery; the *Rosetta Stone*,
dating from 195BC; the
*Mildenhall Treasure*, a
collection of 4th-century silver;
the famous display of Egyptian
mummies; and the exquisite
12th-century *Lewis Chessmen*.

Original documents are on
show in the British Library, a
separate institution within the
British Museum building.

Each year special exhibitions
focus more detailed attention on

**KEY: BRITISH MUSEUM**

**Basement**
1. Greek & Roman
2. Western Asiatic

**Ground Floor**
3. Greek & Roman
4. Western Asiatic
5. Egyptian

6. British Library
7. Oriental
8. Special Exhibits

**Upper Floor**
9. Greek & Roman
10. Western Asiatic
11. Egyptian

12. Prints & Drawings
13. Oriental
14. Romano-British
15. Medieval & Later
16. Special Exhibits

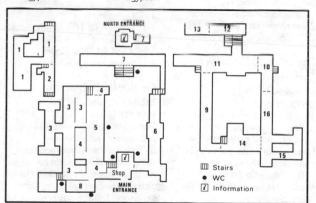

certain aspects of the collections.

*Open Mon–Sat 10–5; Sun 2.30–6 (Closed Good Fri, May Day, 24–26 Dec & 1 Jan). Admission free.*

## Cabinet War Rooms

Clive Steps, King Charles Street, SW1
**MAP REF 22F**
The most important surviving part of the underground emergency accommodation provided to protect the Prime Minister and his Cabinet against air attacks during World War II. Some rooms have been left intact; others are restored to their wartime appearance.

*Open Tue–Sun, also Etr Mon, Spring & Summer BHs, 10–5.50 (last admission 5.15) (Closed Good Fri, May Day, 24–26 Dec & 1 Jan). Admission charge.*

## Courtauld Institute Galleries

Woburn Square, WC1
**MAP REF 15H**
The galleries of London University contain the most important collection of Impressionist and Post Impressionist pictures in Britain. There are also collections of Old Master drawings, early Italian paintings, and works by Goya and Rubens. The exhibitions are changed regularly to bring out pictures from reserve.

*Open Mon–Sat 10–5; Sun 2–5 (Closed Etr, Xmas & most BH). Admission charge.*

## Dulwich College Picture Gallery

College Road, SE21
**DISTRICT MAP**
The oldest public picture gallery in England, this is also one of the most beautiful galleries in London, containing a notable collection of Old Masters.

*Open Tue–Sat 10–1 & 2–5; Sun 2–5 (Closed Mon). Admission charge.*

Safe from the Blitz – the Cabinet War Rooms

## Geffrye Museum

Kingsland Road, E2
**DISTRICT MAP**
Occupying the former almshouses of the Ironmongers' Company, this museum consists of a series of period room settings from the Elizabethan age to 1939.

*Open Tue–Sat 10–5; Sun 2–5; BH Mons 10–5 (Closed Mon, Good Fri, 24–26 Dec & 1 Jan). Admission free.*

## Geological Museum

Exhibition Road, SW7
**MAP REF 26D**
The exhibits in this national museum of earth sciences include a piece of the Moon, and the largest exhibition on basic earth science in the world – *The Story of the Earth*. The regional geology of Britain, and ore

deposits of the world are displayed. The museum is perhaps most famous for its beautiful collection of gem stones, showing them in their parent rock, in natural crystal, and in their final cut state.

*Open Mon–Sat 10–6; Sun 2.30–6 (Closed Good Fri, May Day, 24–26 Dec & 1 Jan). Admission free.*

## Guinness World of Records

The Trocadero, Piccadilly Circus, W1
**MAP REF 22B**
This museum brings to life many of the records contained in the famous *Guinness Book of Records*.

*Open daily from 10am (last admission 10pm) (Closed Xmas Day). Admission charge.*

## Hayward Gallery

The South Bank Complex, SE1
**MAP REF 23H**
Opened in 1968, this purpose-built, ultra-modern building houses brilliantly-arranged touring exhibitions which are put on by the Arts Council.

*Details of current exhibitions and their opening times can be obtained from the national press. Admission charge.*

## Horniman Museum

London Road, SE23
**DISTRICT MAP**
Displays from different cultures, natural history collections – including living creatures – and musical instruments from all parts of the world can be seen.

*Open Mon–Sat 10.30–6, Sun 2–6 (Closed 24–26 Dec). Admission free.*

## IBA Broadcasting Gallery

70 Brompton Road, SW3
**MAP REF 27G**
This permanent exhibition recreates nearly a century of television and radio.

*Open for tours only, Mon–Fri at 10, 11, 2 & 3 (Children under 16 only allowed access if part of an organised group). Admission free.*

## Imperial Collection (Crown Jewels of the World)

Central Hall, SW1
**MAP REF 25L**
On show are over 150 reproductions of crowns, tiaras and jewellery, including the Crown of Charlemagne and the Vatican Crown. Many pieces on show are the only copies, as the originals were lost or destroyed in wars or revolutions.

*Open Jan–Sep, Mon–Sat 10–6; Oct–Dec, Mon–Sat 11–5 (Closed Good Fri & Xmas). Admission charge.*

## Imperial War Museum

Lambeth Road, SE1
**MAP REF 30D**
Housed in the former Bedlam Hospital, this museum illustrates and records all aspects of the two world wars and other military operations involving Britain and the Commonwealth since 1914. An extremely varied collection of exhibits is on display, ranging from tanks and aeroplanes to weapons and uniforms.

*Open Mon–Sat 10–5.30, Sun 2–5.50 (Closed Good Fri, May Day, 24–26 Dec & 1 Jan). Admission free.*

## Kenwood House (The Iveagh Bequest)

Hampstead Lane, NW3
**DISTRICT MAP**
The House at Kenwood was enlarged for Lord Mansfield in 1767 by the great architect Robert Adam. It was bequeathed to the nation in 1927 by the first Earl of Iveagh, and it makes a magnificent setting for his collection of English and Dutch masterpieces; they include works by Frans Hals, Vermeer, Rembrandt, Reynolds, and Turner.

The 200-acre grounds of Kenwood House contain a lakeside platform where open-air concerts are held during the summer.

*Open daily Apr–Sep 10–7; Feb, Mar & Oct 10–5; Nov–Jan 10–4. Admission free (charges for special exhibitions and concerts).*

## The London Dungeon

28–34 Tooley Street, SE1
**MAP REF 25H**
The world's only medieval horror museum. Vast dark vaults house strange and horrifying scenes from Britain's unsavoury past. Viewing takes about one hour.

*Open daily Apr–Sep 10–5.30; Oct–Mar 10–4.30 (Closed Xmas). Admission charge.*

## The London Experience

The Trocadero Centre, Piccadilly Circus, W1
**MAP REF 22B**
A multi-screen audio visual display in sound, vision and light, which takes visitors back through time to experience London's past history. Scenes include the Plague, the Great Fire of London, the hunt for Jack the Ripper, London through the wars, and its pageantry, markets and people.

*Open daily 10.20am–10.20pm (Closed Xmas Day). Admission charge.*

Stargazing is made easy at the London Planetarium

## London Planetarium

Marylebone Road, NW1
MAP REF 13L
Representations of the heavens are projected here on to a great copper dome, to an accompanying commentary.
*Open daily 11 – 4.30 (Closed 25 Dec). Admission charge.*

## London Silver Vaults

Chancery Lane, WC2
MAP REF 16F
A fine collection of antiques and modern silverware in an underground location. Visitors can browse and traders are happy to talk about their wares, look up hallmarks and explain histories.
*Open Mon – Fri 9 – 5.30; Sat 9 – 12.30. Admission free.*

## London Toy and Model Museum

October House, 21 – 23 Craven Hill, W2
MAP REF 19G
Victorian building housing one of the finest collections of commercially made toys and models with an emphasis on trains, cars, and boats. Extensive garden railway.
*Open Tue – Sat 10 – 5.30; Sun 11 – 5 (Closed PH ex BH Mons). Admission charge.*

## London Transport Museum

The Piazza, Covent Garden, WC2
MAP REF 23G
A unique collection of vehicles associated with 150 years of public transport in London. It includes trams, trolley-buses, horse-drawn and motor buses, steam locomotives, and railway coaches; and a selection of signs, tickets, posters, and models.
*Open daily 10 – 6 (last admission 5.15) (Closed Xmas). Admission charge.*

## Madame Tussaud's

Marylebone Road, NW1
MAP REF 13L
Founded in Paris, Mme Tussaud's Wax Exhibition settled in London in the early 19th century. It contains a large collection of famous historical and contemporary figures, new versions of the tableaux, and the

grim Chamber of Horrors. It is always very popular, so be prepared to queue.

*Open daily 10 – 5.30 (Closed 25 Dec). Admission charge.*

## Museum of London

London Wall, EC2
**MAP REF 17J**
London's newest and most exciting large museum, created in 1976 by merging the collections of the former London and Guildhall Museums. The museum is devoted entirely to London and its people, presenting by way of exhibitions and tableaux the story of its development and life. Open plan and arranged in chronological order, the museum affords a continuous view from prehistory to the 20th century.

Among the objects on display are such diverse items as a medieval hen's egg; the graphic audio-visual reconstruction of the Great Fire of 1666; two immaculate Georgian shopfronts; relics from the Great Exhibition of 1851; a beautifully preserved Victorian pub façade; a 1936 Ford motor car; and the Lord Mayor's State Coach.

The main entrance of the Museum opens directly on to the pedestrian walkway linking the Barbican development with the rest of the City.

*Open Tue – Sat 10 – 6; Sun 2 – 6 (Closed BH & Xmas). Admission free.*

## Museum of Mankind

6 Burlington Gardens, W1
**MAP REF 21L**
A department of the British Museum, this absorbing collection embraces the art and material culture of tribal, village and other pre-industrial societies from most areas of the world except Western Europe.

*Open Mon – Sat 10 – 5; Sun 2.30 – 6 (Closed Good Fri, May Day, 24 – 27 Dec & 1 Jan). Admission free.*

## National Army Museum

Royal Hospital Road, SW3
**MAP REF 27M**
Contains a permanent chronological display of the history of the British, Indian,

Objects from every part of the capital's history are gathered at the Museum of London

and Colonial forces from 1485.

*Open Mon – Sat 10 – 5.30; Sun 2 – 5.30 (Closed Good Fri, May Day, 24 – 26 Dec & 1 Jan). Admission free.*

### KEY: MUSEUM OF LONDON

**Lower Level**
1. Late Stuart London
2. Georgian London
3. Early 19 C. London
4. Imperial Capital
5. 20 C. London
6. Treasury
7. Lord Mayor's Coach

**Upper Floor**
8. Special Exhibits
9. Thames Prehistory
10. Roman London
11. The Dark Age
12. Medieval London
13. Tudor London
14. Early Stuart London
15. Great Fire 1666

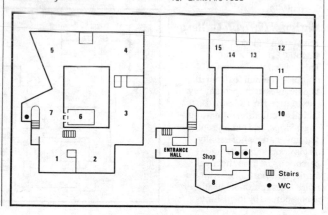

### The National Gallery

Trafalgar Square, WC2
MAP REF 22E

The gallery houses one of the world's finest collections of masterpieces of European painting from the 13th to the 19th centuries. The main collection is arranged chronologically, but changes are made in the arrangement of the rooms from time to time.

Italian paintings occupy the west rooms; Leonardo's cartoon *The Virgin and Child* is one of the most outstanding works in this section. Paintings of the Dutch and Flemish schools occupy the rooms of the north-west extension and include the works of Rembrandt, Rubens, Vermeer and Van Dyck. French and Spanish works, including some by Velazquez, Goya, Manet, and Renoir can be found in the east rooms. A selection of British paintings from Hogarth to Turner includes Gainsborough's *Mr and Mrs Andrews* and Constable's famous *Haywain*.

There are lunchtime lectures and regular guided tours.

*Open Mon – Sat 10 – 6; Sun 2 – 6 (Closed Good Fri, May Day, 24 – 26 Dec & 1 Jan).*
*Admission free.*

### National Maritime Museum

DISTRICT MAP
See page 74.

### National Portrait Gallery

2 St Martin's Place, WC2
MAP REF 22E

This collection of portraits of notable personalities from the Middle Ages to the present day was founded in 1856. It also includes sculpture, miniatures, engravings, and photographs. The gallery does not usually display portraits of living persons apart from the royal family. The portraits, arranged more or less chronologically, are accompanied by furnishings,

The National Gallery portico gives the best views of Trafalgar Square

**KEY: NATIONAL GALLERY**

1. Entrance Hall
2. Early Italian
3. Italian, 16 C.
4. Dutch
5. Flemish
6. Orange St Theatre
7. Special Exhibits
8. Early Northern
9. Italian after 1600
10. French before 1800
11. British
12. Spanish
13. French after 1800

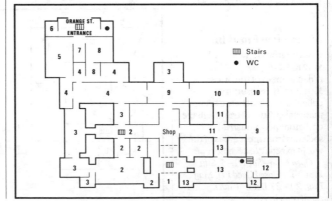

**KEY: NATURAL HISTORY MUSEUM**

| | |
|---|---|
| 1. Birds | 12. Fossil Fishes |
| 2. Insects | 13. Fossil Sea Reptiles |
| 3. Marine Invertebrates | 14. Ecology |
| 4. Whales | 15. Fossil Mammals |
| 5. Human Biology | 16. African Mammals |
| 6. Dinosaurs | 17. Origin of Species |
| 7. Spiders | 18. Mammals |
| 8. Fishes & Reptiles | 19. Man's place in Evolution |
| 9. Special Exhibits | 20. Minerals, Rocks & Gemstones |
| 10. Fossil Invertebrates | 21. Meteorites |
| 11. Wildlife in Danger | 22. British Natural History |

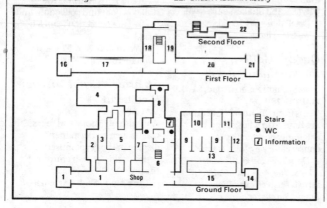

The Natural History Museum

maps, weapons and other items to set them in their historical context.

*Open Mon – Fri 10 – 5; Sat 10 – 6; Sun 2 – 6 (Closed Good Fri, May Day, 24 – 26 Dec & 1 Jan). Admission free (charges for special exhibitions).*

## National Postal Museum

King Edward Building, King Edward Street, EC1
**MAP REF 17J**
Contains probably the finest and most comprehensive collection of postage stamps in the world. There are also proof sheets of every British stamp since 1840.

*Open Mon – Thu (ex BH) 10 – 4.30, Fri 10 – 4. Admission free.*

## Natural History Museum

Cromwell Road, SW7
**MAP REF 26E**
This museum was opened in 1881 to house the natural history exhibits of the British Museum. Sir Hans Sloane's mid-eighteenth century collections form the nucleus of the exhibits now on view, which include animals, birds, reptiles, plants, fossils, and minerals. The Dinosaur and British Natural History Galleries are of particular interest.

*Open Mon – Sat 10 – 6, Sun 2.30 – 6 (Closed Good Fri, May Day, 24 – 26 Dec & 1 Jan). Admission charge from April 1987.*

## North Woolwich Old Station Museum

Pier Road, E16
**DISTRICT MAP**
Imposing restored station building with three galleries of photographs, models, and an original turntable pit. Each Sunday a locomotive is in steam.

*Open Mon – Sat 10 – 5; Sun & BH 2 – 5 (Closed Xmas). Admission free.*

Sir John Soane's Museum is one of the most unusual museums in London and might be described as a 'cabinet of curiosities'.

## Royal Academy of Arts

Burlington House, Piccadilly, W1
**MAP REF 21L**
An annual Summer Exhibition of works of living artists has been held here since 1769. Other exhibitions of international importance take place as announced in the Press.
*Open daily 10 – 6. Admission charge.*

## Royal Air Force Museum

NW8
**DISTRICT MAP**
Over 40 aircraft are included in these galleries devoted to military aviation history.
*Open Mon – Sat 10 – 6, Sun 2 – 6 (Closed Good Fri, May Day, 24 – 26 Dec & 1 Jan). RAF Museum – admission free; Battle of Britain and Bomber Command Museums – admission charge.*

## Royal College of Music Museum of Instruments

Prince Consort Road, SW7
**MAP REF 26D**
Among the 500 musical instruments housed here are the Donaldson collection of rare keyboard pieces, some dating from the 15th century; the Ridley woodwind collection; and the Tagore collection from S E Asia.
*Open Mon & Wed 11 – 4.30. Admission charge.*

## St. Bride's Crypt Museum

Fleet Street, EC4
**MAP REF 24A**
A wealth of history and relics can be seen on permanent display in the crypt museum beneath this 'parish church of the press'.
*Open Mon – Sat 9 – 5; Sun 9 – 8. Admission free.*

## The Photographers' Gallery

5/8 Great Newport Street, WC2
**MAP REF 22D**
As well as monthly exhibitions, the gallery aims to show the best of the many types of professional photography – from reportage and advertising to the purely creative.
*Open Tue – Sat 5 – 7. Admission free.*

## Pollock's Toy Museum

1 Scala Street, W1
**MAP REF 15J**
In two charming interconnected houses are displayed dolls, teddy bears, board games, toy theatres, and mechanical toys from all over the world. There is also a shop.
*Open Mon – Sat 10 – 5 (Closed Good Fri, Etr Mon, Spring BH Mon, Summer BH Mon & Xmas). Admission charge.*

## The Public Records Office

Chancery Lane, WC2
**MAP REF 16F**
This is the chief repository for the national archives. The Search Rooms contain records from the Norman Conquest to the present day. Among the famous documents on display are the *Domesday Book*, letters from Cardinal Wolsey and Guy Fawkes, and Shakespeare's will.
*Open Mon – Sat 10 – 6. Admission charge.*

## Queen's Gallery Buckingham Palace

Buckingham Palace Road, SW1
**MAP REF 28D**
Items from the Royal Collection are housed in a building originally designed as a conservatory by John Nash.
*Open Tue – Sat & BH Mon 11 – 5; Sun 2 – 5 (ex for short periods between exhibitions). Admission charge.*

Engines from the age of steam are among the thousands of exhibits at the Science Museum

### Sir John Soane's Museum

13 Lincoln's Inn Fields, WC2
MAP REF 16C
A fine 1813 house contains the collection of pictures, sculptures, and antiquities founded by the original architect of the Bank of England building. There are paintings by Hogarth, notably his *Rake's Progress*, and more than 20,000 architectural drawings.

*Open Tue–Sat 10–5 (Closed Sun, Mon, BHs & August). Admission free.*

### Science Museum

Exhibition Road, SW7
MAP REF 26D
The extensive collections illustrate the development of engineering and industry throughout the ages. Of all London museums, this is the one most loved by children. There are knobs to press, handles to turn, and all sorts of exhibits that light up, rotate, and make noises.

There are galleries dealing with astronomy, printing, chemistry, nuclear physics, navigation, photography, electricity, communications. The exhibits include a superb collection of model ships, and forming part of the new Exploration of Space Gallery, the *Apollo 10 Space Capsule*.

In the huge new wing of the ground floor devoted to road and rail transport may be seen *Puffing Billy*, the world's oldest steam locomotive, and George Stephenson's *Rocket*. The Wellcome collections of medicine and medical history are on the 5th and 6th floors.

*Open Mon–Sat 10–6; Sun 2.30–6 (Closed Good Fri, May Day, 24–26 Dec & 1 Jan). Admission free.*

**KEY: SCIENCE MUSEUM**

1. Development of Motive Power
2. Hot Air, Gas & Oil Engines
3. Exploration
4. Transport
5. Fire Fighting
6. Hand & Machine Tools
7. Iron & Steel
8. Glass
9. Telecommunications
10. Textile Machinery
11. Plastics
12. Agriculture
13. Gas
14. Meteorology
15. Time Measurement
16. Mapmaking
17. Astronomy
18. Weighing, Measuring & Lighting
19. Chemistry
20. Printing & Papermaking
21. Nuclear Power & Physics
22. Computing
23. Navigation
24. Sailing & Marine Engineering
25. Docks & Diving
26. Optics
27. Heat & Temperature
28. King George III Collection
29. Photography & Cinematography
30. Electricity & Magnetism
31. Geophysics & Oceanography
32. Clothes for the Job
33. Aeronautics

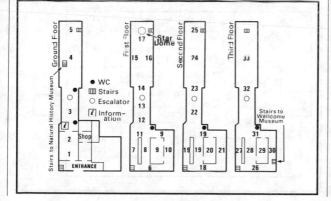

The sedate exterior of the Tate Gallery contrasts with the often controversial works shown inside

## The Tate Gallery

Millbank, SW1
**MAP REF 29L**
Opened in 1897, the gallery houses the national collections of British painting of all periods, modern foreign painting and modern sculpture. There is also a large collection of contemporary prints. Hogarth, Blake, Turner, Constable and the Pre-Raphaelites are particularly well represented, and the English mastery of landscape painting is superbly illustrated. All schools of painting and sculpture are represented in the modern and foreign collections which trace the development of art from Impressionism to the present day. The Tate is especially renowned for its modern works of art, buying some almost before they are finished, so reflecting the constantly changing emphasis of contemporary art.

For exhibition purposes, rooms are rehung, so the layout may change.

*Open Mon – Sat 10 – 5.50; Sun 2 – 5.50 (Closed Good Fri, May Day, 24 – 26 Dec & 1 Jan). Admission free; admission charge to special exhibitions.*

## The Thomas Coram Foundation for Children

40 Brunswick Square, WC1
**MAP REF 15L**
The Foundation was formed in 1739 with the granting of a royal charter to Captain Thomas Coram to open a Foundling Hospital for destitute children. At the instigation of William Hogarth, various works of art were presented to the Foundation to attract the public and raise funds. The building now houses the vast number of exhibits which have been presented to the Foundation over the years.

*Open Mon – Fri, 10 – 4 (Closed BH). (Advisable to check). Admission charge.*

**KEY: TATE GALLERY**

1. 16 C. – 18 C.
2. Exotic & Sublime
3. Blake
4a. Closed at present
4b. British 19 C
5. British Watercolours
6, 7 & 8 British 19 C
9. Pre-Raphaelites
10. Late Victorian
11. 20 C sculpture, art since 1970, etc
12. Cubism, Futurism, Vorticism
13. British Painting 1880 – 1920
14. Aspects of European Art 1910 – 1930
15. Impressionism, Post-Impressionism, Matisse, Bonnard
16. Abstraction c.1910 – 40
17. Surrealism
18. Recent Acquisitions
19. European c. 1940 – 60
20. German art c.1900 – 40 and Abstract Expressionism
21. Dubuffet, etc
22. Rothko
23. Giacometti etc
24. Print Room Gallery

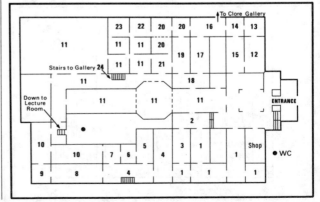

## *Victoria and Albert Museum*

Cromwell Road, SW7
MAP REF 26E
The national museum of
art and design covering all
countries, periods and styles.
Exhibits range from great works
of art to items designed simply to
entertain and amuse: from the
huge 16th-century *Great Bed of
Ware*, to Hilliard's exquisite
portrait miniature *Young Man
leaning against a Tree*. The
maze-like interior contains two
types of galleries: the primary
ones, which display a variety of
exhibits giving a comprehensive
picture of a period or civilization;
and subject galleries, with
specialised exhibitions.

Open Mon – Sat (except Fri)
10 – 5.50; Sun 2.30 – 5.50
(Closed Fri, Good Fri, May Day,
24 – 26 Dec & 1 Jan).
*Donation.*

One of the galleries in the
Victoria and Albert Museum, a
treasure-house of beautiful
objects

### KEY: VICTORIA AND ALBERT MUSEUM

1. Continental 17 C.
2. Continental 18 C.
3. Continental 19 C.
4. Woodwork Collection
5. Raphael Cartoons
6. Eastern & Asian Art
7. Medieval Treasury
8. Dress Collection
9. High Renaissance
10. Sculpture
11. Boilerhouse Project
12. Prints & Photographs
13. Renaissance Italy
14. Morris Room
15. Gamble Room
16. Poynter Room
17. Renaissance N. Europe
18. Medieval Tapestries
19. Carpets
20. Spanish Art
21. Gothic Art
22. Victorian Cast Court
23. Fakes & Forgeries
24. Italian Cast Court
25. English Renaissance
26. British 1650 – 1750
27. Carvings & Bronzes
28. Stained Glass
29. Armour & Ironwork
30. Musical Instruments
31. British Art
32. Theatre Museums
33. Silver
34. Enamel & Metalwork
35. 20 C. Collection
36. Tapestries etc
37. Fans
38. Jewellery
39. Library
40. Glass Vessels

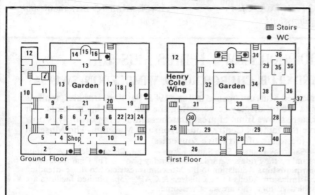

The Victoria and Albert houses beautiful and intriguing objects

## Wallace Collection

Hertford House, Manchester Square, W1
MAP REF 14C
An outstanding collection of works of art which includes pictures by Titian, Rubens, Gainsborough, and Delacroix, together with an unrivalled representation of 18th-century French art. There is also a large, varied display of decorative arts.
*Open Mon – Sat 10 – 5; Sun 2 – 5 (Closed Good Fri, May Day, 24 – 26 Dec & 1 Jan). Admission free.*

## The Wellington Museum

Apsley House, 149 Piccadilly, W1
MAP REF 21J
The original Adam mansion of 1771 – 78 was altered by the Duke of Wellington after the Battle of Waterloo. Exhibits include famous paintings, silver, porcelain, decorations and personal relics of the first Duke. There is an amusing collection of political caricatures.
*Open Tue – Thu, Sat 10 – 6; Sun 2.30 – 6. Admission charge.*

## William Morris Gallery

Water House, Lloyd Park, Forest Road, E17
DISTRICT MAP
As well as exhibits of William Morris fabrics, wallpapers, and furniture, there are also ceramics, work by the Century Guild, Pre-Raphaelite pictures, and sculpture by Rodin.
*Open Tue – Sat 10 – 1 & 2 – 5, and 1st Sun in each month, 10 – noon & 2 – 5 (Closed Mon & PH). Admission free.*

## Wimbledon Lawn Tennis Museum

Church Road, SW19
DISTRICT MAP
The only one of its kind in the world, this museum traces the development of the game over the last century.
*Open Tue – Sat 11 – 5, Sun 2 – 5 (Closed Mon & BH). Admission charge.*

# *ENTERTAINMENT*

However you like to be entertained, you will find something to suit your taste in London. There is always a wide variety of plays and musicals to choose from in the theatres; a host of cinemas show the latest releases, classic oldies, and the more obscure movies which you missed the first time round; and there is music everywhere, from jazz in cafes and folk music in church crypts, to the usual concert venues. Full details of all current and forthcoming concerts, together with theatre and cinema programmes, can be found in the entertainments section of London's evening newspaper, *The Standard*, and in specialist London magazines such as *Time Out*, *What's On*, and *City Limits* – on sale at bookstalls and newsagents.

## BOOKING

Tickets can be booked, of course, at the box offices of the individual theatres and concert halls. Many now accept credit card booking, which means you can telephone the box office to reserve your seats, quote your credit card number, and then collect the tickets half-an-hour before the performance begins. Some places have special phone numbers for credit card bookings, and these are pre fixed *cc* in the listings which follow. Or you can use the services of ticket agencies such as Keith Prowse (tel: (01) 741 9999); or try First Call (tel: (01) 240 7200), a new telephone booking service mainly for credit card holders wanting theatre and concert tickets. It is open 24 hours a day, seven days a week.

## ARTS CENTRES

Amongst the most exciting venues in London, these centres offer several different types of entertainment under one roof. Even if you only go once, you cannot but be aware of the creativity generated by the other activities; they are, anyway, pleasant places to go for an evening meal, snack, or drink, as they all offer refreshments of one sort or another.

## Barbican Centre

Barbican, EC2
MAP REF 17I
Tel: box office (01) 628 8795; recorded information on events (01) 628 9760; *cc* (01) 638 8891

It is best to allow plenty of time to find where you want to go within this massive new complex; the free guide *Welcome to the Barbican Centre* will help get you to your seats on time. **The Barbican Theatre** (levels 3–6), London home of the Royal Shakespeare Company, presents modern drama and classic revivals as well as regular productions of Shakespeare's plays. Beneath, on level 1, more experimental works, as well as the classics, are presented in the studio theatre called the Pit.

In the **Barbican Hall** on levels 5 and 6, the London Symphony Orchestra – whose home this is – offers three one-month-long seasons annually. During the rest of the year, there is visiting opera, classical, jazz, and folk concerts.

**Cinema 1**, on level 1, shows current general releases, as well as important international films which may not get a showing elsewhere.

Whenever you go to the Barbican, even on Sunday mornings, you will find frequent free entertainment – mostly of a musical nature – in the foyers on most levels. Refreshments of one sort or another can also be found on all levels. Particularly pleasant is the Waterside Café on level 5, where you can sit outside overlooking the artificial lake.

## *Institute of Contemporary Arts (ICA)*

12 Carlton House Terrace, SW1
MAP REF 22E
Tel: (01) 930 0493; recorded information (01) 930 6393

You must be a member – if only for a day – in order to enjoy the ICA's facilities. The cinema shows foreign, avant-garde, and unusual films in the evenings and at weekend matinees, and there is a Children's Cinema Club at weekends. The theatre stage often changes shape in order to suit its different productions, which are mostly of a new and experimental nature. There are regular lunchtime debates between artists, writers, critics and the public, and evening lectures on cultural issues.

*The Centre is open from noon to 11pm, Tue to Sun.*

## *Riverside Studios*

Crisp Road, W6
DISTRICT MAP
Tel: (01) 748 3354

This small but most rewarding

Home of the 'Proms' – the Royal Albert Hall

centre for the arts in Hammersmith was formerly a BBC studio. Now a fine mixture of drama, dance, and music can be enjoyed in its theatre from Monday to Saturday; there is usually a one-off concert or show on Sundays. For participators, there are regular jazz, tap, and modern dance classes. Its huge, welcoming foyer houses a bar, and a self-service café where you can buy food at any time.

*Open 10am – 11pm, Mon – Sat; 10.30am – 10.30pm Sun.*

## MUSIC

London is one of the most exciting music centres in the world. International stars of ballet, opera, and classical music have long been drawn to the footlights of London's theatres. Jazz, folk, and pop enthusiasts are similarly well catered for.

## CONCERT HALLS

***The Barbican Hall*** *(see page 113)*

### Royal Albert Hall

Kensington Gore, SW7
**MAP REF 26D**
Tel: (01) 589 8212; *cc* (01) 589 9465
This famous Victorian building on the edge of South Kensington is perhaps best known for the Sir Henry Wood Promenade Concerts ('The Proms') – performed daily from mid-July to mid-September – whose last night is traditionally full of patriotic fervour. It is also the venue for concerts ranging from classical to pop throughout the rest of the year, and for a varied mixture of other events.

### St John's

Smith Square, SW1
**MAP REF 29K**
Tel: (01) 222 1061
This 18th-century church holds regular lunchtime and evening concerts: from solo recitals to choral works. Become a Friend for advance booking and discounts. Lunchtime concerts are at 1pm on Mondays and at 1.15pm on alternate Thursdays.

*Other churches, in the City, hold regular lunchtime concerts or recitals; they include the following. Tel: (01) 606 3030 for full details of venues and programmes, and to check times.*
***All Hallows-by-the-Tower***,
Byward Street, EC3
1pm Mondays; 12.15pm and 1.15pm Thursdays
***Holy Sepulchre***, Holborn Viaduct, EC1
1.15pm Tuesdays, Wednesdays, Fridays; 1.20pm Thursdays
***St Bride***, Fleet Street, EC4
1.15pm Wednesdays
***St Lawrence Jewry***, Gresham Street, EC2
1pm Mondays & Tuesdays
***St Martin-in-the-Fields***,
Trafalgar Square, WC2
1.05pm Mondays & Tuesdays

*St Mary-le-Bow*, Cheapside, EC2
1.05pm Thursdays
*St Mary Woolnoth*, Lombard
Street, EC3
1.05pm Fridays
*St Michael-upon-Cornhill*,
Cornhill, EC3
1pm Mondays
*St Olave*, Hart Street, EC3
1.05pm Wednesdays &
Thursdays
*St Paul's Cathedral*, EC4
12.30pm Fridays
*Southwark Cathedral*, Borough
High Street, SE1
1.10pm Mondays

## The South Bank Arts Complex

SE1
MAP REF 23I1
This includes three concert halls
(central phone number
(01) 928 3191; cc (01)
928 8800).

The Royal Festival Hall, built
in 1951 as part of the Festival of
Britain, is a 3,000-seat concert
hall staging orchestral and
choral programmes. The foyers,
which are open from noon every
day, hold exhibitions as well as
bars, a café, and a restaurant.
These facilities are shared with
the **Queen Elizabeth Hall**, which
stages symphony and orchestral
concerts as well as other
cultural events such as Poetry
International, and the **Purcell
Room**, whose smaller concert
hall is ideal for chamber music
and solo performances. The
complex has a prime position
overlooking the Thames.

## Wigmore Hall

36 Wigmore Street, W1
MAP REF 14C
Tel: (01) 935 2141
The intimate atmosphere of this
small hall is perfect for its
presentations of chamber music
and solo recitals by singers and
instrumentalists. It is supposed
to have the best acoustics for
guitar playing in London. There
are short Sunday morning
concerts during the summer.

**OPERA AND BALLET**

## The London Coliseum

St Martin's Lane, WC2
MAP REF 22E
Tel: (01) 836 3161; cc
(01) 240 5258
The Coliseum was built in 1904,
and was at first used primarily as
a music hall. It is easily identified
by the giant electrical globe on
the roof which twinkles into the
sky each evening. One of the
largest theatres in London, it
was the first to install a
revolving stage, and Sarah
Bernhardt, Lillie Langtry, and
Ellen Terry have all trodden its
boards. Since 1968 the
Coliseum has been the home of
the English National Opera
Company, who always sing in
English. Their varied season
lasts from August to May;
visiting opera companies fill in
while the ENO go off on their
summer tours. There is a
bookstall in the foyer which is
open all day.

## Royal Opera House

Covent Garden, WC2
MAP REF 23G
Tel: (01) 240 1066; recorded
information (01) 240 1911
The present building is the third
theatre of its name on the site,
and opera has flourished here
since 1847. It is the home of the
Royal Opera Company; in 1911
Thomas Beecham brought ballet
to the theatre and it became the
headquarters of the Royal Ballet
Company in 1956. The very best
names in the world of ballet and
opera can be seen here in
suitably lavish settings and
productions. It is advisable to
book well in advance, although
you can queue on the day for a
limited number of cheaper
amphitheatre tickets.

## Sadler's Wells

Rosebery Avenue, EC1
MAP REF 16D
Tel: (01) 278 8916; recorded
information (01) 278 5450

The well or natural spring,
discovered by Richard Sadler in
1683 and developed as a spa, is
still preserved within the
theatre. Famous for the
performances of the clown Joe
Grimaldi in the early 19th
century, and for its
Shakespearean productions a
few years later, the building was
renovated by Lilian Baylis and
re-opened in 1931. Sadler's
Wells then acquired fame as a
ballet and operatic centre and it
was here that the Royal Ballet
first achieved world-wide status
under the guidance of its artistic
director Ninette de Valois.

It is now the home of the
English-singing New Sadler's
Wells Opera and also the
London base of the Sadler's
Wells Royal Ballet (the touring
one). Visiting opera and dance
companies frequently perform
here.

**OPEN-AIR MUSIC**

During the summer, military
bands offer free lunchtime
entertainment in the Royal
Parks, and in certain City parks
and squares.
*Royal Parks*: military and brass
bands play free most lunchtimes
in Hyde Park, St James's Park,
and Regent's Park. Phone
(01) 211 3000 for information.
*City sites* (phone the City
Information Centre on
(01) 606 3030 for details).
*Finsbury Circus Gardens*,
Moorgate, EC2: lunchtime band
concerts, usually Wednesdays.
*Lincoln's Inn Fields*, WC2:
military bands, usually Tuesday
and Thursday lunchtimes.
*Paternoster Square*, EC4: military
bands, daily, lunchtimes.
*St Paul's Steps*, EC4: sit in full
view of St Paul's and listen to a
full military band concert;
usually Thursdays.
*Tower Place*, EC3: military bands,
usually Fridays.
*Victoria Embankment Gardens*,
SW1: riverside setting for
military bands, massed bands,

and light orchestras, most lunchtimes of the week.

*Other sites:*
*Battersea Park Concert Pavilion*, SW11 (tel: (01) 633 1707). Imaginative programme of musical events, lunchtime and evenings.

*Holland Park Court Theatre*, W8 (tel: (01) 633 1707). A small open-air theatre which stages opera and ballet and concerts during July.

*Kenwood*, Hampstead Lane, NW3 (tel: (01) 348 1286). Leading orchestras give symphony concerts in this beautiful setting by the lake on Saturday evenings during June and July. To be seen to be 'in', take a picnic.

*Parliament Hill*, NW3 (tel: (01) 485 4491). Massed bands play beside the lake on Saturday evenings during the summer.

## ROCK AND JAZZ

As well as frequent – and sometimes huge – rock concerts (Wembley Arena is a notable venue), and internationally-recognised jazz clubs, many pubs in London hold informal, often free, sessions. Information about these from the London magazines – see page 113 – or phone the Jazz Centre Society on (01) 580 8532. Here is a small selection of regular venues.

### Dingwall's
Camden Lock, Chalk Farm Road, NW1
**DISTRICT MAP**
Tel: (01) 267 4967
This music club holds a mixture of rock and jazz gigs every evening with jazz at lunchtime on Sundays.

### Dominion Theatre
Tottenham Court Road, W1
**MAP REF 15J**
Tel: (01) 580 9562
This large cinema stages seasons of live rock which are publicised well in advance.

### Half Moon
93 Lower Richmond Road, SW15
**DISTRICT MAP**
Tel: (01) 788 2387
Big-name bands play rock, pop, or jazz in this pub every night and at lunchtime on Sundays.

### Hammersmith Odeon
Hammersmith Broadway, W6
**DISTRICT MAP**
Tel: (01) 748 4081
This huge cinema is given over entirely to concerts with internationally-known stars.

### The Latchmere
503 Battersea Park Road, SW11
**DISTRICT MAP**
Tel: (01) 228 4011
Rock and pop sessions at this pub on Monday to Thursday evenings, and jazz at lunchtime on Sundays.

### The Marquee
90 Wardour Street, W1
**MAP REF 22A**
Tel: (01) 437 6603
One of the first of the London rock clubs, you can hear music here every evening from 7pm.

### 100 Club
100 Oxford Street, W1
**MAP REF 15J**
Tel: (01) 636 0933
Jazz and dancing every evening from 7.30 to midnight.

### Rock Garden
The Piazza, Covent Garden, WC2
**MAP REF 23G**
Tel: (01) 240 3961
Live rock in the basement of this hamburger joint every night.

### Ronnie Scott's
47 Frith Street, W1
**MAP REF 22D**
Tel: (01) 439 0747
International jazz at its best; open 8.30pm to 3am Monday to Saturday.

## THEATRE

More than 400 years after live theatre was first presented in London, there are now about 40 commercial theatres open in the West End of London and two major subsidised companies, the National Theatre and the Royal Shakespeare Company, all combining to give entertainment of unrivalled quality and variety.

## BOOKING

The Half-Price Ticket Booth in Leicester Square, a chalet-type building opposite the Swiss Centre, is open to personal callers only and sells tickets from 12 – 2pm for matinee performances and from 2.30pm – 6.30pm for evening shows. Tickets are for that day only; a booking fee is charged. See also page 113.

## A SELECTION OF FAMOUS THEATRES

### Criterion
Piccadilly, W1
**MAP REF 22B**
Tel: (01) 930 3216; *cc* (01) 379 6565
The strange lay-out of this listed building means that you even go underground to the Upper Circle. The foyer is decorated with the original Victorian tiles.

### Her Majesty's
Haymarket, SW1
**MAP REF 22E**
Tel: (01) 930 6606; *cc* (01) 930 4025
Founded by Sir Herbert Beerbohm Tree in 1897, this pavilioned theatre is crowned by a Baroque copper dome.

### Lyric Hammersmith
King Street, W6
**DISTRICT MAP**
Tel: (01) 741 2311
This is almost an arts centre in itself. The theatre, with its lavish recreation of an Victorian

auditorium, is on the second and third floors, and stages classic, modern, and fringe productions.

## The National Theatre

South Bank, SE1
MAP REF 23L
Tel: (01) 928 2252; cc
(01) 928 5933

Part of the South Bank Arts complex, the National was opened in 1976 and in the few years since has won for itself a world-wide reputation for the quality of its productions of new, classic, foreign, and experimental plays. The building in fact houses two theatres which share the same facilities: the open-staged Olivier, and the smaller Lyttleton, with its proscenium arch. A few seats are held back for sale to personal callers from 10am on the day of the performance. Even if you are not going to a play, the National is a lovely place to browse among the bookstalls and exhibitions, listen to live music in the Lyttleton foyer every evening, or have a drink in the various bars on every floor. You can even enjoy a guided tour of the whole building, including backstage: phone (01) 633 0880 to book.

## Palladium

8 Argyll Street, W1
MAP REF 21K
Tel: (01) 437 7373

This famous music hall opened in 1910. Spectacular revues took over in the 1920s, and the famous Crazy Gang Shows enjoyed permanent residency until after the War. In 1946 the Palladium returned to a policy of top-name variety shows. In the '60s it was famous for television's *Sunday Night at the London Palladium*. Christmas entertainment has always been a speciality here, and once a year there is all the glitter and attraction of the Royal Command Performance.

## The Old Vic

Waterloo Road, SE1
MAP REF 23M
Tel: (01) 928 7616; cc
(01) 261 1821

Also known as the Royal Victoria Theatre, this building was erected in 1818. It was noted for lurid melodramas until 1880 when Emma Cons acquired the premises and made them the home of classical plays and opera – a tradition which was carried on by her niece, Lilian Baylis. For many years famous for its Shakespearean productions, the Old Vic was the headquarters of the National Theatre Company until it transferred to the South Bank in 1976.

## Open Air Theatre

Regent's Park, NW1
MAP REF 13K
Tel: (01) 486 2431; cc
(01) 379 6433

This theatre has been in operation since 1932, braving the rigours of the British climate with the aid of a wet-weather marquee to stage summer performances of Shakespeare. The present auditorium was built in 1975, and the wooded surroundings provide an ideal setting for such plays as *A Midsummer Night's Dream* and *As You Like It*.

## Royal Court

Sloane Square, SW1
MAP REF 27L
Tel: (01) 730 1745

Ever since its opening in 1870, the Royal Court has specialised in innovative plays. The farces of Arthur Pinero were performed here in the 1890s, followed by premiere productions of some of Shaw's plays at the beginning of the century. Probably the most famous and controversial of recent avant-garde plays, the English Stage Company's production of John Osborne's *Look Back in Anger*, ran here in

1956. Since 1969 the small Theatre Upstairs has specialised in particularly new and experimental work.

## Savoy

Strand, WC2
MAP REF 23H
Tel: (01) 836 8888; cc
(01) 379 6219

This theatre, now incorporated in the famous Savoy Hotel, was commissioned by the great D'Oyly Carte and it was here that his productions of Gilbert and Sullivan's comic operas were staged between 1881 and 1889. It was the first public building in the world to be lit by electricity, and now presents a variety of plays and musicals.

## Shaftesbury

Shaftesbury Avenue, WC2
MAP REF 15M
Tel: (01) 379 5399; cc
(01) 741 9999

This theatre was acquired in 1983 by a company of some of the best of British comedy actors, and is now a Theatre of Comedy, showing works of all sorts from classical to modern, farcical to sophisticated.

## Theatre Royal Drury Lane

Catherine Street, WC2
MAP REF 23G
Tel: (01) 836 8108

The Theatre Royal is situated on one of the oldest theatre sites in London. The first building, dating from 1663, was destroyed by fire and replaced by one designed by Wren. A third building opened in 1794 under the management of Richard Sheridan, but this too burnt down. The present theatre is the largest in London, with sumptuous furnishings and surroundings, a portico and Ionic colonnade at the rear, and numerous monuments to former exponents of the dramatic art.

### Theatre Royal
Haymarket, SW1
MAP REF 22E
Tel: (01) 930 9832
Quality plays are presented at this theatre, designed by John Nash and opened in 1821, as befits its grand exterior.

### Young Vic
66 The Cut, SE1
MAP REF 23M
Tel: (01) 928 6363
This is basically a young people's repertory company where the emphasis is put on classics and established plays.

### OTHER WEST END THEATRES
*Adelphi*, Strand, WC2 (tel: (01) 836 7611)
*Albery*, St Martin's Lane, WC2 (tel: (01) 836 3878; *cc* (01) 379 6565)
*Aldwych*, Aldwych, WC2 (tel: (01) 836 6404)
*Ambassadors*, West Street, WC2 (tel: (01) 836 1171; *cc* (01) 741 9999)
*Apollo*, Shaftesbury Avenue, W1 (tel: (01) 437 2663)
*Apollo*, Victoria, 17 Wilton Road, SW1 (tel: (01) 828 8665; *cc* (01) 630 6262)
*Astoria*, Charing Cross Road, WC2 (tel: (01) 734 4287)
*Barbican*, Barbican, EC2 (tel: (01) 628 8795; *cc* (01) 638 8891)
*Comedy*, Panton Street, SW1 (tel: (01) 930 2578; *cc* (01) 839 1438)
*Donmar Warehouse*, Earlham Street, WC2 (tel: (01) 836 3028; *cc* (01) 379 6565)
*Duchess*, Catherine Street, WC2 (tel: (01) 836 8243; *cc* (01) 741 9999)
*Duke of York's*, St Martin's Lane, WC2 (tel: (01) 836 5122; *cc* (01) 836 9837)
*Fortune*, Russell Street, WC2 (tel: (01) 836 2238; *cc* (01) 741 9999)
*Garrick*, Charing Cross Road, WC2 (tel: (01) 836 4601; *cc* (01) 379 6433)

*Globe*, Shaftesbury Avenue, W1 (tel: (01) 437 1592)
*ICA Theatre*, Carlton House Terrace, SW1 (tel: (01) 930 0493)
*Jeanetta Cochrane*, Theobalds Road, WC1 (tel: (01) 242 7040)
*King's Head*, Upper Street, N1 (tel: (01) 226 1916)
*Lyric*, Shaftesbury Avenue, W1 (tel: (01) 437 3686; *cc* (01) 434 1050)
*Mayfair*, Stratton Street, W1 (tel: (01) 629 3036)
*Mermaid*, Puddle Dock, EC4 (tel: (01) 236 5568)
*New London*, Drury Lane, WC2 (tel: (01) 405 0072; *cc* (01) 404 4079)
*Palace*, Shaftesbury Avenue, W1 (tel: (01) 437 6834; *cc* (01) 379 6131)
*Phoenix*, Charing Cross Road, WC2 (tel: (01) 836 2294; *cc* (01) 741 9999)
*Piccadilly*, Denman Street, W1 (tel: (01) 437 4506; *cc* (01) 379 6565)
*Prince Edward*, Old Compton Street, W1 (tel: (01) 437 6877; *cc* (01) 439 8499)
*Prince of Wales*, Coventry Street, W1 (tel: (01) 930 8681; *cc* (01) 930 0844)
*Queen's*, Shaftesbury Avenue, W1 (tel: (01) 734 1166)
*St Martin's*, West Street, WC2 (tel: (01) 836 1443)
*Strand*, Aldwych, WC2 (tel: (01) 836 4143)
*Vaudeville*, Strand, WC2 (tel: (01) 836 9987)
*Victoria Palace*, Victoria Street, SW1 (tel: (01) 834 1317; *cc* (01) 828 4735)
*Westminster*, Palace Street, SW1 (tel: (01) 834 0283)
*Wyndhams*, Charing Cross Road, WC2 (tel: (01) 836 3028; *cc* (01) 379 6565)

### CINEMAS
*ABC 1 & 2*, Shaftesbury Avenue, WC2 (tel: (01) 836 8861)
*Cannon (Baker Street)*, Marylebone Road, NW1 (tel: (01) 935 9772)

*Cannon*, Charing Cross Road, WC2 (tel: (01) 437 4815)
*Cannon*, Haymarket, SW1 (tel: (01) 839 1527)
*Cannon Moulin*, Great Windmill Street, W1 (tel: (01) 437 1653)
*Cannon*, Oxford Street, W1 (tel: (01) 636 0310)
*Cannon*, Panton Street, SW1 (tel: (01) 930 0631)
*Cannon (Piccadilly Circus)*, Piccadilly, W1 (tel: (01) 437 3561)
*Cannon Premier*, Swiss Centre, Leicester Square, WC2 (tel: (01) 437 2096)
*Cannon*, Tottenham Court Road, W1 (tel: (01) 636 6148)
*Cannon Royal*, Charing Cross Road, WC2 (tel: (01) 930 6915)
*Curzon (Mayfair)*, Curzon Street, W1 (tel: (01) 499 3737)
*Curzon (West End)*, Shaftesbury Avenue, WC2 (tel: (01) 439 4805)
*Dominion*, Tottenham Court Road, W1 (tel: (01) 580 9562)
*Empire*, Leicester Square, WC2 (tel: (01) 437 1234)
*Leicester Square Theatre*, Leicester Square, WC2 (tel: (01) 930 5252)
*Lumiere*, St Martin's Lane, WC2 (tel: (01) 836 0691)
*Metro*, Rupert Street, W1 (tel: (01) 437 0757)
*Minema*, 145 Knightsbridge, SW1 (tel: (01) 235 4225)
*National Film Theatre*, South Bank, SE1 (tel: (01) 928 3232)
*Odeon*, Haymarket, SW1 (tel: (01) 930 2738)
*Odeon*, Leicester Square, WC2 (tel: (01) 930 6111)
*Odeon*, Marble Arch, W2 (tel: (01) 723 2011)
*Plaza 1, 2, 3 & 4*, Regent Street, W1 (tel: (01) 437 1234)
*Prince Charles*, Leicester Place, WC2 (tel: (01) 437 8181)
*Renoir*, Brunswick Square, WC1 (tel: (01) 837 8402)
*Screen on Baker Street*, Baker Street, W1 (tel: (01) 935 2772)
*Warner West End 1, 2, 3 & 4*, Cranbourn Street, WC2 (tel: (01) 439 0791)

### Wembley Stadium

Empire Way, Wembley
DISTRICT MAP
Built in 1923 as part of the British Empire Exhibition, this 100,000-capacity stadium is most famous as the staging ground of *the* football match of the year – the FA Cup Final (held in May). Also used for the football Littlewood's Cup Final and international matches, it is every footballer's dream to 'go to Wembley'.

A host of other events take place here each year, including the Rugby League Challenge Cup Final, women's hockey internationals, schoolboy internationals, the Gaelic Games, pop festivals, speedway championships, and regular twice-weekly greyhound racing. In 1934 an indoor sports building, the Empire Pool and Sports Arena, was built, and though no longer used for swimming, the arena is frequently adapted to stage ice shows and ice hockey, boxing (the ABA Championships are held here in May), badminton (All England Championships in March), tennis (the Benson & Hedges World Doubles Championship in November), gymnastics, basketball, cycling, and horse shows (the Horse of the Year Show in October). For most of these events, it is almost impossible to get in unless you have tickets in advance: apply in the first instance to the Wembley Stadium Box Office, tel: (01) 902 1234.

### ASSOCIATION FOOTBALL

Football is so old a sport that no-one is quite sure of its origins. It has always been popular in England, and was well-established in London by the 17th century when street games were regularly played between rival groups of apprentices in Covent Garden, Cheapside, and the Strand.

The football season runs from August to May.

### LONDON'S FOOTBALL CLUBS

### Arsenal

Arsenal Stadium, Highbury, N5
DISTRICT MAP
Arsenal have won the FA Cup five times, the most recent being in 1979. They have achieved a total of eight League Championships, including four between 1931 and 1935. In 1971 they were the second team this century to win the League and Cup double.

### Brentford

Griffin Park, Braemar Road, Brentford
DISTRICT MAP
Brentford have spent most of their time in the lower echelons, apart from a spell in the First Division just before and after World War II.

### Charlton Athletic

Selhurst Park, Whitehouse Lane, SE25
DISTRICT MAP
Charlton Athletic played in the first post-war Cup Final in 1946. Their player Bert Turner scored for each side in Derby County's 4–1 victory and the ball burst. Charlton redeemed themselves the following year, beating Burnley 1–0. The ball burst again.

### Chelsea

Stamford Bridge, Fulham Road, SW6
DISTRICT MAP
Chelsea, perhaps London's most fashionable club, won the League Championship in 1955 and the FA Cup in 1970. This was the first Wembley final to require a replay. The following year they beat Real Madrid in the European Cup-Winners Cup Final, again in a replay.

### Crystal Palace

Selhurst Park, Whitehouse Lane, SE25
DISTRICT MAP
Crystal Palace, then in the Third Division, reached the semi-final of the FA Cup in 1976. Palace, as they are known, won the Second Division Championship in 1979 to gain long-sought promotion to the First Division.

### Fulham

Craven Cottage, Stevenage Road, SW6
DISTRICT MAP
Fulham, a Second Division club, went to Wembley in 1975 for an all-London FA Cup final against West Ham, but found their First Division opponents too much for them, losing 2–0.

### Millwall

The Den, Cold Blow Lane, New Cross, SE14
DISTRICT MAP
Millwall have yet to gain promotion to the First Division, having spent most of the last two decades in the Second Division.

### Orient

Leyton Stadium, Brisbane Road, E10
DISTRICT MAP
Orient's fine Cup form in 1954, when they reached the 6th round as a Third Division side, was surpassed in 1978 when they reached the semi-final – only to lose to Arsenal.

## Queen's Park Rangers

South Africa Road, W12
DISTRICT MAP
Queen's Park Rangers' supreme
moment came in 1967 when
they appeared in the first
Wembley League Cup Final – a
Third Division club facing First
Division opponents, West
Bromwich Albion. Rangers were
losing 0 – 2 but staged a
dramatic fight-back to win 3 – 2.

## Tottenham Hotspur

748 High Road, N17
DISTRICT MAP
Tottenham Hotspur have
consistently been the most
successful London club over the
last two decades, their total of
seven FA Cup triumphs
including wins in 1961, 1962,
1967, 1981 and 1982. In 1961
they were the first team this
century to achieve the League
and Cup double in the same
year. Spurs, as they are
popularly known, became the
first English club to win a
European trophy when they
defeated Athletico Madrid 5 – 1
in the 1962 – 63 European Cup-
Winners Cup Final. Since then
they have added two League
Cup Final victories (1971 and
1973) as well as winning the
EUFA Cup in 1972 and 1984.

## West Ham United

Boleyn Ground, Green Street,
Upton Park, E13
DISTRICT MAP
West Ham United have never
been League Champions but
they won the FA Cup in 1964
and 1975, and defeated Munich
1860 in the European Cup-
Winners Cup Final at Wembley
in 1965.

## Wimbledon

Plough Lane Ground,
45 Durnsford Road, SW19
DISTRICT MAP
Wimbledon were elected to the
Football League in 1977 after
three consecutive Southern

League Championships. Earlier
that year they had a splendid FA
Cup run. Ten years later, they
have reached the First Division.

### ATHLETICS

## Crystal Palace National Sports Centre

Crystal Palace Park, Sydenham,
SE19
DISTRICT MAP

## New River Sports Centre

White Hart Lane, Wood Green,
N22
DISTRICT MAP

## Parliament Hill Fields

Gospel Oak, NW3
DISTRICT MAP

## Victoria Park

Victoria Park, E9
DISTRICT MAP

## West London Stadium

Wormwood Scrubs, W12
DISTRICT MAP
London has witnessed many
great moments in athletics
history, including the staging of
the 14th Olympic Games at
Wembley in 1948. Built at the
beginning of this century, the
White City Stadium was the
venue for the 4th Modern
Olympic Games and was
London's principal athletics
stadium for more than half a
century.
  In 1964 the Crystal Palace
National Sports Centre opened
and the White City finally ended
its long and honourable
association with athletics. The
purpose-built Sports Centre at
Crystal Palace has an all-
weather track and covered
accommodation for spectators,
and stages all manner of
athletics ranging from major
international matches to county
championships.

### THE BOAT RACE

The Boat Race, a contest
between two crews of eight

rowers and one coxswain
representing the universities of
Oxford and Cambridge, is one of
the most famous sporting events
in the world. The first Boat Race
took place at Henley-on-Thames
in 1829, but in 1845 the event
was moved to its present
location in London. The course
runs on the Thames from
Putney to Mortlake, a distance
of over 4 miles, and it takes place
annually on a Saturday shortly
before Easter. Thousands of
people watch from the towpath
along the course; no tickets are
required, though many pay for
the privileged positions near the
finish at Duke's Meadows,
Chiswick, or on floating barges.

### CRICKET

## Lord's Ground

St John's Wood Road, NW8
MAP REF 12D

## The Oval

Kennington, SE11
MAP REF 30C
Cricket, first played in Tudor
times, is still one of the most
widely-played games in
England. Even the smallest
village will probably have its
team and its own ground where
the quiet of a Sunday afternoon
is broken only by the slap of
leather on willow and a gentle
ripple of applause.
  The game of cricket
accompanied the British to the
colonies and it became equally
popular in Australia, New
Zealand, the West Indies, India,
and Pakistan. It is these
countries who play England in
the Test Matches, which are
played here and in their own
countries. A Test Match is
usually five days long and there
can be as many as six in a series.
Nowadays England will also
play one-day Tests against
visiting international sides.
  Cricket is widely played in
London, on commons and
playing fields, but the two major

venues are Lord's Cricket Ground and The Oval at Kennington. Lord's is probably the most famous cricket ground in the world and is home to two clubs – Middlesex County CC who play their county matches here, and the famous Marylebone Cricket Club, perhaps even better known by its initials, MCC. Lord's is a traditional venue for Test Matches, and the first-ever Test was played here in 1880. Many other matches are played at Lord's, including the finals of the Gillette Cup and the Benson & Hedges Cup, and the annual match between Eton and Harrow.

The Oval is the home ground of Surrey County CC, and is usually the site of the final Test in a series.

The cricket season runs from April to September.

## TENNIS

### All England Lawn Tennis and Croquet Club

Church Road, Wimbledon, SW19
DISTRICT MAP
'Wimbledon' – for tennis fans the world over, the name resounds with the excitement and magic of that summer fortnight when top players from across the globe converge in London to compete for the most coveted prizes in lawn tennis. In the last week of June and the first week in July, the All England Lawn Tennis and Croquet Club hosts, in effect, the world tennis championships on grass. Over 2,000 members of staff cater for the 300,000-plus spectators who attend throughout the fortnight, and almost as coveted as the prizes and trophies is a ticket to the Centre Court for one of the final matches. Near-continuous TV coverage of the Wimbledon fortnight sweeps the whole country with tennis-

madness, and 'Wimbledon' has become one of those great British institutions which everybody loves – or simply learns to live with. It is best to apply for tickets – which are allocated by a ballot system – in about October, or queue for standing room on the day.

There are also various other tournaments held in the London area; those which are held immediately before Wimbledon fortnight – for example, at Queen's Club, Palliser Road, W14 – include top international players.

## THE LONDON MARATHON

Since its first running in 1981, the London Marathon has grown into the biggest in the world and attracts thousands of overseas runners as well as entries from all over Britain. In 1986, 22,000 people took part – chosen from over 85,000 who applied – and the runners now annually raise over £4 million to help a wide range of charities. Top international marathon runners regularly take part, as was proved when Ingrid Kristiansen set a new women's world record time for the 1985 race. The course, which is over the traditional marathon distance of 26 miles 385 yds, starts at Greenwich, winds its way through London's dockland, the Isle of Dogs, along the embankments of the Thames, through the City, and finishes at Westminster Bridge in Central London. The 1987 race is scheduled to take place on Sunday 10 May. Thousands of people turn out to watch, lining the route all along the way. There are special spectator areas at the most popular places to watch: along Charlton Way and Shooters Hill Road in Greenwich for the start, and all along The Mall and Birdcage Walk in St James's Park for the finish on Westminster Bridge. Each year on marathon day it

seems as if the whole of London turns out in festive and carnival mood, and great fun is had by competitors and spectators alike.

## GREYHOUND RACING

### Catford
Greyhound Stadium, SE6
DISTRICT MAP

### Hackney Wick
Waterden Road, E15
DISTRICT MAP

### Harringay
Green Lanes, N4
DISTRICT MAP

### Walthamstow
Chingford Road, E4
DISTRICT MAP

### Wembley
Stadium Way
DISTRICT MAP

### Wimbledon
Plough Lane, SW19
DISTRICT MAP
'Going to the dogs' has always been a popular pastime, especially with East End Londoners. Pure-bred greyhounds chase after an artificial hare on an electrified rail at speeds of up to 40mph. Races, either on the flat or over hurdles, are over varying distances and attract a good deal of betting and prize money. The more famous tracks are at Harringay and Walthamstow. Several of the tracks have restaurants overlooking the races. Most greyhound racing takes place in the evening.

## HORSE RACING

Racecourses near London include: *Ascot*, Berkshire – famous for its Royal meeting in June; *Epsom*, Surrey – stages the world-famous Derby in June; *Kempton Park*, Sunbury-on-Thames, Middlesex; *Lingfield*

Twickenham, where the great matches in the rugby calendar are played

*Park*, Surrey; *Sandown Park*, Esher, Surrey – famous for the Whitbread Gold Cup; *Windsor*, Berkshire.

The flat-racing season extends from March to November, steeplechasing from August to June.

### RUGBY UNION FOOTBALL

Rugby Football may have been born when, in 1823, W W Ellis picked up a soccer ball and ran with it – but there is no doubt it was nursed to maturity in London. Guy's Hospital claims to have the world's oldest Rugby Club, formed in 1843. Blackheath Club, the first group to come together specifically for the purpose of playing Rugby (in 1858), Richmond (founded 1861) and Harlequins (founded 1866) played important roles in shaping the game as it is now played.

The Twickenham ground (Whitton Road, Twickenham, Middlesex), is the HQ of the Rugby Football Union, controlling body of the sport. Fixtures to look out for at

Twickenham are internationals (which are well publicised), the Oxford v Cambridge match in early December, the RFU 'John Player' Club Competition final in April, and the Inter-Services Championships played during March and April.

The major clubs in London which play matches every week during the season (September – April) include:

### Blackheath RFC

Rectory Field, Charlton Road, SE3
DISTRICT MAP

### Harlequin RFC

Stoop Memorial Ground, Craneford Way, Twickenham
DISTRICT MAP

### London Irish RFC

Pavilion, The Avenue, Sunbury-on-Thames
DISTRICT MAP

### London Scottish RFC

Richmond Athletic Ground, Richmond, Surrey
DISTRICT MAP

### London Welsh RFC

Old Deer Park, Kew Road, Richmond, Surrey
DISTRICT MAP

### Metropolitan Police RFC

Police Sports Club, Ember Court, Embercourt Road, East Molesey, Surrey
DISTRICT MAP

### Richmond RFC

Richmond Athletic Ground, Richmond, Surrey
DISTRICT MAP

### Rosslyn Park RFC

Priory Lane, Upper Richmond Road, Roehampton, SW15
DISTRICT MAP

### Saracens RFC

The Pavilion, Bromley Sports Ground, Green Road, N14
DISTRICT MAP

### Wasps RFC

Repton Avenue, Wembley
DISTRICT MAP

### SPEEDWAY

### Hackney Wick

Waterden Road, E15
(Fridays, 8pm)
DISTRICT MAP

### Wimbledon

Plough Lane, SW19
(Thursdays, 7.45pm)
DISTRICT MAP
Introduced to Britain in the 1920s, speedway has grown to be one of the most popular of all spectator sports. This highly-specialised form of motorcycling is now usually held within large football or greyhound stadiums. With thrills, spills, and the roar of machines under brilliant floodlighting, speedway racing is very exciting entertainment. The highly-powered 500cc bikes run on pure methanol, and have no brakes, and a great deal of skill and daring is needed to execute the long, broadside drifts on the sweeping curves at each end of the track, sending showers of the loose shale surface into the air.

# **K**EY TO ACCOMMODATION AND EATING

Hotels, guesthouses, farmhouses and inns.
(fictional example)

**Establishment Name**
Where the name appears in *italics*, this indicates that particulars have not been confirmed by the proprietor in time for this edition.

**Classification & merit award**

**Name of hotel group** (if applicable)

**Annexes**
If annexe rooms are shown, this indicates that their standard is acceptable. They may, however, lack some of the facilities available in the main building. If you are offered an annexe room, check facilities and charges before booking.

★ ♨ Lydford House (Guest accom)
☎(0253) 239 Telex no 67737
Closed Xmas Day & Boxing Day
*Set in 3 acre grounds and has own riding school. Former home of Victorian artist William Widgery.*
13rm(9⇄1🛏) Annexe: 15rm (11⇄4🛏);
®
sB&B£14.50 sB&B⇄🛏£16 dB&B£28
dB&B⇄🛏£32🛏
30P⇔ ❋() nc 5yrs
❖Lunch £5.50 Dinner £6.50&alc Wine
£3.40 Last dinner 8pm
Credit cards ① ② ⑤

**Credit Cards**
The numbered boxes indicate the credit cards which the establishment will accept.

| | |
|---|---|
| ① | Access/Euro/Mastercard |
| ② | American Express |
| ③ | Barclays/VISA |
| ④ | Carte Blanche |
| ⑤ | Diners |

**Specific Details**
To interpret details of opening times, prices, facilities etc consult 'Symbols and Abbreviations' below.

**Star Classifications and Subjective Awards**
The majority of hotels are indicated by black stars and offer traditional hospitality and service in traditional accommodation.

★ Hotels and inns generally of small scale with good facilities and furnishings; adequate bath and lavatory arrangements. Meals are provided for residents, but their availability to non residents may be limited.

★ ★ Hotels offering a higher standard of accommodation, with 20% of the bedrooms containing a private bathroom or shower with lavatory.

★ ★ ★ Well appointed hotels with more spacious accommodation with two thirds of the bedrooms containing a private bathroom/shower with lavatory. Fuller meal facilities are provided.

★ ★ ★ ★ Exceptionally well appointed hotels offering a high standard of comfort and service with all bedrooms providing a private bathroom/shower with lavatory.

★ ★ ★ ★ ★ Luxury hotels offering the highest international standards.

♨ Used to denote AA Country House hotels, often secluded, but not always rurally situated, where a relaxed, informal atmosphere and personal welcome prevail. However, some of the facilities may differ from those found in urban hotels of the same classification.
**Red Star Hotels**
These hotels are considered by the AA to be of outstanding merit within their classification. The award is reviewed annually.
**Rosette Award for Food**
This award highlights those hotels where it is judged that food can be specially recommended.

❸ Indicates that the food is a higher standard than is expected for its classification.
❸❸ Indicates excellent food and service irrespective of its classification.
❸❸❸ Outstanding food and service irrespective of its classification.

**Merit Awards**

These are subjective awards given to hotels where a particular aspect is very good and significantly better than that implied by the hotel's star classification. Three types of award are given:

H   Hospitality, friendliness and service
B   Bedrooms
L   Lounges, bars and public areas.

Guesthouses, farmhouses and inns have to apply to the AA for listing, and, if successful, are regularly inspected, having to maintain minimum standards and meet stipulated criteria.

**Opening Dates**

Unless otherwise stated, the establishments are open all year. Hotels show inclusive dates when they are closed (i.e. closed Xmas) whereas guesthouses, farmhouses and inns give inclusive dates when they are fully open (i.e. Apr–Oct). Although some establishments are open all year, they may at times offer a restricted service during the less busy months, this may mean there is a reduction in meals and/or accommodation.

**Disabilities**

Members with any form of disability should notify proprietors so that appropriate arrangements can be made to minimise difficulties, particularly in the event of an emergency. The AA *Travellers' Guide for the Disabled* is available free to members.

## Symbols & Abbreviations

### English

| | |
|---|---|
| ✕ | Restaurant, classification |
| ★ | Hotel classification |
| ○ | Hotel likely to open during the currency of this guide |
| ⚑ | Country-house hotel |
| HBL | Merit award |
| ❸ | Rosette award |
| GH | Guesthouse |
| FH | Farmhouse |
| INN | Inn |
| ✳ | 1986 prices |
| ☎ | Telephone |
| ⇄ | Private bathroom with own WC |
| ⋔ | Private shower with own WC |
| ® | Tea/coffee-making facilities in bedrooms |
| ✖ | No dogs allowed overnight in bedrooms |
| ✗ | Bedrooms and/or area set aside for non-smokers |
| P | Open parking for cars |
| ⚠ | Garage or covered space |
| ₱ | No parking on premises |
| ⇔ | No coach parties accepted |
| ⌧ | Indoor swimming pool |
| ⌐ | Outdoor swimming pool |
| ♙♙₁₈ | 9-hole or 18-hole golf course |
| ⚲ | Tennis court(s) |
| ⌁ | Fishing |
| ∪ | Riding stables on premises |
| ♧ | Special facilities for children |
| ♿ | The hotel can accommodate disabled persons |
| alc | *à la carte* |
| TV | Monochrome television |
| CTV | Colour television |
| Etr | Easter |
| fb | Family bedrooms |
| fr | from |
| MAP | National grid reference |
| mdnt | Midnight |
| nc | No children, *eg* no children under . . . years of age |
| rm | Letting bedrooms in main-building |
| RS | Restricted service |
| → | Entry continued overleaf |

| | |
|---|---|
| Plan | Number gives location of hotel or guesthouse: on town plan |
| sB&B | Single room including breakfast per person per night |
| sB&B⇄ | Single room with private bath and WC and breakfast per person per night |
| sB&B⋔ | Single room with private shower and wc and breakfast per person per night |
| dB&B | Double room (2 persons) including breakfast |
| dB&B⇄ | Double room (2 persons) with private bath and wc and breakfast |
| dB&B⋔ | Double room (2 persons) with private shower and wc and breakfast |
| ⧫ | This symbol shows that the hotel offers cheaper off-season weekends |
| ♋ | Type of cooking. If this symbol is not shown, the type of cooking is English, Scottish or Welsh according to the part of Britain in which the hotel is situated |
| ♲ | Afternoon tea |
| ⎏ | Morning coffee |
| CFA | Conference facilities available |
| Wine | Minimum price of full bottle of wine (*eg 70cl*) |
| xmas | Special Christmas programme for residents |
| V | Vegetarian meals offered |
| T | Direct dial telephones in rooms |
| ❀ | Garden over $\frac{1}{2}$ acre |
| ⌸ | Four-poster bed |
| ☽ | Night porter |
| ⊞ | Air conditioning throughout |
| B&b | Bed and breakfast per person per night |
| Bdi | Inclusive dinner bed and breakfast. When B&b prices not shown, rate always charged whether dinner taken or not |
| ⋈ | Bed and breakfast for £8 or under |
| W | Weekly terms |
| Ł | No lunches included in weekly price |
| Ṁ | No main meals included in weekly price |
| LDO | Time last dinner has to be ordered |
| Lic | Licensed |
| hc | Number of bedrooms with hot and cold water |
| ♨ | Full central heating |

## Français

| | |
|---|---|
| ✕ | Classement des Restaurants |
| ★ | Classement des Hotels |
| ○ | Hótels qui doivent ouvrir prochainement |
| ⚑ | Hôtel de Campagne |
| HBL | Symboles de merites speciaux |
| ❀ | Rosettes |
| GH | Guesthouse |
| FH | Farmhouse |
| INN | Inn |
| ✳ | Prix 1986 |
| ☎ | téléphone |
| ⇨ | salle de bain privée avec WC particulier |
| 🏠 | Douche privée avec WC particulier |
| ® | Possibilité de fair ele thé/le café dans les chambres |
| 🐕 | Défense de garder des chiens pendant la nuit dans les chambres |
| ✗ | Chambres et/ou section de restaurant réservee(s) aux non-fumeurs |
| P | Stationnement pour voitures |
| ⚠ | Garage á ciel ouvert á espaces couverts |
| P | Pas de stationnement sur place |
| 🚌 | Les groupes en car ne seront pas admis |
| ⊡ | Piscine à l'intérieur |
| ⌐ | Piscine à l'extérieur |
| 🏌 | Terrain de golf à 9 trous ou 18 trous |
| 🎾 | Court(s) de tennis |
| 🎣 | Péche |
| ○ | Ecuries d'équitation sur les lieux |
| 🧸 | Facilités speciales pour enfants |
| ⚘ | L'hôtel peut recevoir des invalides |
| alc | *à la carte* |
| TV | TV en noir et blanc |
| CTV | TV en couleurs |
| Etr | Plaquen |
| fb | Chambre de famille |
| fr | à partir de |
| MAP | Repère du quadrillage de carte national |
| mdnt | Minuit |
| nc | Enfants pas admis, par ex. enfants audessous de . . . ans pas admis |
| rm | Location de chambres dansle bâtiment principal |
| RS | Service limité |
| → | Suite au verso |
| Plan | Le numéro indiquel'emplacement del'hôtel ou du restaurant sur le plan de la ville |
| sB&B | Chambre à un lit et petit déjeuner par personne et par nuit |

| | |
|---|---|
| sB&B⇨ | Chambre à un lit avec bain et WC particuliers, et petit déjeuner par personne et par nuit |
| sB&B🏠 | Chambre à un lit avec douche privée et WC particulier et le petit déjeuner par personne la nuitée |
| dB&B | Chambre à deux lits (2 personnes) avec petit déjeuner |
| dB&B⇨ | Chambre à deux lits (2 personnes) avec bain et WC particuliers, et petit déjeuner |
| dB&B🏠 | Chambre à deux (deux personnes) avec douche privée et WC particulier et le petit déjeuner |
| 🚩 | Ce symbole indique que l'hotel offre des week-ends à prix réduit hors saison |
| ♀ | Categorie de cuisine. Si ce symbole ne figure pas, la cuisine est anglaise, écossaise ou galloise, seionla région de la Grande Bretagne ou l'hôtel se trouve |
| ♥ | Thé l'apres-midi |
| ☕ | Café le matin |
| CFA | Installations de conference |
| Wine | Prix minimum d'une bouteille de vin (70cl) |
| xmas | Programme spécial de Noel pour les clients |
| V | Menu végétarien offert |
| T | Téléphone dans la chambre, direct avec l'extérieur |
| ✤ | Jardin de plus de 0.20ha |
| 🛏 | Lits à quatre montants |
| D | Concierge de nuit |
| ⊞ | Conditionnement d'air intégral |
| B&b | Chambre et petit déjeuner par personne et par nuit |
| Bdi | Dîner, chambre petit déjeuner compris. Si des prix B&b ne sont pas indiqués, le tarif est toujours facturé, que l'on prenne le dîner ou non |
| ᵐ | Chambre et petit déjeuner pour mois de £8 |
| W | Tarif á la semaine |
| £ | Le tarif hebdomadaire ne comprend pas le déjeuner |
| M | Le tarif hebdomadaire ne comprend pas de repas principaux |
| LDO | Le dîner est á commander avant cette heure |
| Lic | Licence de boissons alcoholiques |
| hc | Nombre de chambres avec eau chaude et froide |
| ♨ | Chauffage central intégal |

Prix

Cartes de crédit

## Deutsch

| | |
|---|---|
| ✕ | Restaurantklassifikation |
| ★ | Hotelklassifikation |
| ○ | Hotel wird wahrend de aufzeit dieses Fuhrers eroffnet |
| ⚑ | Landgut-Hotel |
| HBL | Verdienst-Symbole |
| ❀ | Rosetten |
| GH | Guesthouse |
| FH | Farmhouse |
| INN | Inn |
| ✳ | 1986 Preise |
| ☎ | Telefon |

| | |
|---|---|
| ⇨ | Privatbadezimmer mit eigener WC |
| 🏠 | Privatdusche mit eigener WC |
| ® | Tee/Kaffee moglichke enim Zimmer |
| 🐕 | Hundeverbotim Zimmer wahrend der Nacht |
| ✗ | Zimmer bzw. Restaurant abschnitt für Nichtraucher |
| P | Parken im Freien |
| ⚠ | Garegen bzw. überdachtes Parken |
| P | Parken an Ortund Stelle |
| 🚌 | Reisebusgesellschaften nicht aufgenommen |
| ⊡ | Hallenbad |
| ⌐ | Freibad |

| | |
|---|---|
| ♌9 ♌18 | Golfplatz mit 9 oder 18 holes |
| ⚲ | Tennisplatz (Platze) |
| ↗ | Angeln |
| ∪ | Reitstall an Ort und Stelle |
| ⚘ | Sonderdienstleistungen für Kinder |
| ♿ | Fur Körperbehinderte geeignet |
| alc | *à la carte* |
| TV | Schwarzweissfernsehen |
| CTV | Farbfernsehen |
| Etr | Ostern |
| fb | Familienzimmer |
| fr | Von |
| MAP | Planquadratangabe |
| mdnt | Mitternacht |
| nc | Kinder nicht aufgenommen z. B. Kinder unter Jahren nicht aufgenommen |
| rm | Zimmeranzahlim Hauptgebäude |
| RS | Beschrankle Dienstleislungen |
| → | Fortsetzung siehe umseitig |
| Plan | Nummer gibt die Lage des Hotels am Stadtplan an |
| sB&B | Ubernachtungin einem Einzeizimmer mit Frühstuck pro Person |
| sB&B⇄ | Einzelzimmer mit Privatbad und WC und Frühstuck pro Person pro Nacht |
| sB&B♒ | Einzelzimmer mit Privatdusche und WC und Frühstuck pro Person pro Nacht |
| dB&B | Doppelzimmer (2 Personen) mit Frühstück |
| dB&B⇄ | Doppelzimmer (2 Personen) mit Privatbad und WC mit Frühstück |
| dB&B♒ | Doppelzimmer (2 Personen) mit Privatdusche und WC und Frühstück |
| 🏠 | Betrieb gibt Wochener dermassigung fur Vorund Nachsaison |

| | |
|---|---|
| ☺ | Küch, Wenn dieses Zeichen nicht aufgefürht wird, ist die Küche englisch, schottish oder walisischjenach der Gegend, wo das Hotel sich befindet |
| ♈ | Nachtmittagstee |
| ♋ | Kaffee vormittags |
| CFA | Tagungseinrichtungen vorhanden |
| Wine | Mindestpreis fur eine Flasche Wein (dh 70cl) |
| xmas | Sonderweihnachtsprogramm fur Gäste |
| V | Vegetansche Kost vorhanden |
| T | Zimmertelefon mit Aussenverbindung uber Telefonzentrale |
| ✿ | Garten grósser als 0.20ha |
| 🛏 | Himmelbett |
| ☽ | Nachtportier |
| ▦ | Klimaanlage durchaus |
| B&b | Über nachtung mit Frühstück pro Person |
| Bdi | Übernachtung einschl. Frühstück und Abendessen. Wenn Preis für Zimmer & Frühstück nicht angegeben, werden die Halbpensionspreise immer in Rechnung gestelt, ob eingenommen oder nicht |
| ⋈ | Bett mit Frühstück für unter £8 |
| W | Wochenpreis |
| £ | Mittagessenspreis nicht im Wochenpreis eingeschlossen |
| M | Keine Hauptessen im Wochenpreis eingeschlossen |
| LDO | Letze Bestellzeit für Abendessen |
| Lic | Ausschank alkoholischer Getränke |
| hc | Zimmer mit Warm-und Kaltwasser |
| 🌡 | Vollfernheizung |

# ACCOMMODATION AND EATING

Places are listed below in postal district order, commencing East, then North, South and West, with a brief indication of the area covered.

**E1 Stepney** *and east of the Tower of London*
★★★★**Tower Thistle** St Katherine's Way (Thistle) ☎01 488 4134 Telex no 885934
*Located on the north bank of the Thames, overlooking the Tower of London and Tower Bridge, this large hotel offers comfortable accommodation to a large variety of clients.*
826⇄ 🛏(35fb) ⌧ in 24 bedrooms CTV in all bedrooms T ⌧
*sB⇄ 🛏£65  f 85 dB⇄ 🛏£78–£99 (room only) 🚭
Lift Ɒ ⊞ 120P 80⚿ (charged) ℃FA
♡International ♡ ☑ *Lunch fr £14.95&alc Dinner fr £14.95&alc Wine £7
Last dinner 10pm
Credit cards ①②③④⑤

✕**Blooms** 90 Whitechapel High St ☎01-247 6001
*Busy but friendly strictly Kosher restaurant with modestly priced menu.*
Closed Sat Dinner not served Fri
♡Kosher 150 seats 80P
Credit cards ①③

**E14 Poplar**
✕**Good Friends** 139/141 Salmon Ln ☎01-987 5541
*Simple restaurant specializing in nicely prepared Cantonese cuisine.*
Closed 24–26 Dec
♡Cantonese V 12 seats *Lunch £8–£12alc Dinner £8–£12alc Wine £4.50 Last dinner 11pm
Credit cards ①②③⑤

**EC1 City of London**; *Barbican, Clerkenwell, Farringdon*
✕**La Bastille** 116 Newgate St ☎01-600 1134
*This small, intimate, city restaurant has some good wood carvings, and the portraits of Victorian judges on the walls set the atmosphere. A sound standard of French provincial cuisine is provided, the menu changing daily.*
Closed 1 wk Aug & 2 wks Dec
Dinner not served
♡French 55 seats S% Lunch £15.50–£18 Wine £6.50
Credit cards ①②③④⑤

✕**Three Compasses** 66 Cowcross St ☎01-253 3368
*There has been an inn on this site since the 18th century, and the present building, though modernised, retains some of its original character. The comfortably-appointed first-floor restaurant offers a short menu of interesting international dishes with friendly, informal service.*
Closed 1 wk after Xmas & last 2 wks Aug
Dinner not served
♡International V 40 seats *Lunch £5–£15&alc Wine £4.50 Last lunch 2.15pm
 nc 8yrs Live music Sun
Credit cards ①②③

**EC2 City of London**; *Bank of England, Liverpool Street Station*
●✕✕✕**Le Poulbot** 45 Cheapside ☎01-236 4379 Telex no 8813079
*(Rosette awarded for lunch only)*
*Very popular basement restaurant with an intimate, plush atmosphere. There is a short fixed-price menu, which changes daily, and the chef's individuality and flair is most evident, along with excellent presentation and good blending. Service is efficient and unobtrusive.*
Closed Sat, Sun & Bank Hols
Dinner not served
♡French 45 seats S% *Lunch £24.50 Wine £9.80 Last lunch 3pm  nc 4yrs
Credit cards ①②③④⑤

✕✕**Baron of Beef** Gutter Ln, Gresham St ☎01-606 9415
*Spacious, panelled basement restaurant specialising in English cuisine.*
Closed Sat & Sun
70 seats S% Lunch £25–£30alc Dinner £25–£30alc Wine £9.60
Last dinner 9pm
Credit cards ①②③⑤

**EC3 City of London;** *Monument, Tower of London*
✕✕**Shares** 12–13 Lime St ☎01-623 1843
*A modern, tastefully furnished lunch-time restaurant with a small bar.*
Closed Bank Hols Dinner not served
♡International 74 seats S% *Lunch £22.50–£24 Wine £7.75
Credit cards ①②③⑤

**EC4 City of London;** *Blackfriars, Cannon Street and Fleet Street*
✕**Le Gamin** 32 Old Bailey ☎01-236 7931 Telex no 8813079
*Small tables and chairs in a large, airy basement create a French cafe-style atmosphere. Half a bottle of wine is included in the fixed-price of the short menu of carefully prepared dishes, representing good value and contributing to the restaurant's popularity.*
Closed Sat, Sun & Bank Hols
Dinner not served
♡French V 120 seats S% *Lunch £17.75 Wine £5.10
Last lunch 2.30pm
Credit cards ①②③④⑤

✕**Ginnan** 5 Cathedral Pl ☎01-236 4120
*Simple modern Japanese restaurant with small party room.*
Closed Sun & Bank Hols
Dinner not served Sat
♡Japanese 60 seats *Lunch £4.80–£5.20 Dinner £16–£18 Wine £7 Last dinner 10pm
Credit cards ①②③⑤

**N1 Islington**
✕✕**Frederick's** Camden Passage ☎01-359 2888
*Dating back to the 18th century, and originally called 'The Gun', this very popular and well appointed restaurant was renamed in honour of Prince Augustus Frederick who died in 1813. The enterprising menu is changed fortnightly but always includes some delectable puddings, and the formal service is very efficient.*
Closed Sun, Boxing Day, New Years Day, Good Fri & Etr Mon
♡International V 150 seats S% Lunch £17–£18alc Dinner £17–£18alc Wine £4.65 Last dinner 11.30pm
Credit cards ①②③④⑤

●✕**Annas Place** 90 Mildmay Park ☎01-249 9379
*This small, bustling restaurant cum wine bar, simply furnished and prettily decorated, provides a blackboard menu of excellent Swedish fare at very reasonable cost. The informal atmosphere is enhanced by cheerful young staff, supervised by Anna herself.*
Closed Sun, Mon, 2 wks Xmas, 2 wks Etr & Aug
♡Swedish & Continental 52 seats S% *Lunch £10–£14alc Dinner £12–£14alc Wine £4.95 Last dinner 10.15pm

✗**Mr Bumbles** 23 Islington Grn ☎01-354 1952
*Large brick fireplace and ceiling beams give the atmosphere of a country kitchen.*
Closed Mon
♀Greek V 60 seats S% Lunch £6&alc Dinner £9alc Last dinner 11.30pm ⚑
Credit cards ① ② ③ ⑤

✗**M'sieur Frog** 31A Essex Rd ☎01-226 3495
*Proprietor provides well prepared food in this friendly informal Bistro restaurant.*
Closed 1 wk Xmas & 3 wks Aug
Lunch not served Dinner not served Sun
♀French 63 seats S% Dinner fr £15.95alc Wine £4.95 Last dinner 11.15pm ⚑
Credit cards ① ③

✗**Portofino** 39 Camden Passage ☎01-226 0884
*Simple, Italian restaurant, where the walls are decorated with hanging bottles.*
Closed Sun, Bank Hols, Good Fri & Xmas
♀French & Italian V 65 seats Last dinner 11.30pm Live music Thu–Sat
Credit cards ① ② ③ ⑤

**N6 Highgate**
✗✗**Bayleaf Tandoori** 2 North Hill ☎01-340 1719
*This smart, modern Indian restaurant has canopied windows and a walled frontage with attractive flower beds. The cuisine is that of North India. Tandoori dishes being the speciality.*
♀Indian V 100 seats Lunch £7–£10alc Dinner £7–£10alc Wine £4.50 Last dinner 11.15pm ⚑

✗✗**San Carlo** 2 High St, Highgate ☎01-340 5823
*Good modern Italian restaurant with patio.*
Closed Mon & Bank Hols
♀Italian V 100 seats S% Lunch £15alc Dinner £20alc Wine £6.25 Last dinner 11.30pm 30P Live music nightly
Credit cards ① ② ③ ④ ⑤

✗**China Garden** 12 Shepherds Hill ☎01-348 8606
Lunch not served
♀Pekinese & Szechuan V 70 seats S% *Dinner £10–£15&alc Wine £4.90 Last dinner 10.45pm ⚑
Credit cards ① ② ③

**N8 Hornsey**
✗**M'sieur Frog** 36 The High St ☎01-340 2116
*An imaginative menu of well-prepared French provincial dishes is offered by this small, simple, French-style bistro.*
Lunch not served
♀French 44 seats Last dinner 11pm ⚑
Credit cards ① ③

**N14 Southgate**
✗**L'Oiseau Noir** 163 Bramley Rd ☎01-367 1100
*This restaurant combines simple elegance*

with a warm, friendly atmosphere and offers a regularly-changed and reasonably-priced menu of honest and well-prepared French dishes.*
Closed Mon
Dinner not served Sun
♀French V 62 seats *Lunch £7.95–£15&alc Dinner fr £14&alc Wine £5.50 Last dinner 11pm
Credit cards ① ② ③ ④ ⑤

**N16 Stoke Newington**
✗**Eleganza** 70 High St ☎01-254 1950
*A small, simple restaurant specialising in Pekinese cuisine of a good standard.*
Lunch not served Sun
♀Pekinese V 55 seats Lunch £4–£10&alc Dinner £7–£10&alc Wine £5 Last dinner 11.30pm ⚑ nc 4 yrs
Credit cards ① ② ③ ⑤

**NW1 Regent's Park; Baker Street, Euston and King's Cross stations**
○**Hotel Ibis Euston**
Cordington St ☎01-759 4888
300⇌🍴
Expected to open summer 1987

✗✗**Viceroy of India** 3–5 Glentworth St ☎01-486 3401
*Modern, well-appointed North Indian restaurant with marble pillars, statues and well-prepared authentic cooking.*
Closed Xmas Day
♀North Indian V 125 seats
Last dinner 11.30pm ⚑
Credit cards ① ② ③ ④ ⑤

✗**Asuka** Berkeley Arcade, 209A Baker St ☎01-486 5026
*This small, contemporary and very neat Japanese restaurant features a Suishi Bar and speciality dishes cooked at the table. Authentic fish cuisine figures prominently on the menu, quality materials are used throughout, and attentive, helpful staff will guide you in your choice of meal.*
Closed Sun & 24 Dec–5Jan
Lunch not served Sat
♀Japanese 62 seats S% *Lunch £5.50–£6.95&alc Dinner £18.90–£45&alc Wine £8 Last dinner 10.30pm ⚑
Credit cards ① ② ③ ⑤

✗**One Legged Goose** 17 Princess Rd, Regent's Pk ☎01-722 9665
*Good Swedish food is a feature of this small friendly restaurant.*
Closed 1st 3 wks Jan
Lunch not served Sat
Dinner not served Sun
V 50 seats Lunch £12alc Dinner £12alc Wine £5.25 Last dinner 11pm ⚑
Credit cards ① ③

✗**Sagarmatha** 339 Euston Rd ☎01-387 6531
*Posters and pictures of Nepal set the tone of this compact little restaurant which specialises in Nepalese cuisine. The atmosphere is friendly and informal, the manager is ready to help you in your choice.*

♀Indian & Nepalese V 55 seats *Wine £3.95 Last dinner 11.45pm ⚑
Credit cards ① ② ③ ⑤

**NW3 Cricklewood, Willesden**
✗**Quincy's** 84 675 Finchley Rd ☎01-794 8499
*Flair and imagination are evident in the cooking at this restaurant, where dishes from a short but interesting menu are served in a friendly, informal atmosphere under the personal supervision of the owner.*
Closed Mon & 1st 2 wks Jan
Lunch not served Sat
♀English & French V 30 seats *Lunch £8.50–£10.50 Dinner £13.75 Wine £6 Last dinner 10.30pm ⚑
Credit cards ① ③

✗**Yeti** 68 Cricklewood Broadway ☎01-452 4789
*This small, intimate restaurant specialises in North Indian and Nepalese cuisine, the quality of cooking owing much to the skilful blending of spices. Guests can relax in a friendly, informal atmosphere.*
♀Indian & Nepalese V 50 seats S% Lunch £4–£10&alc Dinner £5–£10&alc Wine £4.80 Last dinner mdnt 20P
Credit cards ① ② ③ ⑤

**NW3 Hampstead and Swiss Cottage**
★ ★ ★ B **Holiday Inn** Swiss Cottage
King Henry's Rd. (Holiday Inns) ☎01-722 7711 Telex no 267396
*A modern hotel with spacious comfortable bedrooms, large public lounge area and numerous sporting facilities.*
291⇌🍴(174fb) ✗ in 52 bedrooms
CTV in all bedrooms T S%
*sB&B⇌🍴£86.45–£91.05
dB&B⇌🍴£105.05–£114.25 🍴
Lift ▦ 50P 75 ⚠ ⌂ (heated) sauna bath solarium gymnasium table tennis pool table Live music nightly ⚠ xmas
♀International V ♥ ♫ *Lunch fr £13.50 Dinner fr £15 Wine £8.25 Last dinner 10.30pm
Credit cards ① ② ③ ④ ⑤

★ ★ ★ **Charles Bernard** 5 Frognal ☎01-794 0101 Telex no 23560
*Friendly and well-managed modern hotel with pleasant bedrooms, public rooms and restricted lunch arrangements.*
57 ⇌ CTV in all bedrooms ® T ✗ S%
*sB&B⇌£43.70–£48.20
dB&B⇌£57.50–£63.25 🍴
Lift ♪ CTV 20P 🚗
♀English & French ♥ ♫ S% *Bar lunch £6alc Tea £2 Dinner £8.50alc Wine £4.80 Last dinner 9.30pm
Credit cards ① ② ③ ④ ⑤

★ ★ ★ **Post House** Haverstock Hill (Trusthouse Forte) ☎01-794 8121 Telex no 262494
*Popular modern hotel with well-equipped bedrooms.*
140 ⇌ CTV in all bedrooms ®
sB&B⇌£57.50 dB&B⇌£74.50 🍴
Lift ♪ 70P xmas

♻ Last dinner 10.30pm
Credit cards 1 2 3 4 5

★ ★ ★Swiss Cottage 4 Adamson Rd
☎01-722 2281 Telex no 297237
*Elegantly furnished hotel with a spacious
lounge and good quality antiques.*
65rm (45⇔20▥)(4fb) CTV in all
bedrooms T ✻ sB&B⇔▥ £36.50–£66
dB&B⇔ £55–£73 Continental
breakfast ⊟
Lift Ɔ 5P ♨ sauna bath
♢ Continental ♡ ♏ Lunch £6&alc Tea
£1.25 Dinner £10&alc Wine £5.50
Last dinner 9pm
Credit cards 1 2 3 4 5

★★Bunny's 9 Pond St ☎01-435 1541
*Basement restaurant serving Edwardian
classic French dishes, and ground floor is a
smart fish restaurant. Well-prepared
dishes are served with flair and
imagination.*
Closed Mon Lunch not served Mon–Sat
♢French 75 seats ✻Lunch £7.95
Dinner £10.50–£12.50&alc Wine
£5.65 Last dinner 11.15pm ♪ ✗ Live
music Sun lunch
Credit cards 1 2 3

⊛✗✗Keats 3 Downshire Hill ☎01-
435 3544
*(Rosette awarded for dinner only)*
*This intimate French restaurant cultivates
a literary air, its lilac-painted walls decked
with bookshelves and prints. Cuisine of a
high standard is complemented by a very
good wine list, and special gastronomique
evenings are organised.*
Closed Sun
♢French V 50 seats S% Lunch £9alc
Dinner £20alc Wine £13 Last dinner
11pm ♪ nc 7yrs
Credit cards 1 2 3 5

✗Finches 250 Finchley Rd ☎01-
435 8622
*Good honest cooking and value for money
can be found at this friendly, intimate little
restaurant where the menu combines
English and French cuisine.*
♢English & French V 45 seats Last
dinner 10.45pm ♪
Credit cards 1 2 3 4 5

✗Green Cottage II 122A Finchley Rd
☎01-794 3833
*Offering over 40 dishes made completely
from vegetables and vegetable substances,
this claims to be the first vegetarian
Chinese restaurant in Europe. Bright, air-
conditioned surroundings, informal
atmosphere and helpful staff all add to the
guest's enjoyment of his meal.*
Closed Tue & Xmas Day
♢Chinese V 80 seats Last dinner
11.15pm
Credit cards 1 2 5

✗Hawelli Tandoori 102 Heath St
☎01-431 0172
*A smart, modern Indian restaurant,
tastefully decorated and furnished,
specialising in North Indian cuisine of a
high standard. Service is by willing,*

*friendly staff and the atmosphere is relaxed
and informal.*
Closed Xmas Day
♢Tandoori V 75 seats Last dinner
11.15pm 1P ✗
Credit cards 1 2 3 5

✗Peachey's 205 Haverstock Hill ☎01-
435 6744
*There is a continental aura about this
appealing and intimate little restaurant
which offers an interesting French menu
with daily 'specials', backed by a
comprehensive wine list. Visitors are
assured of a warm welcome and helpful
service.*
Closed Bank Hols, 10 days Xmas & 4
days Etr
Lunch not served Sat
Dinner not served Sun
♢French V 38 seats S% Lunch fr
£8.95&alc Dinner fr £8.95&alc Wine
£5.45 Last dinner 11.30pm ♪
Credit cards 2 3 5

✗Wakaba 31 College Cres ☎01-
586 7960
*This small, two-section Japanese
restaurant provides an informal, intimate
atmosphere in which to enjoy a good
variety of well-prepared and authentic
dishes.*
Closed Mon, 4 days Xmas, 4 days Etr &
1 wk Aug Lunch not served
♢Japanese V 38 seats Last dinner
11pm
Credit cards 1 2 3 5

**NW4 Hendon**

★★★Hendon Hall Ashley Ln
(Kingsmead) ☎01-203 3341 Telex no
8956088
*Georgian house (once the home of David
Garrick) has been refurbished to provide
comfortable modern accommodation.*
52 rm (49⇔3▥) CTV in all bedrooms
⑪ ⊟
Lift Ɔ CTV 65P CFA ♣ Live music &
dancing Sat xmas
♢English, American & French V ♡ ♏
Last dinner 10.15pm
Credit cards 1 2 3 5

**NW6 Kilburn**

✗La Frimousse 75 Fairfax Rd ☎01-
624 3880
*Situated close to Swiss Cottage, this smart,
attractive restaurant produces original
French cuisine from excellent raw
materials.*
Closed Sun
♢French 46 seats S% ✻Lunch fr £9.95
Dinner fr £21.50 Wine £6.75 Last
dinner 11pm ♪ nc 6yrs
Credit cards 1 2 3 5

✗Peter's Bistro 63 Fairfax Rd ☎01-
624 5142
*Green awning and fresh plants make the
frontage of this restaurant very
impressive. Inside, the relaxed and
intimate atmosphere provides the ideal
setting for a well-cooked meal chosen from
the bistro-type menu.*
Lunch not served Sat

Dinner not served Sun
V 48 seats S% Lunch £20alc Dinner
£22.50alc Wine £6.95 Last dinner
11.30pm ♪ nc 12yrs
Credit cards 1 2 3 5

✗Sheridan's 351 West End Ln ☎01-
794 3234
Closed Mon, 1–15 Jan & 18 Aug–2 Sep
Lunch not served Tue–Sat
♢English & French V 4 seats ✻Lunch
£8.50 Dinner £13alc Wine £6 Last
dinner 11pm ♪
Credit cards 1 2 3 4 5

✗Vijay 49 Willesden Ln ☎01-
328 1087
*Small Indian restaurant specialising in the
vegetarian cuisine of southern India.*
Closed Xmas
♢Southern Indian V 74 seats Last
dinner 10.45pm
Credit cards 1 2 3 5

**NW7 Mill Hill**

★★TraveLodge M1 Scratchwood
Service Area (Access from Motorway
only) (Trusthouse Forte) ☎01-
906 0611 Telex no 8814796
*The restaurant facilities (mainly grills) are
located in the adjacent service area.*
100⇔(12fb) CTV in all bedrooms ®
sB&B⇔£39.50 dB&B⇔£51 ⊟
Ɔ 120P CFA
♢Mainly grills
Credit cards 1 2 3 4 5

✗✗Good Earth 143–145 Broadway,
Mill Hill ☎01-959 7011
*Smart, modern restaurant specialising in
very good Cantonese cuisine.*
♢Chinese V 100 seats ✻Lunch
£10–£16&alc Dinner £10 £16&alc
Wine £5 Last dinner 11.30pm 10P

**NW8 St John's Wood**

★★★Ladbroke Westmoreland (&
Conferencentre) 18 Lodge Rd
(Ladbroke) ☎01-722 7722 Telex no
23101
*Pleasant, modern hotel with well-equipped
bedrooms.*
347⇔(15fb) ✗ in 10 bedrooms CTV in
all bedrooms ® T S% sB⇔£69–£79
dB⇔£85–£95 (room only) ⊟
Lift Ɔ ⊞ 35P 4S ⚐ (£1.50 per day)
CFA Live music Mon–Fri xmas
V ♡ ♏ S% Lunch £5–£11&alc Tea fr
£1.75 Dinner £11.50&alc Wine £8.95
Last dinner 9.45pm
Credit cards 1 2 3 4 5

✗✗Lords Rendezvous 24 Finchley Rd
☎01-722 4750
*Modern, elegant Chinese restaurant.*
Closed Xmas Day & Boxing Day
♢Chinese V 100 seats ✻Lunch
£13–£20&alc Dinner £13–£20&alc
Wine £5.50 Last dinner 11.15pm ♪
Credit cards 1 2 3 5

✗✗Oslo Court Prince Albert Rd ☎01-
722 8795
*A traditional, comfortable restaurant
overlooking Regent's Park.*

Dinner not served Sun
♀French V 55 seats Last dinner 11pm
👂
Credit cards ① ② ③ ④ ⑤

✕L'Adventure 3 Blenheim Ter ☎01-624 6232
*Small, well-run French restaurant serving traditional dishes in intimate, friendly atmosphere.*
Lunch not served Sat
Dinner not served Sun
♀French 36 seats Last dinner 11pm
Credit card ②

✕Fortuna Garden 128 Allitsen Rd ☎01-586 2391
*This friendly Chinese restaurant specialises in Peking cuisine but also serves other dishes designed to please the European palate. The food is authentic and well-prepared, and the staff are cheerfully pleasant.*
♀Pekinese V 80 seats Last dinner 11.30pm 👂
Credit cards ① ② ③ ⑤

**NW10 Harlesden, Willesden**
✕Khas Tandoori 39 Chamberlayne Rd ☎01-969 2537
*Colourful and modern, this North Indian restaurant produces Tandoori dishes of a very high standard. Willing, friendly staff help to make eating there an enjoyable experience.*
Closed Xmas Day
♀North Indian V 44 seats Last dinner mdnt 👂
Credit cards ① ② ③ ⑤

✕Kuo Yuan 217 High Rd, Willesden ☎01-459 2297
*Spacious restaurant offering well-prepared Pekinese dishes in a relaxed friendly atmosphere.*
Lunch not served Mon–Fri
♀Pekinese V 120 seats Last dinner 11pm 👂

**NW11 Golders Green**
✕✕Luigi's 1–4 Belmont Pde, Finchley Rd ☎01-455 0210
*The proprietor's personal supervision and the good Italian cooking create a friendly atmosphere in this well-appointed restaurant.*
Closed Mon, Xmas Day & Good Fri
♀Italian V 80 seats ✳Lunch £5&alc
Dinner £10–£15alc Wine £4.90 Last dinner 10.30pm 👂
Credit cards ① ② ③ ⑤

**SE1 Southwark, Waterloo**
✕RSJ's 13a Coin St ☎01-928 4554
*Small popular French restaurant offering well-prepared dishes at reasonable prices.*
Closed Sun Lunch not served Sat
♀French 48 seats ✳Lunch £15alc
Dinner £15alc Wine £5.95 Last dinner 11pm 👂

✕South of the Border Joan St ☎01-928 6374
*Very informal restaurant on two floors*

*featuring some interesting South Pacific dishes on its international menu.*
Lunch not served Sat
♀Australasian, Indonesian & South Pacific V 80 seats S% Lunch
£18–£20alc Dinner £15–£16alc Wine £5 Last dinner 11.30pm 👂
Credit cards ① ② ③ ⑤

**SE10 Greenwich**
✕✕Mean Time 47–49 Greenwich Church St ☎01-858 8705
*Personally supervised restaurant with efficient and friendly service in a pleasant relaxed atmosphere.*
Closed 25, 26 Dec & Good Fri
Lunch not served Sat
♀English & Continental V 100 seats
Lunch £13.50alc Dinner £13.50alc
Wine £5.50 Last dinner 11pm 👂 ✗
Credit cards ① ② ③ ⑤

✕✕Spread Eagle 2 Stockwell St ☎01-853 2333
*A charming restaurant with great character has resulted from the conversion of an old coaching inn. Intimate alcoves are surrounded by authentic photographs and pictures, while the cheerful waiters who serve the food have a good knowledge of the French cuisine involved.*
Closed Sun Lunch not served Sat
♀French V 60 seats S% Lunch
£6–£9.75 Dinner £15alc Wine £7 Last dinner 10.45pm 👂
Credit cards ① ② ③ ⑤

✕Le Papillon 57 Greenwich Church St ☎01-858 2668
*Well-prepared French and English cuisine is available in this small, intimate oak-panelled restaurant.*
Lunch not served Sat
Dinner not served Sun
♀French 36 seats Lunch fr £4.95&alc
Dinner £12.50alc Wine £5.50
Last dinner 10.30pm 👂
Credit cards ① ② ③ ⑤

✕Mr Chung 166 Trafalgar Rd ☎01-858 4245
*Small, brightly decorated, modern restaurant with friendly and intimate atmosphere.*
♀Pekinese 50 seats Last dinner 11.30pm
Credit cards ① ② ③ ⑤

**SE11 Kennington**
★★London Park Brook Dr, Elephant & Castle (Consort) ☎01-735 9191 Telex no 919161
*Reasonably priced large hotel with small, adequately-appointed bedrooms.*
364rm(34⇄258 fil)(15fb) CTV in all bedrooms S% ✳sB&B£22.50
sB&B⇄fil £27.50–£29.50
dB&B£37.50 dB&B⇄fil £45
Lift Ɗ 15P (charge) CFA *xmas*
♀English & French ✆ ⚘ S% ✳Lunch
£7alc Dinner £6.95&alc Wine £4.75
Last dinner 8.45pm
Credit cards ① ② ③ ④ ⑤

**SE13 Lewisham**
✕Curry Centre 37 Lee High Rd ☎01-852 6544
*Informal friendly service, and typical Indian decor are found at this simple restaurant.*
♀Indian 60 seats Last dinner 11.45pm
Credit cards ① ② ③ ⑤

**SW1 Westminster;** *St James's Park, Victoria Station, Knightsbridge, Lower Regent St*
**Five Red Stars Berkeley Hotel**
Wilton Pl, Knightsbridge ☎01-235 6000 Telex no 919252
*In the 14 years since it was opened this hotel has become firmly established, having an international reputation and a clientele who return year after year to enjoy the superb service offered in this elegant and dignified hotel. Yet with most of the more mundane facilities discreetly out of sight and the absence of a bar, it retains an English atmosphere reminiscent of the Old Berkeley. However, with its chic, modern decor in the restaurant and Buttery, it has also kept pace with modern trends. Even so, with marbled floor and two luxurious sitting rooms, attractive decor that includes crystal chandeliers and gorgeous flower arrangements, it conveys an air of luxury reminiscent of past times. Air-conditioned bedrooms reach the same high standards. All the usual five-star facilities are provided and the room service can be particularly commended. Notable in London is the roof-level swimming pool with a roof that can be opened in the summer. Chef Schmidt provides good French cooking in the main restaurant while in the Perroquet there is a hot/cold buffet at lunch-times and a more formal menu at night.*
160⇄fil CTV in all bedrooms T ✗ S%
✳sB⇄fil £150 dB⇄fil £185 (room only)
Lift Ɗ 🅿 50 ♿ (charge) 🚗 🏊 (heated) sauna bath solarium
♀French & Italian ✆ ⚘ S% ✳Lunch
£30alc Tea fr £2.50 Dinner £35alc
Wine £7.50 Last dinner 10.45pm
Credit cards ① ② ③ ⑤

★★★★★L Hyatt Carlton Tower
Cadogan Pl ☎01-235 5411 Telex no 21944
*Improvements continue at this luxurious modern hotel where bedrooms have recently been upgraded and where the refurbished lounge is proving an attraction, particularly when afternoon tea is served. For a more substantial meal, guests can choose between the fine roast beef of the Rib Room and the first-class, creative food served in the elegant Chelsea Room.*
221⇄fil ✗ in 2 bedrooms CTV in all bedrooms T sB⇄fil £140.15–£166.65
dB⇄fil £176.80–£206.70 (room only) 🅿
Lift Ɗ 🅿 40 ♿ (£6.50) CFA ✿ ⚘ sauna bath solarium gymnasium
♀English & French ✆ ⚘ Lunch fr £17.50 High Tea fr £6.75 Dinner fr

£17.50 Wine £8.50 Last dinner 11pm
Credit cards ① ② ③ ④ ⑤

★ ★ ★ ★ **B Hyde Park** Knightsbridge
(Trusthouse Forte) ☎01-235 2000
Telex no 262057
*Traditional, elegant and very English in
style, this hotel is small enough to permit
personal and friendly service. Except for
those on the top floor, the bedrooms are,
arguably, the best of any London hotel.*
180⇄ 1🛏 CTV in all bedrooms T
sB&B⇄£144 dB&B⇄£168
Lift 🄳 ᵖ CFA 🚗
⌖ ⌣ Last dinner 10.30pm
Credit cards ① ② ③ ④ ⑤

★ ★ ★ ★ **Sheraton Park Tower** 101
Knightsbridge ☎01-235 8050 Telex no
917222
*Circular-shaped hotel with large, well
appointed bedrooms and friendly service.*
295⇄ CTV in 265 bedrooms T 🍴 S%
*sB⇄£127.65–£143.75
dB⇄£144.90–£161 (room only) 🍴
Lift 🄳 🎦 ᵖ 🚗 xmas
⌣ ⌖ *Lunch £10.75 Tea £4.75
Dinner £16.75&alc Wine £8 Last
dinner mdnt
Credit cards ① ② ③ ④ ⑤

**Four Red Stars Goring Hotel**
Beeston Pl, Grosvenor Gdns ☎01-
834 8211 Telex no 919166
*Family-owned since it opened in 1910, it
is Mr George Goring who is now
responsible for maintaining the unique
atmosphere, which is special to those
hotels where the proprietor personally
runs it. From the moment you step inside
you sense that you will be well cared for by
the courteous and solicitous staff, everyone
you meet, porters receptionists, waiters or
chamber maids, will greet you with a
smile. Such a welcome change! The interior
is smartly traditional with a black and
white marble floor, plasterwork ceilings
and crystal chandeliers, all beautifully
maintained. The lounge is in two parts, the
upper overlooking the pretty gardens and
has a bar counter. A gas log fire burns,
there are flowers and magazines as well as
comfortable easy chairs to offer solid
comfort in peaceful surroundings. Clean
and comfortable bedrooms vary in size but
are all one could wish for as is the prompt
room service. In the elegant dining room,
the staff serve you well from the good value
fixed price or à la carte menus and the
fairly traditional cooking is consistently
good.*
90⇄ 🏠 CTV in all bedrooms T 🍴 S%
sB&B⇄ 🏠£82 dB&B⇄ 🏠£129
Lift 🄳 10P 4🄰 (open £4.50 covered
£6) 🚗
⌖English & French V ⌣ ⌖ Lunch
£12–£14.50&alc Tea £5 Dinner fr
£16&alc Wine £7.50 Last dinner 10pm
Credit cards ① ② ③ ⑤

★ ★ ★ ★ **Cavendish** Jermyn St
(Trusthouse Forte) ☎01-930 2111
Telex no 263187
*Comfortable, modern hotel with efficient*

*friendly service.*
253⇄ CTV in all bedrooms T
sB&B⇄£89 dB&B⇄£117 🍴
Lift 🄳 10P 80🄰 CFA xmas
⌣ ⌖ Last dinner 11pm
Credit cards ① ② ③ ④ ⑤

❋ ★ ★ ★ ★ **HB Duke's** St James Pl
(Prestige) ☎01-491 4840 Telex no
28283
*This small hotel has been tastefully and
elegantly refurbished to provide
comfortable accommodation. The service is
very professional, yet the hotel retains an
informal, relaxing atmosphere. The cuisine
is English and French and the cooking is of
a very high standard.*
52⇄(16fb) 1🛏 CTV in all bedrooms T
🍴*sB⇄£110 dB⇄£145–160 (room
only)
Lift 🄳 ᵖ 🚗
⌖English & French ⌣ ⌖ *Lunch
£16.50&alc Tea £2 Dinner £25alc
Wine £7.50 Last dinner 10pm
Credit cards ① ② ③ ④ ⑤

★ ★ ★ ★ **Holiday Inn Chelsea** 17–25
Sloane St (Holiday Inns) ☎01-
235 4377 Telex no 919111
*Modern hotel with good leisure facilities
and helpful staff.*
198⇄ 🏠(22fb) CTV in all bedrooms T
🍴 S% *sB⇄ 🏠£93 dB⇄ 🏠£112
(room only)
Lift 🄳 🎦 ᵖ 🚗 CFA ⊒ (heated) xmas V
⌣ ⌖ S% *Wine£7.40 Last dinner
10.30pm
Credit cards ① ② ③ ④ ⑤

★ ★ ★ ★ **Royal Westminster Thistle** 49
Buckingham Palace Rd (Thistle) ☎01-
834 1821 Telex no 916821
*Extensive refurbishment of all bedrooms
and public areas has now been completed,
so that the hotel offers excellent
accommodation with impressive lobby and
lounge and a brasserie restaurant.*
135⇄ 🏠(38fb) 🗡 in 30 bedrooms
CTV in all bedrooms T 🍴*sB⇄ 🏠 fr
£85 dB⇄ 🏠 fr £105 (room only) 🍴
Lift 🄳 🎦 ᵖ 🚗
⌖International ⌣ ⌖ *Lunch fr
£14.95&alc Dinner fr £21.95&alc
Wine £7 Last dinner 11pm
Credit cards ① ② ③ ④ ⑤

★ ★ ★ ★ **H Stafford** 16–18 St James's Pl
(Prestige) ☎01-493 0111 Telex no
28602
*Small, comfortable, secluded hotel with
elegant restaurant and lounges.*
62⇄ 1🛏 CTV in all bedrooms T 🍴
Lift 🄳 6🄰 🚗
⌖French V ⌣ ⌖ S% *Lunch £16
Dinner £18 Wine £9 Last dinner 10pm
Credit cards ① ② ③ ⑤

★ ★ ★ **Lowndes Thistle** 19 Lowndes St
(Thistle) ☎01-235 6020 Telex no
919065
*A modern and somewhat exclusive hotel in
Belgravia with elegant Adam-style sitting
area and particularly attractive bedrooms.*
80⇄ 🏠 🗡 in 32 bedrooms CTV in all

bedrooms T 🍴*sB⇄ 🏠£85–£105
dB⇄ 🏠£115–£135 (room only) 🍴
Lift 🄳 ᵖ 🚗
⌖International ⌣ ⌖ *Lunch fr
£13.75&alc Dinner fr £13.75&alc
Wine £7 Last dinner 9.30pm
Credit cards ① ② ③ ④ ⑤

★ ★ ★ **L Royal Horseguards Thistle**
Whitehall Court (Thistle) ☎01-889
3400 Telex no 917096
*Modern very comfortable hotel with an
attractive restaurant.*
284⇄ 🏠 🗡 in 25 bedrooms CTV in
bedrooms ® T 🍴*sB⇄ 🏠£70–£105
dB⇄ 🏠£85–£135 (room only) 🍴
Lift 🄳 ᵖ CFA 🚗
⌖International ⌣ ⌖ *Lunch
£12.50&alc Dinner £12.50&alc Wine
£7.50 Last dinner 10pm
Credit cards ① ② ③ ④ ⑤

★ ★ ★ **L Rubens** Buckingham Palace
Rd ☎01-834 6600 Telex no 916577
*Modernised hotel with nicely-appointed
rooms.*
191rm(173⇄18🏠)(5fb) 🗡 in 11
bedrooms CTV in all bedrooms T
*sB&B⇄ 🏠£63.75 dB&B⇄ 🏠£93.50
🍴
Lift 🄳 🎦 ᵖ xmas
⌖International V ⌣ ⌖ *Lunch
£10.50 Tea 85p–£3.45 Dinner
£10.50&alc Wine £6.95 Last dinner
10pm
Credit cards ① ② ③ ④ ⑤

**One Red Star Ebury Court Hotel**
26 Ebury St ☎01-730 8147
*This hotel occasionally attracts the odd
criticism from people who think it a bit
small and cramped, but these criticisms are
insignificant among the whole-hearted
praise showered upon it. The Tophams,
who have owned it since pre-war days have
altered it and enlarged it over the years in
an endearingly quaint way. Mrs Topham's
influence is seen in the prettily decorated
bedrooms which vary in size considerably
but are well kept. Those in the front are
double glazed. There are two cosy little
sitting rooms – one with television – a
sandwich bar and the club bar where
guests can obtain temporary membership.
In the basement is the restaurant which
serves conventional style cooking of a good
standard. Here, as in the rest of the hotel,
you will be attended to by many long-
serving staff who do their best to make you
feel at home. Altogether a charmingly old-
fashioned sort of hotel at sensible prices.*
39rm(12⇄) 4🛏 T *sB&B£34
dB&B£54 dB&B⇄£64
Lift 🄳 CTV ᵖ 🚗
⌖English & French V Lunch £10.50alc
Dinner £12alc Wine £4.55
Last dinner 9pm
Credit cards ① ③

✕ ✕ ✕ **Auberge De Provence** (St James
Court Hotel) Buckingham Gate ☎01-
834 6655 Telex no 919557
*A pleasantly cool restaurant with white
walls, arches and hanging plants, which
specialises in French regional cooking*

131

*skilfully prepared under the direction of consultant/chef Jean André Chanal. Service by the young French staff is good.*
♡French V 80 seats S% ✳Lunch fr £15 Dinner £25alc Wine £7.60 Last dinner 11pm ▸
Credit cards ①②③⑤

✕✕✕**Dolphin Brasserie** Rodney House, Dolphin Sq/Chichester St ☎01-828 3207
*Following a change of management, the restaurant has been reopened with a new decor and a new chef. Set price and à la carte menus are offered, the standard of cuisine and accompanying wine list both being of a good standard and giving value for money. Management and service are friendly and willing.*
♡British & French V 100 seats ✳Lunch £12&alc Dinner £14.50&alc Wine £6.20 Last dinner 10.45pm ▸ Live music Mon–Sat
Credit cards ①②③⑤

✕✕**L'Amico** 44Horseferry Rd ☎01-2224680
*Extensive basement Italian restaurant with several separate rooms.*
Closed Sat & Sun
♡Italian V 70 seats S% ✳Lunch £16alc Dinner £16alc Wine £5.50 Last dinner 10.30pm P nc 4yrs
Credit cards ①②③⑤

✕✕**Le Caprice** Arlington House, Arlington St ☎01-629 2239
*Modern, French restaurant, with large plants, and featuring photographs by David Bailey.*
Lunch not served Sat
Dinner not served 24Dec–2Jan
♡French 70 seats Lunch £14alc Dinner £14alc Wine £5 Last dinner mdnt ▸ nc 5yrs Live music nightly
Credit cards ①②③⑤

❊✕✕**Gavvers** 61 Lower Sloane St ☎01-730 5983 Telex no 8813079
*(Rosette awarded for dinner only)*
*A Roux Brothers enterprise, the restaurant offers a very popular, value-for-money, fixed-price menu, the charge covering not only half a bottle of wine but also service and VAT. Surroundings are comfortable and the young French staff charmingly attentive.*
Closed Sun & Bank Hols
Lunch not served
♡French 60 seats S% ✳Dinner £18.75 Last dinner 11pm ▸
Credit cards ②⑤

❊✕✕**Ken Lo's Memories of China** 67 Ebury St ☎01-730-7734
*Kenneth Lo, acclaimed for his book on Chinese cooking, includes both classical and regional dishes on the menu of this elegant restaurant.*
Closed Sun & Bank Hols
♡Chinese 80 seats Lunch fr £15.50 Dinner £19.50–£28 Wine £6 Last dinner 10.45pm ▸
Credit cards ①②③⑤

❊✕✕**Le Mazarin** 30 Winchester St ☎01-828 3366
*(Rosette awarded for dinner only)*
*Chef/patron Rene Bajard continues to impress guests with his 'new classic cuisine', beautifully cooked and presented in cosy, candle-lit, basement surroundings. The fixed-price menu offers excellent value for money, there is an interesting wine list, and service is efficient, friendly and well-organised.*
Closed Sun, Bank Hols & 1 wk Xmas
Lunch not served
♡French V 55 seats S% Dinner £15.50–£22.50 Wine £7 Last dinner 11.30pm ▸
Credit cards ①②⑤

❊✕✕**Mijanou** 143 Ebury St ☎01-7304099
*In a smart little restaurant fronted by her husband Neville, Sonia Blech continues to provide enjoyable dishes with a French influence.*
Closed Sat, Sun, 1 wk Etr, 3 wks Aug & 2 wks Xmas
♡French 30 seats Lunch £10.75&alc Dinner £26.50&alc Wine £6.50 Last dinner 11pm ▸ ✗
Credit cards ①②⑤

✕✕**Pomegranates** 94 Grosvenor Rd ☎01-828 6560
*Cuisine from at least 14 countries features in this basement restaurant.*
Closed Sun & Bank Hols
Lunch not served Sat
♡International 50 seats ✳Lunch £12–£17.50 Dinner £12.50–£19.50 Wine £7.50 Last dinner 11.15pm ▸
Credit cards ①②③④

❊✕✕**Salloos** 62–64 Kinnerton St ☎01-235 4444
*An amiable atmosphere prevails in this first-floor, family-run restaurant, tucked away in a quiet corner off Knightsbridge. Menus feature the subtler, Pakistani, style dish, such as the seldom-encountered Indian Cheese Soufflé.*
Closed Sun & Bank Hols
♡Pakistani V 70 seats Lunch £12–£20&alc Dinner £15–£20&alc Wine £6 Last dinner 11.15pm ▸
Credit cards ①②③④⑤

✕✕**Tate Gallery** Millbank Embankment ☎01-834 6754
*Brightly decorated, popular restaurant with interesting menu featuring old English dishes, and excellent wine list.*
Closed Sun, 24–26 Dec, New Year's Day, Good Fri & May Day
Dinner not served V 120 seats Last lunch 3pm ▸ ✗

❊✕**Ciboure** 21 Eccleston St ☎01-730 2505
*This bright, modern and well-appointed French restaurant offers a high standard of cooking, fish dishes being particularly impressive; service is professional but informal in style.*
Closed Sun Lunch not served Sat

♡French 36 seats Lunch £14–£15 Dinner £18alc Wine £6.30 Last dinner 11.30pm ▸ nc 10yrs
Credit cards ①②③⑤

✕**Eatons** 49 Elizabeth St ☎01-730 0074
*Continental cuisine is featured in this small, friendly French-stle restaurant.*
Closed Sat, Sun & Bank Hols
♡Continental 40 seats S% Lunch £15.50alc Dinner £15.50alc Wine £6.50 Last dinner 11.15pm ▸
Credit cards ①②③⑤

✕**La Fantaisie Brasserie** 14 Knightsbridge Gn ☎01-589 0509
*Mirrored panels and soft pink walls give this popular 'estamet' a serene and elegant atmosphere befitting the lightness and subtlety of the food. The thoughtfully-constructed menu features popular, modern dishes, prepared with attention to detail and excellently presented. Staff are smart, unobtrusively friendly and efficient.*
Closed Sun, Xmas & New Year
♡French 54 seats ✳Lunch £14alc Dinner £15alc Wine £5.40 Last dinner 10.30pm ▸
Credit cards ①②③⑤

✕**Le Poule au Pot** 231 Ebury St ☎01-730 7763
*Friendly French restaurant featuring interesting authentic dishes.*
Closed Sun Lunch not served Sat
♡French 50 seats Last dinner 11.15pm
Credit cards ①②③④⑤

✕**Tent** 15 Eccleston St ☎01-730 6922
*The decor of this small French restaurant is in keeping with the name. The regular clientele is attracted by friendly service, an informal atmosphere and a good standard of cuisine, though the menu is not very extensive.*
Closed Sat
♡French 45 seats S% ✳Lunch £12 Dinner £12 Wine £6.25 Last dinner 11.30pm ▸
Credit cards ①②③

✕**Le Trou Normand** 27 Motcomb St ☎01-235 1668
*This contemporary seafood restaurant is a little piece of Normandy set down in London. The Cuisine Normande, featuring Plats du Jour, fresh lobsters, traditional cheeses and desserts, is high in standard and reasonable in price, whilst a taste of luxury is offered in the Oyster and Champagne Bar in the basement.*
Closed 23 Dec–3 Jan
♡French 36 seats ✳Lunch £16alc Dinner £22alc Wine £8 Last dinner 11.30pm ▸
Credit cards ②③⑤

**SW3 Chelsea,** *Brompton*
❊**Four Red Stars The Capital**
Basil St, Knightsbridge ☎01-589 5171
Telex no 919042
*'There are few hotels that can provide so*

*much of one's ideal in a hotel' says one of
our most experienced inspectors. And he is
right! David Levin's gem of a hotel, a short
distance from Harrods, provides formal yet
friendly and welcoming service, good food
and comfortable bedrooms, some of which
are outstanding. The latter are individually
decorated to a high standard and are
beautifully done although compact in size.
On the ground floor are the public rooms,
recently refurbished by Nina Campbell
(she also did Hambleton Hall). There is the
cosy little lounge with its green colour
scheme in which to relax, the lively bar
and the stylishly elegant restaurant: very
chic with its terracotta and cream-
festooned curtains and immaculate table
appointments. Peter Schultz is the fine
Restaurant Manager who will look after
you here while you sample the delicious
cooking from the hands of chef Brian
Turner. He follows the modern French
style, but he has not forgotten his roots
and some of his dishes have an endearing
earthy quality. One such was a ragout of
duck livers and giblets with a red wine
sauce. Other dishes to gain acclaim were
the perfectly cooked salad of sea food,
terrine of rabbit, quenelles of smoked fish
and the pigeon breasts with saurkraut and
red wine sauce. Vegetables are nicely
cooked as are the toothsome puddings. Just
a little more attention to detail should
enable them to earn a second rosette next
year.*

60⇌ CTV in all bedrooms T S%
sB⇌fr£100 dB⇌£120–£140 (room
only)
Lift D 📶 12⚠ (£8 per day) 🐾
♀French V ✿ ⚿ S% ✴Lunch
£16.50–£19.50&alc Tea £4.50 Dinner
£18.50&alc Wine £10.75 Last dinner
10.30pm
Credit cards ① ② ③ ④ ⑤

★ ★ ★HL **Basil Street** Basil St,
Knightsbridge ☎01-581 3311 Telex no
28379
*Antique furniture and plenty of flowers
create a country house atmosphere here.*
95rm(69⇌) CTV in all bedrooms T
sB&B£39.80 sB&B⇌£69 dB&B£64.50
dB&B⇌f93.50 Continental breakfast
📦
Lift D 🎏 CFA 🐾
♀International V ✿ ⚿ Lunch
£9.75–£10.75 Tea £3 High Tea £4.50
Wine £6.75 Last dinner 9.45pm
Credit cards ① ② ③ ⑤

◉✕✕✕✕**Waltons** 121 Walton St
☎01-584 0204
*Elegantly luxurious comfort is enhanced
by discreet management supervision and
professionally formal service. Attention to
detail is good, and standards of cuisine are
reliable but never dull, for the chef's skill
and artistry transform best-quality
ingredients into some adventurous dishes.
The beautifully flavoured sauces, often
textured with cream, are particularly
noteworthy.*
Closed Bank Hols
♀International 65 seats Lunch

£11&alc Dinner £17.50&alc Wine
£7.50 Last dinner 11.30pm 🐾 nc 2yrs
Credit cards ① ② ③ ④ ⑤

✕✕✕**Zen Chinese** Chelsea Cloisters,
Sloane Av ☎01-589 1781
*The Chinese Zodiac is the background to an
interesting menu including old Buddhist
dishes and other delicacies.*
♀Chinese 120 seats Last dinner
11.15pm
Credit cards ① ② ③ ④ ⑤

✕✕**Avoirdupois** 334 Kings Rd ☎01-
352 6151
*Well-prepared, varied and imaginative
menu served in friendly atmosphere with
soft, live music.*
♀English & French V 140 seats Last
dinner 11.45pm Live music nightly
Credit cards ① ② ③ ⑤

✕✕**Daphne's** 112 Draycott Av ☎01-
589 4257
*Warm cosy restaurant with fine French
and English cooking.*
Closed Sun & Bank Hols
Lunch not served Sat
♀English & French 96 seats ✴Lunch
£12alc Dinner £17alc Wine £6 Last
dinner 11.30pm 🐾
Credit cards ① ② ③ ⑤

◉✕✕**English Garden** 10 Lincoln St
☎01-584 7272
*Well-researched Old English recipes,
cooked with considerable skill, are featured
in a fashionable conservatory, English-
garden setting.*
Closed 25 & 26 Dec
V 65 seats S% Lunch £20alc Dinner
£27.50alc Wine £7.50 Last dinner
11.30pm 🐾
Credit cards ① ② ③ ⑤

◉✕✕**English House** 3 Milner St ☎01-
584 3002
*This elegant, well-appointed restaurant
serves thoroughly researched traditional
English dishes; supervision and service are
excellent.*
Closed 25, 26 Dec & Good Fri
V 40 seats S% Lunch
£10.50–£12.50&alc Dinner
£17.50&alc Wine £7 Last dinner
11.30pm 🐾
Credit cards ① ② ③ ⑤

✕✕**Le Français** 259 Fulham Rd ☎01-
352 4748
*This small, intimate restaurant features
French regional menus (which are
changed weekly) and classical dishes.
Skilful and very enterprising cooking,
coupled with friendly and efficient service,
makes a meal here particularly good value
for money.*
Closed Sun
♀French 65 seats S% Lunch £11–£20
Dinner £20–£25 Wine £10.50 Last
dinner 10.45pm 🐾
Credit cards ② ③

✕✕**Good Earth** 233 Brompton Rd
☎01-584 3658

*Modern Cantonese restaurant offering
well-prepared authentic dishes in a friendly
informal atmosphere.*
Closed 24–27 Dec
♀Chinese V 105 seats S%
✴Lunch£5–£11&alc Dinner
£7–£16&alc Wine £5 Last dinner
11.15pm 🐾
Credit cards ① ② ③ ⑤

✕✕**Good Earth** 91 King's Rd ☎01-
352 9321
*Modern restaurant on two floors decorated
with fine murals. Staff are helpful and
friendly, serving some interesting set
gourmet dishes.*
♀Pekinese V 80 seats Last dinner
11.45pm 🐾
Credit cards ① ② ③ ④ ⑤

✕✕**Mario** 260–262A Brompton Rd
☎01-584 1724
*Well-managed contemporary Italian
restaurant with authentic cuisine and
home-made pasta.*
Closed Bank Hols
♀Italian 80 seats ✴Lunch fr £8.50&alc
Dinner £12–£14alc Wine £6.25 Last
dinner 11.30pm 🐾
Credit cards ① ② ③ ⑤

✕✕**Menage à Trois** 15 Beauchamp Pl
☎01-589 4252
*The basement restaurant is a 'fun' place to
dine in an intimate atmosphere with live
piano music and open fires. The menu is
restricted to starters and puddings –
though no-one checks how many of these
you have! – and the success of this original
idea owes much to the innovative
preparation of quality ingredients. Service
by a team of delightful young ladies adds
another dimension to your enjoyment.*
Closed Sun
V 70 seats Lunch£14–£17&alc Dinner
£18–£25&alc Wine £5.95 Last dinner
11.30pm 🐾 Live music wkly
Credit cards ① ② ③ ⑤

✕✕**Meridiana** 169 Fulham Rd ☎01-
589 8815
*Well-managed and efficient contemporary
Italian restaurant featuring open air
balcony terrace, interesting authentic and
home-made pasta.*
♀Italian V 120 seats ✴Lunch
£17.50alc Dinner £18.50alc Wine
£5.50 Last dinner mdnt 🐾 Live music
nightly
Credit cards ① ② ③ ⑤

✕✕**St Quentin** 243 Brompton Rd
☎01-589 8005
*Stylish Brasserie serving adventurous,
tempting food.*
Closed 1 wk Xmas
♀French 80 seats Lunch £9.50 Dinner
£12.90 Wine £6.20 Last dinner mdnt
🐾
Credit cards ① ② ③ ⑤

✕✕**San Frediano** 62 Fulham Rd ☎01-
584 8375
*This long-established and popular Italian
restaurant provides an authentic*

*atmosphere and traditional cuisine. Amenities are limited, though of an acceptable standard, and the value for money that the restaurant provides amply compensates for any short-fall.*
Closed Sun
♡Italian V 85 seats Lunch £15alc Dinner £15alc Wine £4.70 Last dinner 11.15pm ⚑
Credit cards ① ② ③ ⑤

✕✕**Tandoori** 153 Fulham Rd ☎01-589 7749
*An intimate atmosphere is created by subdued lighting in this cosy basement restaurant. Pleasant waiters serve good quality curries and Tandoori dishes.*
Closed 25 & 26 Dec
♡Indian V 65 seats Lunch £12alc Dinner £15alc Wine £5.20 Last dinner mdnt ⚑
Credit cards ① ② ③ ④ ⑤

✸✸✕✕**Tante Claire**
68 Royal Hospital Rd ☎01-352 6045
*After a few teething troubles last autumn following the opening of the enlarged and refurbished premises, Pierre Koffman is back on form. The restaurant now has a sitting area, and the whole is very much improved with the fresh colour scheme in pastel shades. The Head Waiter, Jean-Pierre, with his young brigade, attends to you exceedingly well with interested and proficient service. The à la carte menu offers an interesting choice of delicious dishes while at luncheon there is still the fantastic value fixed-price lunch and another short list of fish dishes of the day. Mr Koffman succeeds admirably with fish. delicate cooking, subtle flavours and exquisite sauces make them truly memorable. He cooks in the modern French style but without copying the French masters as so many do. His style is his own and despite the refined quality there is a subtle earthiness that probably comes from his background in south-west France. Dishes like his stuffed pigs trotter, made famous on TV, and his roast pigeon with a selection of cereals show this. Dishes that have particularly pleased our inspectors have included a brandade of salt cod with caviar accompanied by a lovely fresh-tasting tomato sauce, and blinis (buckwheat yeast pancake) and the balotine of foie gras, full of wonderful flavour and with some poached leeks in a delicious mustardy vinaigrette. Fish dishes such as the fillet of bass with chopped black olives and salsifi with a butter sauce was delightfully piquant. Meat dishes include the delicious roundels of spring lamb with parsley charlotte and garlic-flavoured sauce, and saddle of rabbit dressed on a cabbage leaf with julienne of cabbage and primeur carrots and again a subtly-flavoured sauce. Vegetables can lack heat, perhaps the price of over presentation, but are always properly cooked. His desserts are ambrosian as evinced by his sandwich of caramel mousse with tuile-like pastry, garnished with pink grapefruit segments and with a grapefruit syrup; also by that old favourite, biscuit glacé flavoured with*

*praline and with a zestful cullis of raspberries. Great attention is paid to detail – there is sometimes a hot beignet with the petits fours. Pierre Koffman can be one of the four best chefs in the country, but unfortunately the third rosette remains elusive. Never mind, on a good day you can eat as well here as anywhere in Britain.*
Closed Sat, Sun, 2 wks Xmas/New Year, 2 wks Etr & 3 wks Aug/Sep
♡French 38 seats S% Lunch £19&alc Dinner £32alc Wine £7 Last dinner 11pm ⚑
Credit cards ② ⑤

✕**Choy's** 172 Kings Rd ☎01-352 9085
*Long-established family Chinese restaurant with friendly atmosphere and particularly good vegetables.*
♡Cantonese V 60 seats S% ✻Lunch £5–£15&alc Dinner £10–£15&alc Wine £5 Last dinner mdnt ⚑
Credit cards ① ② ③ ⑤

✸✕**Dans** 119 Sydney St ☎01-352 2718
*This busy restaurant, painted in delicate pastel shades, decked with hanging baskets and standing in a garden, offers simple dishes of outstanding quality; the atmosphere is cheerful and the service unobtrusive but attentive.*
Closed Sat, Sun & Bank Hols
♡English & French V 50 seats Last dinner 11.15pm
Credit cards ② ③ ⑤

✕**Dumpling House** 9 Beauchamp Pl ☎01-589 8240
*Peking and Szechuan dishes are the specialities of this popular restaurant. An extensive and authentic menu can be enjoyed in a casually friendly atmosphere, the special set dinners representing particularly good value for money.*
♡Peking & Szechuan V 46 seats Lunch £8 Dinner £8 Wine £5.50 Last dinner 11.30pm ⚑
Credit cards ① ② ③ ⑤

✸✕**Ma Cuisine** 113 Walton St ☎01-584 7585
*This small, well-appointed restaurant offers impeccably-cooked, inventive and imaginative dishes, efficiently served by friendly staff.*
Closed Sat, Sun, Xmas, New Year, 1 wk Etr & 14 July–14 Aug
♡French 32 seats Wine £7.25 Last dinner 11pm ⚑ nc 10yrs
Credit cards ② ⑤

✕**Mes Amis** 31 Basil St ☎01-584 4484
*Popular restaurant featuring a good selection of traditional dishes.*
♡International 90 seats Lunch £15alc Dinner £18alc Wine £6.95 Last dinner 11pm ⚔
Credit cards ① ② ③ ④ ⑤

✕**Poissonnerie** 82 Sloane Av ☎01-589 2457
*Popular and well-appointed Oyster Bar and oak-panelled fish restaurant, featuring high quality fresh seasonal dishes.*
Closed Sun, 24 Dec–2 Jan & Bank Hols
♡French V 100 seats Wine £6.50 ⚑
Credit cards ① ② ③ ⑤

✕**Le Suquet** 104 Draycott Av ☎01-581 1785
*Very popular Sea Food French restaurant with formidable range of dishes.*
♡French 50 seats Last dinner 11.30pm ⚑
Credit cards ②

### SW4 Clapham
✕**Maharani Indian** 117 Clapham High St ☎01-622 2530
♡Indian V 76 seats ✻Lunch £8alc Dinner £10alc Wine £3.50 Last dinner mdnt ⚑ ⚔
Credit cards ① ② ③ ⑤

### SW5 Earl's Court
★★★**London International** 147 Cromwell Rd, Kensington (Swallow) ☎01-370 4200 Telex no 27260
*Large, friendly hotel with well-equipped bedrooms.*
417 ⇔ (36fb) CTV in all bedrooms T S% sB&B⇔£52–£57 dB&B⇔£62–£68 Continental breakfast ➡ Lift ⅅ ⅉ
♡English & French ✧ ⅏ S% ✻Lunch £8alc Tea £1.05–£2.95 High Tea £3.50–£5.25&alc Dinner £10.95&alc Wine £6.50 Last dinner mdnt
Credit cards ① ② ③ ⑤

★★**Hogarth** Hogarth Rd (Inter Hotel) ☎01-370 6831 Telex no 8951994
*This modern hotel has well-equipped, attractive bedrooms and modest public areas. The standards of service are generally acceptable and plain food is available.*
85 rm(67⇔18🏠)(10fb) CTV in all bedrooms ⓡ T Continental breakfast ➡ Lift ⅅ 18⚠
♡Mainly grills ✧ Last dinner 9.30pm
Credit cards ① ② ③ ⑤

✕✕**Pontevecchio** 256 Old Brompton Rd ☎01-373 9082
*Reservations are advisable at this very lively and popular restaurant, where you can enjoy a range of authentic Italian dishes, including some home-made pasta, in a fashionable forecourt setting where the friendly and attentive service is personally superintended by the patron.*
♡Italian 100 seats ✻Lunch £15alc(incl wine) Dinner £15alc(incl wine) Wine £6.50 Last dinner 11.30pm ⚑
Credit cards ① ② ③ ⑤

✕✕**Tiger Lee** 251 Old Brompton Rd ☎01-370 2323 Telex no 919660
*The elegantly modern Chinese restaurant specialises in seafood and offers dishes with such evocative names as 'Shadow of a Butterfly'. The attentive and professional service is excellent and there are some fine French wines on the wine list.*

Lunch not served
♥Cantonese 56 seats Dinner
£22–£25&alc Wine £8.80 Last dinner
11pm ✱ ✗
Credit cards ①②③⑤

✗**L'Aquitaine** 158 Old Brompton Rd
☎01-373 9918
Closed Sun
♥French 100 seats S% Lunch
£11.50–£14.50 Dinner £18alc Wine
£7.50 Last dinner 1.30am ✱
Cabaret Tue & Fri
Credit cards ①②③⑤

✗**L'Artiste Affamé** 243 Old Brompton
Rd ☎01-373 1659
French bistro-style restaurant.
Closed Sun, 24–26 Dec & Bank Hols
♥French V 80 seats Last dinner
11.15pm ✱
Credit cards ①②③⑤

✗**New Lotus Garden** 257 Old
Brompton Rd ☎01-370 4450
Popular Chinese restaurant with Colonial
atmosphere, good service and authentic
speciality cooking
Closed Xmas
♥Pekinese 55 seats Last dinner
12.30am ✱
Credit cards ①②③⑤

✱✗**Read's** 152 Old Brompton Rd
☎01 373 2445
Small well-managed restaurant featuring
skilful imaginative cooking complemented
by subtlety and flair.
Closed 2 wks Xmas–New Year
Dinner not served Sun
V 45 seats Last dinner 11pm
Credit cards ①②③⑤

**SW6 Fulham**
✱✗✗**Gastronome One** 311–313 New
Kings Rd ☎01-731 6381
Split level basement French restaurant
featuring 'Nouvelle' dishes
Closed Sun lunch not served Sat
♥French V 70 seats S% Lunch
£12.50–£16.50 Dinner
£16.50–£18.50 Wine £7 Last dinner
11.30pm ✱ ✗
Credit cards ①②③⑤

✱✗**L'Hippocampe** 131A Munster Rd
☎01-736 5588
Closed Sun, 24 Dec–31 Jan
Lunch not served Sat
♥French 35 seats Lunch
£4.50–£8.50&alc Dinner £20alc Wine
£5.20 Last dinner 11pm ✱
Credit cards ①②③

✗**Mao Tai Szechuan** 58 New Kings Rd
☎01-731 2520
♥Chinese & Szechuan V 90 seats S%
✱Lunch £12.50alc Dinner £12.50alc
Wine £5.20 Last dinner 11.45pm ✱
Credit cards ①②③⑤

✱✗**Perfumed Conservatory** 182
Wandsworth Bridge Rd
☎01-731 0732

Fashionable restaurant and cocktail bar
specialising in original and imaginative
British cooking.
Closed Sun & Mon, Xmas
Lunch not served Sat
40 seats ✱Lunch £15–£17.50 Wine £6
Last dinner 11.30pm ✱ nc 10yrs
Credit cards ①②③

✗**Trencherman** 271 New Kings Rd
☎01-736 4988
Supervised by the Patron Jean-Paul
Grillon, this small cosy Bistro features
authentic regional dishes.
♥French 30 seats Last dinner
10.45pm ✱
Credit cards ②③④⑤

**SW7 South Kensington**
★★★**Gloucester** 4–18 Harrington
Gdns (Rank) ☎01-373 5842 Telex no
917505
Modern, well managed hotel with
comfortable, well-equipped bedrooms, good
service and choice of restaurants.
531⇌(2fb) ✗ in 10 bedrooms CTV in
all bedrooms ⓡ in 473 bedrooms T S%
✱sB⇌fr£87 dB⇌fr£101 (room only)
� Lift Ⓓ ⊞ 100Ⓐ (£5.75 per day)
CFA sauna bath solarium xmas
♥English & Continental V ✧ ⌘ ✗ S%
✱Lunch £9.45&alc Tea
£1.50–£2.50&alc High Tea £5&alc
Dinner £10–£25&alc Wine £7.50 Last
dinner 12.30am
Credit cards ①②③④⑤

★★★**L Rembrandt** Thurloe Pl ☎01-
589 8100 Telex no 295828
A professionally-managed hotel, with
modern, well-equipped bedrooms, the
Rembrandt offers extensive 24-hour
services, the congenial 'Masters'
restaurant and an outstanding health and
fitness club.
200⇌(25fb) CTV in all bedrooms T ✗
Continental breakfast ➮
Lift Ⓓ ✱ sauna bath solarium
gymnasium ✧ ⌘ Last dinner 9.30pm
Credit cards ①②③④⑤

✗✱✗**Bombay Brasserie** Courtfield
Close, Gloucester Rd ☎01-370 4040
(classification for dinner only)
Part of Bailey's Hotel, this restaurant
serves authentic regional dishes in an
elegant colonial atmosphere
♥Indian V 175 seats Lunch fr £8.50
Dinner £18.50alc Wine £6.25 Last
dinner mdnt
Credit cards ①②③⑤

✱✗✗**Hilaire** 68 Old Brompton Rd
☎01-584 8993
(Rosette awarded for dinner only)
Fashionable, contemporary restaurant
featuring imaginative fixed-price menu.
Closed Sun & Public Hols
Lunch not served Sat
♥French 50 seats Lunch
£13.50–£14.50 Dinner £21–£23
Wine £7.50 Last dinner 11pm ✱
nc 5yrs
Credit cards ①②③⑤

✗**Chanterelle** 119 Old Brompton Rd
☎01-373 5522
This attractive, pine-panelled restaurant
features a fixed-price menu which
represents particularly good value for
money. Reliable standards of cooking are
matched by attentive and friendly service.
Closed 4 days Xmas
♥English & French 45 seats Lunch
£7–£9.50 Dinner £11–£12 Wine
£4.70 Last dinner 11.30pm ✱
Credit cards ①②③⑤

✗**Montpeliano** 13 Montpelier St ☎01-
589 0032
Popular, fashionable Italian restaurant,
featuring authentic cuisine and efficient,
friendly service.
Closed Sun, Xmas Day & Bank Hols
♥Italian V 80 seats Last dinner mdnt
✱ ✗

✗**Zen Too** 53 Old Brompton Rd ☎01-
225 1609
Friendly and well-managed, this
contemporary restaurant is attractively
decorated and appointed in pink. The menu
features a carefully-chosen selection of
Chinese regional dishes, the high standard
of cooking extending to fresh vegetables
and rich sauces. It is advisable to reserve a
table on the ground floor, as the basement
can be depressing.
♥Chinese V 70 seats Last dinner
11.30pm
Credit cards ①②③⑤

**SW8 Battersea**
✱✱✱✗✗**L'Arlequin**
123 Queenstown Rd ☎01-622 0555
Christian Delteil's little restaurant
continues to earn the plaudits of our
members. He follows the modern fashion
but refrains from the admixture of too
many ingredients in a dish. They are
always beautifully balanced and they
always taste essentially 'clean'. His
mousselines are as light as can be, yet
flavoursome, while his fish cooking is
perfect and his sauces just right to
complement the dish without
overpowering it. Among the reports we
have had, persillée de ris de veau etmoutard,
and confit de foie gras au poireaux with
brioche, have been first courses to be
enjoyed; raviolées de fenouil aux
langoustines and a fricassée of scallops
with ginger, among the fish, and succulent
Challans duck with its sapid sauce and
meltingly tender foie gras dressed on a bed
of darfin potatoes, garnished with apples
and grapes with a port wine sauce, have
been highly lauded. Vegetables usually
please but if there is a weak point it is the
puddings. That is judging at the highest
standards however; we are sure you will
enjoy his sorbets, which are among the
best, marquise au chocolat and, if you have
room, the assiette gourmande – a selection.
The wine list is well-chosen. You will be
well looked after by the smart young
brigade. The room is quietly elegant but
gleaming table appointments bright with

*flowers on crisp linen make for an appropriate setting in which to enjoy this delicious cooking. The fixed-price luncheon is something of a bargain.*
Closed Sat, Sun, 1 wk Xmas & 3 wks Aug
♀French 40 seats Lunch fr £12.50 Dinner £40alc Wine £9 Last dinner 11pm ⚑
Credit cards ① ③ ⑤

**❀✕✕Chèz Nico** 129 Queenstown Rd ☎01-720 6960
*This restaurant has been elegantly refurbished with attractive, pleasing decor, and the atmosphere is relaxing and informal.*
Closed Sun, 1 wk Xmas, Bank Hols & 3 wks summer
Lunch not served Sat & Mon
♀French 45 seats S% ✳Lunch £14.50&alc Dinner £28alc Wine £8.95 Last dinner 10.45pm ⚑ nc 7yrs
Credit cards ① ③ ⑤

**✕✕Lampwicks** 24 Queenstown Rd ☎01-622 7800
*The tastefully-decorated, split-level restaurant features a fixed-price menu, the imaginative choice of dishes offering excellent value for money. Careful preparation and skilful cooking in the modern style are complemented by a choice from the Philippe Olivier cheese board.*
Closed Sun, Mon, 2 wks Xmas & last 2 wks Aug
♀French V 30 seats Last dinner 10.30pm ⚑
Credit cards ① ② ③ ⑤

### SW10 West Brompton
**✕✕Brinkley's** 47 Hollywood Rd ☎01-351 1683
*An imaginative menu is offered by this unusual and fashionable French restaurant where meals are served on a covered rear terrace by friendly young staff.*
Closed Sun Lunch not served
♀English & French 60 seats Dinner £12.50–£14 Wine £6 Last dinner 11.30pm ⚑
Credit cards ① ② ③ ⑤

**✕✕Nikita's** 65 Ifield Rd ☎01-352 6326
*Authentic Russian dishes served in friendly candlelight atmosphere complemented by one of the best Vodka lists.*
Closed Sun, Xmas Day, Bank Hols Lunch not served
♀Russian 50 seats S% Dinner £20alc Wine £5.95 Last dinner 11.15pm ⚑ ✗
Credit cards ① ② ⑤

**✕✕L'Olivier** 116 Finborough Rd ☎01-370 4183
*Fashionable basement restaurant with enterprising authentic cuisine at fixed price, and several imaginative à la carte dishes.*
Closed Sun & 2 wks Xmas
♀French 50 seats Lunch fr £20&alc

Dinner fr £20 Last dinner 11.45pm ⚑
Credit cards ① ② ③ ⑤

**✕✕September** 457 Fulham Rd ☎01-352 0206
*Cooking is unpretentious and uncomplicated at this neatly compact restaurant and bar, a wide choice of dishes being accompanied by particularly good vegetables, though the range of desserts is limited. Service is friendly and reliable, and a meal here represents good value for money.*
Closed Sun Lunch not served
♀International V 65 seats ✳Dinner £13.50&alc Wine £6.25 Last dinner 11.30pm ⚑
Credit cards ① ② ③ ④ ⑤

**✕Bagatelle** 5 Langton St ☎01-351 4185
*Sophisticated and fashionable small French restaurant, featuring skilful, imaginative cooking and friendly service, and a rear garden patio.*
Closed Sun & Bank Hols
♀French 60 seats ✳Lunch £12&alc Dinner £17alc Wine £6.20 Last dinner 11pm ⚑
Credit cards ① ② ③ ⑤

**✕Chelsea Wharf** Lots Rd ☎01-351 0861
*This popular, fashionable, riverside restaurant has extensive waterfront views. A menu which changes monthly offers a choice of fixed-price or à la carte meals, and service is friendly and helpful.*
Closed Public Hols
Lunch not served Mon
♀English & French V 90 seats Last dinner 11.30pm 6P
Credit cards ① ② ③ ⑤

**✕La Croisette** 168 Ifield Rd ☎01-373 3694
*Popular, small, French restaurant specialising in shellfish. Good main basement ambience.*
Closed Mon & 2 wks Xmas
♀French 55 seats Last dinner 11.30pm ⚑
Credit card ②

**✕Jake's** 14 Hollywood Rd ☎01-352 8692
*This straightforward but stylish English restaurant has a lively and informal atmosphere which is complemented by thoroughly enjoyable food. Such dishes as breast of duck and home-made salmon fish-cakes are enhanced by herb-based and piquant sauces, whilst vegetables are fresh and simply-cooked. Service is unobtrusively friendly.*
Dinner not served Sun
♀International V 60 seats ✳Lunch £8–£10alc Dinner £12–£14alc Wine £5.50 Last dinner 11.45pm ⚑
Credit cards ① ② ③ ④ ⑤

**✕Van B's** 306B Fulham Rd ☎01-351 0863
*Unusually long and narrow, the first-floor*

*dining room bears a remarkable resemblance to a carriage on the Orient Express, and a good standard of comfort is achieved by skilful lighting and tasteful furnishing. The fixed-price menu offers an enterprising selection of dishes, including home-made ice-cream and sorbet which are very good value for money, and the standards of service are generally acceptable.*
Lunch not served
♀French V 40 seats Dinner £12.50 Wine £6.85 Last dinner mdnt ⚑
Credit cards ① ② ③

### SW11 Battersea
**✕Ormes** 245 Lavender Hill ☎01-228 9824
*Two-level restaurant featuring interesting, imaginative fish dishes.*
Closed Sun Lunch not served
68 seats Last dinner 11pm ⚑
Credit cards ① ② ③ ⑤

**✕Pollyanna's** 2 Battersea Rise ☎01-228 0316
*Fashionable bistro-style decor is complemented by skilful and reliable cooking supervised by the proprietor.*
Closed 24–27 Dec & 1 Jan
Lunch not served Mon–Sat
Dinner not served Sun
♀French V 70 seats Lunch £8.95 Dinner £10.95&alc Wine £5.50 Last dinner mdnt ⚑
Credit cards ① ② ③

### SW13 Barnes
**✕Barnaby's** 39B High St, Barnes ☎01-878 4750
*Small high street restaurant offering French specialities.*
Closed Sun, Bank Hols, 3 wks Sep, 5 days Xmas & Etr
Lunch not served Sat & Mon
♀French 24 seats S% Lunch £14alc Dinner £14alc Wine £5.95 Last dinner 10.15pm ⚑
Credit cards ① ② ③ ⑤

### SW14 East Sheen
**✕Crowthers** 481 Upper Richmond Rd West, East Sheen ☎01-876 6372
*Small family-run, tastefully decorated restaurant offering a fixed-price menu.*
Closed Sun, Mon, Xmas Day, New Year's Eve, 1 wk Feb & 2 wks Aug/Sep
Lunch not served
♀French V 30 seats Lunch £12 Dinner £17.50 Wine £6 Last dinner 11pm ⚑
nc 10yrs
Credit cards ① ②

**✕Janine's** 505 Upper Richmond Rd West, East Sheen ☎01-876 5075
*Small, intimate, candlelit Anglo-French restaurant.*
Closed Mon 2 wks Feb/Mar, 2 wks Sep/Oct Lunch not served Tue–Sat
Dinner not served Sun
♀English & French 34 seats ✳Lunch £9.50–£10.50 Dinner £9.95&alc Wine £4.50 Last dinner 11pm ⚑
Credit cards ① ② ③ ⑤

## SW15 Putney

✕✕**Annia's** 349 Upper Richmond Rd
☎01-876 4456
This unique restaurant, based on a
Swedish country house design, is furnished
with antiques. The menu features a good-
value selection of authentic Swedish
dishes, and Annia creates a relaxing
atmosphere with personal attention.
Closed Mon
♥French & Swedish 30 seats Last
dinner 11.30pm Live music nightly
Credit cards ① ② ③ ⑤

✕**Berts** 34 Upper Richmond Rd ☎01-
874 8839
A highly original and eclectic cuisine is
featured on the fixed-price menu of this
small and very stylish restaurant. Wines
are particularly good value for money, and
service is very friendly and helpful.
Lunch not served except Sun & Xmas
♥English & French V 50 seats Lunch
£7.45&alc Dinner £12.85&alc Wine
£4.95 Last dinner 11pm ✈
Credit cards ① ③

✕**Buzkash Afghan** 4 Chelverton Rd
☎01-788 0599
The atmosphere of this compact, authentic,
Afghan restaurant is created largely by the
traditional weaponry which decorates the
walls, hanging alongside bright, woven
carpets. Quietly attractive, friendly service
makes guests feel comfortable and relaxed,
whilst the food itself, with its aromas of
exotic spices, is no disappointment.
Closed Sun, Xmas Day & Boxing Day
♥Afghan 48 seats S% ✦Lunch £12alc
Dinner £12alc Wine £5.95. Last dinner
11pm ✈
Credit cards ① ② ③ ⑤

✕**Samratt** 18 Lacy Rd ☎01-788 9110
The individuality of this small, air-
conditioned, Indian restaurant and take-
away creates a relaxing atmosphere,
Tandoori special dishes and curries to suit
most tastes are available.
Closed Xmas
♥Indian V 46 seats Last dinner
11.50pm
Credit cards ① ② ③ ⑤

✕**Wild Thyme** 96 Felsham Rd ☎01-
789 3323
An original, fixed-price menu which
changes every six weeks is politely served
in cheerful surroundings at this bright,
conservatory restaurant.
Closed Sun
♥British & French 40 seats Lunch
£11.50 Dinner £16 Wine £5.50 Last
dinner 11pm ✈
Credit cards ① ② ③

## SW16 Norbury

✕**Malean** 1585 London Rd, Norbury
☎01-764 2336
Small family-run Chinese restaurant.
Closed 25–27 Dec
Lunch not served Sun
♥Pekinese & Szechuan V 38 seats Last
dinner 11.45pm ✈
Credit cards ① ② ③ ⑤

## SW19 Wimbledon

○**Cannizaro House** West Side Common
(Thistle) ☎01-937 8033
58 ⇔ ▥ ☎01-937 8033
Due to have opened summer 1986

✕**Les Amoureux** 156 Merton Hall Rd
☎01-543 0567
A converted Post Office with a candlelight
atmosphere and eclectic cuisine.
Lunch not served
♥French V 50 seats S% Dinner
£12.75alc Wine £6 Last dinner 10pm
✈
Credit cards ① ②

## W1 West End

Piccadilly Circus, Soho, St Marylebone
and Mayfair
**Five Red Stars Claridge's,**
Brook St ☎01-629 8860 Telex no
21872
A bastion of tradition, this most elegant of
hotels has been, traditionally, the second
home of Royalty and other discriminating
clients when visiting London. It is very
much in the grand manner, with marbled
floors and a lofty lounge with marbled
pillars where the Hungarian Quartet plays
and where you will be attended by waiters
in knee breeches. An imposing and newly-
restored staircase leads to the upper floors,
suites and bedrooms which are
sumptuously done. The more mundane of
the five-star facilities are discreetly hidden
away and there is no bar, so the
atmosphere is something like that of a
gracious and opulent private house, Mr
Ron Jones, the fairly recently appointed
General Manager, is making his mark here
without making waves to disturb the even
tenor; small improvements like the
staircase and the rearrangement of the
Causerie are the sensible order of the day.
More formal eating than in the Causerie
takes place in the elegantly appointed
restaurant decorated in the style of the
inter war years. Chef Mario Lesnik
presents mostly classical dishes which are
well-cooked. Needless to say the attentive
service matches the cooking; indeed the
proficient service can provide practically
any requirement you may need throughout
the hotel. One of the things that lifts
Claridge's above most of its peers, is the
real friendliness you can experience here; it
is exceptional for this type of hotel.
189 ⇔ ▥ CTV in all bedrooms T ✖ S%
sB⇔ ▥ £105–£150
dB⇔ ▥ £160–£185 (room only)
Lift D ✈ ✦ Live music and dancing
Lunch (Mon–Fri) Dinner (Sun–Thu)
♥British & French V ♥ ⚤ S%
✦Lunch £31alc Tea £6alc Dinner
£35alc Wine £5.30 Last dinner
11.30pm
Credit cards ① ② ③ ④ ⑤

●●**Five Red Stars The Connaught**
Carlos Pl ☎01-499 7070
This hotel does not manifest the more
obvious appurtenances of a five-star hotel,
but the moment you step through the front
door you know that you are somewhere
special, a feeling shared by an international
clientele who return repeatedly to
experience the discreet luxury of a stay
here. It is very English in atmosphere,
with two elegant sitting rooms, a
mahogany staircase rising out of the hall,
the club-like mahogany-panelled
restaurant and the simpler Grill room;
there is also a smart cocktail bar.
Bedrooms are individually decorated and
well up to five-star standard. Nice pieces of
furniture, crystal chandeliers, pictures and
lovely informal flower arrangements
enhance the atmosphere. Catering is of the
utmost importance and chef Michel
Bourdin has shown that it is possible to
produce epicurean cooking for large
numbers. Mainly luxury hotel classical, he
is able to offer something for everyone,
from simple grills and traditional British
dishes to haute cuisine. Mousselines are
light and flavoursome; there are full
flavoured terrines, and sapid combinations
of ingredients on melt-in-the-mouth
pastry. His fish and meat dishes are
always highly commended, also game with
zestful sauces. Mouth-watering puddings
are served, but alas, the talented young
patissier does not have the predecessor's
way with soufflés. Mr Chevalier will look
after you in the restaurant with its 3
course menu priced according to the main
course chosen, plus extras, while in the
Grill Room, where Mr Boro is in charge,
an à la carte menu is provided. In both
cases, dishes in heavy print on the menu
are the gastronomic delights. Mr Zago is
the General Manager and he ensures that
his friendly staff look after you
proficiently; linkmen, reception staff,
porters, waiters, valets and chambermaids
will, without exception, provide smooth-
running service that cannot be beaten in
London.
90 ⇔ ▥ CTV in all bedrooms T ✖
Lift D ✈ ⬤
♥English & French ⚤ Last dinner
10.30pm
Credit cards ①

⬤**Five Red Stars The Dorchester**
53 Park Ln ☎01-629 8888 Telex no
887704
(Rosette awarded only to Terrace Room)
One of the most famous hotels in the
world, this is the epitome of a luxurious
hotel. Unashamedly catering for the rich
and the glamorous, it has a suitable and
sumptuous decor in the public areas: the
promenade lounge with its pillars and gold
leafed ceiling, the cocktail bar with a
singer/pianist, the Spanish-style Grill
room, and the charmingly elegant Terrace
room with dancing. There is also the
rarely-met residents' library, provided not
only with books and games, but also
personal stereo. Another unusual feature
since last year is the 24-hour television
news service beamed direct from the USA.
Bedrooms vary from the fantastic Oliver
Messel suite to more moderately sized
ones. They are air conditioned and provided
with bath gowns and hairdryers as well as
superior toiletries. Valet and room service
is smoothly efficient, as is the service
throughout the hotel by courteous,

*dignified staff. Anton Mosimann is in charge of the catering and he produces excellent food. In the Grill room, it is basically British in a modern interpretation, but in the Terrace room he presents a more refined style of nouvelle cuisine with his own 'cuisine naturelle'. We have found this less successful with meat than with fish, but such dishes without any fat or flour will find favour with the health conscious. Otherwise, oysters Moscovite, feuilleté of calves sweetbreads and crayfish, his version of roast duck with zestful sauce or the best end of lamb with shallots have been highly complimented, as well as the now famous symphony of sea food. Puddings seem to have been a weakness but the tangy fruit terrine with its raspberry coulis was much enjoyed. The wine list is outstanding but expensive.*

280 ↩ 1 ▥ CTV in all bedrooms T ✕ S% *sB↩£115–£145 dB↩£165–£175 (room only) Lift ⅅ 10P 50 ⚠ (£12 per night) CFA 🐾 Live music & dancing 6 nights wkly *xmas* ♀English & French V ♥ ⚖ S% *Lunch £17 Tea £8 Dinner £17&alc Wine £10.70 Last dinner 10.30pm Credit cards ① ② ③ ④ ⑤

★ ★ ★ ★ ★**Churchill** Portman Sq ☎01-486 5800 Telex no 264831 *This modern hotel has become well-established on the London scene over the years. It has luxurious décor with a Regency flavour.* 489↩ CTV in all bedrooms T sB↩£130 dB↩£145 (room only) Lift ⅅ ▦ 75⚠ (charge) CFA 🐾 ✎ (hard) ♀International V ♥ ⚖ S% Lunch £25alc Tea fr £7.50 Dinner £30alc Wine £8.40 Last dinner 11pm Credit cards ① ② ③ ④ ⑤

★ ★ ★ ★ ★**L Grosvenor House** Park Ln (Trusthouse Forte) ☎01-499 6363 Telex no 24871 *Significant improvements in both accommodation and standards of service are now taking place with the help of a committed and more permanent management team at this traditional hotel. The fine facilities available include ballroom, health club, swimming pool, three restaurants and a delightful lounge where traditional afternoon tea is served.* 472↩ CTV in all bedrooms T sB&B↩£124.50 dB&B↩£159 Lift ⅅ 20P 100⚠ CFA ▣ (heated) sauna bath solarium gymnasium ♥ ⚖ Last dinner 11pm Credit cards ① ② ③ ④ ⑤

★ ★ ★ ★ ★**BL Inn on the Park** Hamilton Pl, Park Ln (Prestige) ☎01-499 0888 Telex no 22771 *Possibly the best modern hotel in London, it has splendid suites, excellent bathrooms and two restaurants.* 228↩ 🅧 in 24 bedrooms CTV in all bedrooms T S% sB↩ 🍴 £166.75 dB↩ 🍴 £189.75 (room only)

Lift ⅅ ▦ 80⚠ (£7 per night) 🐾 ♿ *xmas* ♀International V ♥ ⚖ S% Lunch £16.25–£19 Tea fr £8.50 Dinner fr £28 Wine £9.55 Last dinner mdnt Credit cards ① ② ③ ④ ⑤

●●●★ ★ ★ ★ ★ **Inter-Continental** 1 Hamilton Pl, Hyde Park Corner ☎01-409 3131 Telex no 25853 *(Rosettes awarded for Le Soufflé Restaurant)* *In this American owned hotel is the art deco restaurant in red, black and silver, that is the scene for chef Peter Kromberg's talented cooking. Although he has been here for some time, it is only in the last couple of years that we have seen such a big improvement. This year was best of all and we think that the food is now worth a second rosette. The menu is marked by the use of expensive ingredients, but is none the worse for that provided you can afford to eat here. As its name suggests, a range of soufflés are available among the first courses and puddings. But there are other good things too: a recherché dish of ravioli stuffed with a mixture of pigeon puree and foie gras, cooked and served in a soup-like sauce from pigeon stock and morilles was much acclaimed. Fish dishes, like sole fillets with lobster and cucumber in butter sauce, are delicately cooked; among the meat dishes, duck breast stuffed with foie gras and baked in a pastry cage with its impeccable sauce, lamb fillet with blackcurrant sauce, and a 'moneybag' filled with lambs sweetbreads have greatly impressed us. There is a tempting array of mouthwatering puddings. Service is first class under the able supervision of Josef Lanser, who is friendly, proficient and attentive, but they could do with a more knowledgable sommelier than our visits have experienced. For the rest, this modern hotel near Hyde Park Corner, provides good standards of public rooms and bedrooms. They have mini-bars, and in-house movies, and somewhat compact bathrooms.* 491↩ 🍴 🅧 in 6 bedrooms CTV in all bedrooms T ✕ sB↩ 🍴 £163.30 dB↩ 🍴 £180.90 (room only) Lift ⅅ ▦ 120⚠ (charged) CFA sauna bath gymnasium Disco Mon–Sat *xmas* ♀International V ♥ ⚖ 🅧 Lunch fr £15.60&alc Tea fr £4.80 High Tea fr £6.50 Dinner fr £15.60&alc Wine £9.50 Last dinner 1am Credit cards ① ② ③ ④ ⑤

★ ★ ★ ★**London Hilton** 22 Park Ln ☎01-493 8000 Telex no 24873 *This is one of the liveliest and most exciting hotels in London, and many of the bedrooms (especially those overlooking Hyde Park) have spectacular views. Extensive refurbishment continues, including upgrading of the bedrooms and the provision of a new first floor restaurant and a popular lobby lounge. Other facilities include two further restaurants, a new shopping arcade, a disco and three bars.*

501↩ 🍴 🅧 in 23 bedrooms CTV in all bedrooms T *sB↩ 🍴 £126.50–£155.25 dB↩ 🍴 £147.20–£180.55 (room only) Lift ⅅ ▦ ₱ sauna bath solarium Disco 6 nights wkly Live music and dancing 6 nights wkly Cabaret 6 nights wkly *xmas* ♀International V ♥ ⚖ Lunch £15–£20&alc Tea £4–£8&alc Dinner £17–£35&alc Wine £14 Last dinner 1am Credit cards ① ② ③ ④ ⑤

★ ★ ★ ★**May Fair Inter-Continental** Stratton St ☎01-629 7777 Telex no 262526 *Long-established hotel, with friendly service. Facilities include a popular coffee house, elegant restaurant, small cinema and the Mayfair theatre.* 322↩ 🍴 (14fb) CTV in all bedrooms T ✕ sB↩ 🍴 £86–£120 dB↩ 🍴 £115–£145 (room only) Lift ⅅ ▦ ₱ ♿ *xmas* ♀English & French V ♥ ⚖ Credit cards ① ② ③ ④ ⑤

★ ★ ★ ★ ★**L Ritz** Piccadilly (Prestige) ☎01-493 8181 Telex no 267200 *The internationally-famous hotel, in the heart of London, is noted for its fine, ornate public rooms and the elegant restaurant in the Louis XVI style where meals of a high standard are served. The Palm Court is a famous rendezvous for traditional English afternoon tea. Bedrooms are elegant and spacious, and about a third of them are being further upgraded this year.* 128↩ 🍴 CTV in all bedrooms T ✕ S% *sB↩ 🍴 £120–£130 dB↩ 🍴 £140–£190 (room only) 🍽 lift ⅅ ₱ 🐾 Live music and dancing Sat Cabaret Wed–Fri *xmas* ♀English & French ♥ ⚖ S% *Lunch fr £18.75 Tea fr £8.50 Dinner fr £26.25 Wine £8.75 Credit cards ① ② ③ ④ ⑤

**Four Red Stars The Athenaeum** Piccadilly (Rank) ☎01-499 3464 Telex no 261589 *Continual upgrading of the bedrooms at this hotel ensures that they reach a very high standard. They are not a bad size for a modern hotel and the decoration and soft furnishings lend a warmth to the rooms. They have yew, military-type pieces of furniture and are double glazed, very well-equipped and comfortable; within-house movies are available on the television. Room service, like that throughout the hotel, is smoothly proficient. On the ground floor public areas include the club-like panelled bar and a comfortable lounge where you can take your ease after a hard day's work. There is also the elegant restaurant which offers a good value, fixed-price lunch including wine; additionally there is a pre-theatre dinner and a well chosen à la carte menu at night. Cooking is mostly French with a modern influence and is enjoyable. All staff are cheerful, friendly and enthusiastic so that you will enjoy that aspect of your stay. It has a*

pleasing situation overlooking Green Park and is convenient for the West End of London.
112⇄🁢 🛏 in 54 bedrooms CTV in all bedrooms T ✻ (ex guide dogs) S%
sB⇄🁢£118–£130
dB⇄🁢£140–£160 (room only) 🍴
Lift 𝒟 ⊞ 🏴 CFA ⇔ Live music 5 nights wkly *xmas*
♥International V ♥ ♨ 🛏 S% Lunch £16.50–£17.50&alc Tea £4–£6 Dinner £13.50–£15.50&alc Wine £8.50 Last dinner 10.30pm
Credit cards ①②③④⑤

**Four Red Stars Brown's**
Dover St Albemarle St (Trusthouse Forte) ☎01-493 6020 Telex no 28686
*A wealth of old, mellow panelling, pillars and chimney-pieces and moulded ceilings, all set off by lovely flower arrangements and cheerful chintz colours in the lounge, set the scene for this most English of hotels. Started a long time ago as a building offering sets of chambers for the London 'season', it has become a most distinguished hotel and one very popular with Americans. As an old building that has been extended and altered over the years, the bedrooms clearly vary a great deal in size, and the corridors are narrow; nevertheless, they have been modernised to good effect, some with nice old pieces of furniture. The St George's bar is a popular rendezvous for drinks, as is the lounge for coffee and particularly good afternoon teas. L'Apertif restaurant serves fixed-price and à la carte menus and the cooking is chiefly in the modern style. It is with regret that we learned that Barry Larvin, the exceedingly able and pleasant restaurant manager left at the turn of the year. He will be sorely missed but we wish him well running his own restaurant. His manner was the epitome of the friendly, solicitous care that all staff here show towards their guests.*
125⇄ CTV in all bedrooms T
sB&B⇄£108.50 dB&B⇄£148.50
Lift 𝒟 🏴 CFA ⇔ *xmas*
♥ ♨ Last dinner 10pm
Credit cards ①②③④⑤

★★★★**Britannia** Grosvenor Sq ☎01-629 9400 Telex no 23941
*This smart, comfortable hotel has bedrooms which are furnished to a high standard, and room service is efficient. The Carlton restaurant serves noteworthy meals in the modern French style.*
356⇄ 🛏 in 48 bedrooms CTV in all bedrooms T S% ✻sB⇄frf£115
dB⇄frf£126.50 (room only) 🍴
Lift 𝒟 ⊞ 🏴 CFA Live music & dancing nightly *xmas*
♥English, American & Japanese V ♥ ♨ 🛏 S% Lunch fr £14.95 Dinner £14.95–£24.40&alc Wine £9.50 Last dinner 12.30am
Credit cards ①②③④⑤

★★★★**Cumberland** Marble Arch (Trusthouse Forte) ☎01-262 1234 Telex no 22215
*A commercial and tourist hotel with*

limited room service, but good coffee shop facilities.
905⇄ CTV in all bedrooms T
sB&B⇄£78.50 dB&B⇄£105 🍴
Lift 𝒟 🏴 CFA ⇔
♥ ♨ Last dinner 10.30pm
Credit cards ①②③④⑤

★★★★**B Holiday Inn–Marble Arch**
134 George St (Holiday Inns) ☎01-723 1277 Telex no 27983
*Well-appointed hotel with attractive garden-style coffee shop.*
241⇄🁢 (116fb) 🛏 in 36 bedrooms CTV in all bedrooms T ✻ S%
sB⇄🁢 fr£100.05
dB⇄🁢£106.95–£120.75 (room only) 🍴
Lift 𝒟 ⊞ 100▲ CFA ⇔ ☒ (heated) sauna bath solarium gymnasium ⅋
♥International ♥ ♨ S% Lunch £4.50–£12.75&alc Tea fr £1.20 Dinner £4.50–£13.50&alc Wine £8.75
Credit cards ①②③④⑤

★★★**London Marriot** Grosvenor Sq ☎01-493 1232 Telex no 268101
*Modern tastefully-furnished hotel with good restaurant, NCP car park located underneath the building.*
229⇄(61fb) CTV in all bedrooms T ✻ Continental breakfast 🍴
Lift 𝒟 ⊞ CFA *xmas*
♥French V ♥ ♨ Last dinner 1pm
Credit cards ①②③④⑤

★★★**Montcalm** Great Cumberland Pl ☎01-402 4288 Telex no 28710
*The terraced, Georgian building has now been completely modernised throughout and offers formal service in a quiet atmosphere.*
116⇄🁢 (9fb) CTV in all bedrooms T S% ✻sB⇄🁢 fr£115 dB⇄🁢£138 (room only)
Lift 𝒟 ⊞ 🏴 ⇔
♥French ♥ ♨ S% ✻Lunch fr £7.50&alc Dinner fr £17.50&alc Wine £13 Last dinner 11pm
Credit cards ①②③④⑤

★★★★**L Park Lane** Piccadilly ☎01-499 6321 Telex no 21533
*(Rosette awarded for Bracewell's Restaurant)*
*The Palm Court lounge is very well-appointed offering the elegance and atmosphere of the twenties. Bracewell's Restaurant is decorated with 16th-century carved wood panelling and mirrored pillars, which create an elegant, formal atmosphere enhanced by attentive service. There is a choice of table d'hôte and à la carte menus to which a Menu Gastronomique is added in the evening; mouth-watering desserts are much in evidence.*
325⇄ CTV in all bedrooms T S% ✻sB⇄£99.95–£119.95
dB⇄£119.95–£129.95 (room only) 🍴
Lift 𝒟 180▲ (£9 per 24 hrs) CFA
♥International V ♥ ♨ S% ✻Lunch fr £13.50 Tea £2.50–£6 Dinner

£17.50–£19.50 Wine £8 Last dinner 12.30am
Credit cards ①②③⑤

★★★★**Portman Inter-Continental**
22 Portman Sq ☎01-486 5844 Telex no 261526
*Well-appointed modern hotel with efficient and friendly service.*
278⇄ 🛏 in 14 bedrooms CTV in all bedrooms T ✻ sB&B⇄£113.60–£132 dB&B⇄£137.50–£150.15
Continental breakfast
Lift 𝒟 ⊞ CFA ⇔ (hard) Live music & dancing Sun *xmas*
♥ ♨ 🛏 Lunch £14.80&alc Tea £1.20 High Tea £7.50 Dinner £24&alc Wine £7.50
Credit cards ①②③④⑤

★★★★**St George's** Langham Pl (Trusthouse Forte) ☎01-580 0111 Telex no 27274
*A modern hotel whose top floor restaurant gives panoramic views across London.*
85⇄ CTV in all bedrooms ® T sB&B⇄£88.50 dB&B⇄£114.50 🍴
Lift 𝒟 ⊞
♥ ♨ Last dinner 10pm
Credit cards ①②③④⑤

★★★★**Selfridge** Orchard St (Thistle) ☎01-408 2080 Telex no 22361
*A modern hotel with small bedrooms and bathrooms, but comfortable and attractive public lounge and restaurant.*
298⇄🁢 🛏 in 44 bedrooms CTV in all bedrooms T ✻sB⇄🁢£90–£105
dB⇄🁢£125–£165 (room only) 🍴
Lift 𝒟 ⊞ ▲ ⇔ *xmas*
♥International ♥ ♨ ✻Lunch fr £14.50&alc Dinner fr £14.50&alc Wine £7 Last dinner 10pm
Credit cards ①②③④⑤

★★★★**Westbury** New Bond St (Trusthouse Forte) ☎01-629 7755 Telex no 24378
*Comfortable commercial and tourist hotel with attractive wood-panelled lounges.*
240⇄ CTV in all bedrooms T sB&B⇄£104 dB&B⇄£127.50
Lift 𝒟 🏴 CFA ⇔
♥ ♨ Last dinner 11pm
Credit cards ①②③④⑤

★★★**D Berners** Berners St ☎01-636 1629 Telex no 25759
*Ideally situated in the heart of the West End, this hotel has been restored to retain the original beauty of the Edwardian era. Bedrooms are designed to a high standard and well-equipped, whilst both carvery restaurant and cocktail bar are air-conditioned.*
232⇄🁢 (10fb) 🛏 in 41 bedrooms CTV in all bedrooms T ✻ S%
sB⇄🁢£72–£81.50
dB⇄🁢£99–£115 (room only)
Lift 𝒟 🏴 CFA ⅋
V ♥ ♨ S% Lunch £10.75–£11.50 &alc Tea £2.35–£2.50 Dinner £10.75–£11.50&alc Wine £6.50 Last dinner 10pm
Credit cards ①②③⑤

★ ★ ★**L Chesterfield** 35 Charles St
☎01-491 2622 Telex no 269394
*This traditional hotel in the centre of
Mayfair now has the new Butlers
restaurant, which offers an outstanding
buffet lunch in addition to its à la carte
menu. The colourful bedrooms are
furnished to a high standard, and a warm
atmosphere is created by flowers and
antiques in the ground floor public rooms,
which include a wood-panelled library.*
113⇨ 🏠 1⬛CTV in all bedrooms T ✖
*sB⇨ 🏠 fr£95 dB⇨ 🏠 fr£110 (room
only)
Lift 🌙 🅿 🚗
♬International V ♦ ⚲ *Lunch fr
£13.50&alc Tea fr £5.25 Dinner
£19alc Wine £5.25 Last dinner mdnt
Credit cards 1 2 3 5

★ ★ ★**L Clifton-Ford** 47 Welbeck St
☎01-486 6600 Telex no 22569
Closed 24Dec–1 Jan
*This very good hotel offers considerable
comfort and excellent service.*
216⇨ 🏠 CTV in all bedrooms T
*sB&B⇨ 🏠 £72.75
dB&B⇨ 🏠 £97.50 Continental
breakfast 🍴
Lift 🌙 20♿ (£8.50 per day) Live music
nightly
♬International V ♦ ⚲ *Lunch fr
£10.50alc Tea fr £5.50 High Tea fr
£9.20 Dinner fr £10.75&alc Wine £8
Last dinner 10.15pm
Credit cards 1 2 3 5

★ ★ ★**Mandeville** Mandeville Pl ☎01-
935 5599 Telex no 269487
*Possibly one of the best commercial and tourist
hotels. Sound French cuisine in the restaurant.*
165⇨ 🏠 CTV in all bedrooms T S%
*sB&B⇨ 🏠 £71.50 dB⇨ 🏠 £88 (room
only) 🍴
Lift 🌙 🅿
♬International ♦ ⚲ S% *Lunch
£8–£15alc Tea £3.50alc Dinner
£8–£15alc Wine £6 Last Dinner
11.30pm
Credit cards 1 2 3 4 5

★ ★ ★**Mount Royal** Bryanston St,
Marble Arch (Mount Charlotte) ☎01-
629 8040 Telex no 23355
*Set near Marble Arch, overlooking Hyde
Park, this commercial and tourist hotel
provides good coffee shop facilities.*
701⇨ 🏠 (31fb) CTV in all bedrooms ®
T sB&B⇨ 🏠 fr£57.75
dB&B⇨ 🏠 fr£72.50 Continental
breakfast 🍴
Lift 🌙 🅿 CFA *xmas*
♬Mainly grills ♦ ⚲ *Lunch fr
£9.95&alc Dinner fr £9.95&alc Wine
£5.95 Last dinner 11pm
Credit cards 1 2 3 4 5

★ ★ ★**Stratford Court** 350 Oxford St
☎01-629 7474 Telex no 22270
*Small, friendly central hotel.*
140⇨ 🏠 (16fb) CTV in all bedrooms T S%
sB&B⇨ 🏠 £67–£70 dB&B⇨ 🏠 £90–£95
Continental breakfast
Lift 🌙 🅿

♦ ⚲ S% Lunch £8.50–£10&alc Tea
£3 Dinner £8.50–£10&alc Wine £6
Last dinner 9.30pm
Credit cards 1 2 3 4 5

★ ★**Bryanston Court** 56–60 Great
Cumberland Pl ☎01-262 3141 Telex
no 262076
*Part of a terraced row of houses some 300
yards from Marble Arch, this cosy if
somewhat cramped hotel offers compact
bedrooms and showers, efficient service,
dinners better than those in most London
hotels, and prices reasonable for the
location.*
56rm(10⇨46 🏠) CTV in all bedrooms
T ✖ S% *sB&B⇨ 🏠 £42
dB&B⇨ 🏠 £54 Continental breakfast 🍴
Lift 🌙 🅿 🚗
♦ ⚲ S% *Lunch £14alc Tea 75p alc
Dinner £14alc Wine £5.50 Last dinner
10pm
Credit cards 1 2 3 4 5

★ ★**Regent Palace** Glasshouse St,
Piccadilly (Trusthouse Forte) ☎01-
734 7000 Telex no 23740
*Good accommodation in this outstanding
value-for-money hotel, adjacent to
Piccadilly Circus.*
999rm(34fb) CTV in all bedrooms ®
sB&B£34 dB&B£48 🍴
Lift 🌙 🅿 CFA *xmas*
♦ ⚲ Last dinner 9pm
Credit cards 1 2 3 4 5

○**Le Meridien** Piccadilly ☎01-
734 8000
Now open
*This lavishly-restored and elegant hotel
has the outstanding feature of a splendid
leisure club (available to residents as well
as members). Boasting three restaurants,
one in a glass conservatory, it is hard to
believe one is so close to Piccadilly Circus.
Service throughout is friendly and
welcoming.*

✕✕✕✕✕**Cafe Royal (Grill Room)** 68
Regent St ☎01-439 6320 Telex no
27234
*The ornate decor of carved gilt mirrors,
moulded ceilings and plush banquettes
provides an effective backdrop to the
traditionally formal service that
complements sound French cuisine at this
restaurant.*
Closed Sun
♬Cosmopolitan V 65 seats S% Lunch
£25alc Dinner £30alc Wine £9.10 Last
dinner 10.30pm
Credit cards 1 2 3 4 5

✕✕✕✕**Ninety Park Lane** 90 Park
Ln ☎01-409 1290 Telex no 24871
*Luxurious and elegant surroundings
combine here with professional service.*
Closed Sun Lunch not served Sat
♬French V 75 seats S% Lunch
£17.50–£22.50&alc Dinner
£29–£42.50&alc Wine £14 Last
dinner 10.45pm ✗ nc 6yrs Live music
Mon–Sat
Credit cards 1 2 3 4 5

❀❀❀✕✕✕✕**Le Gavroche**
43 Upper Brook St ☎01-408 0881
Telex no 8813079
*Classically based, innovatively interpreted,
Albert Roux and his brigade still provide
the best food in the country, presented with
real artistry. It is a joy in itself to see their
dishes presented for your delectation, and
this in itself stimulates your taste buds as
much as an aperitif (at these prices that
can be worthwhile!) Such standards of
quality in ingredients, cooking and service
do not come cheaply, but for those who
appreciate them we think it provides value
for money, particularly on some special
occasion. From start to finish the attention
to detail is awe-inspiring; even the canapes
to start and the chocolates and petits fours
to finish manifest the same supreme skill
and dedication. Soups, particularly the
sparklingly clear consommé, are superb,
shellfish dishes with their sauces are too,
while mousselines are beautifully light, yet
definite in flavour. But the meat and game
dishes are unsurpassed for strength of
flavour. Roundels of spring lamb, cooked
pink with a glazed sauce flavoured with
mustard and basil, and chicken of old-
fashioned flavour with mussels, shallots
and chopped red capsicums in a saffron
sauce, are a miracle of composition, with
all the individual flavours coming together
beautifully, and where the total effect is
greater than the sum of their parts.
Vegetables and salads are equally good,
particularly the beautiful, oily dressing
with the latter. Desserts are a work of art
in themselves and if you have room try
assiette du chef, a selection of miniature
delights. There is Menu Exceptionel of six
courses and the à la carte menu, while at
luncheon there is a good value fixed-price
menu. The wine list of about 500 is superb
and features vintages back to 1918. Mr
Silvano Geraldin and his brigade of
immaculately attired young men will
attend to you with unfailing attention and
skill in a formal manner. The restaurant is
appropriately furnished with a bar on the
ground floor, and the restaurant
downstairs has an ante room convenient
for smokers.*
Closed Sat, Sun, Bank Hols & 24 Dec–1
Jan Lunch not served 2 Jan
♬French 70 seats S% *Lunch
£19.50–£35&alc Dinner £35&alc
Wine £10.90 Last dinner 11pm 🅿
nc 6yrs
Credit cards 1 2 3 4 5

✕✕✕✕**London Hilton Hotel (Trader
Vic's)** Park Ln ☎01-493 7586 Telex no
24873
*Lively Polynesian restaurant below Hilton
Hotel.*
Closed Xmas Day Lunch not served Sat
♬International 180 seats S% *Lunch
£25–£30alc Dinner £35alc Wine £9
Last dinner 11.45pm 🅿
Credit cards 1 2 3 4 5

✕✕✕**Greenhouse** 27A Hay's Mews
☎01-499 3331
*Modern elegant dining room with a formal*

*but friendly service accompanying English and French cuisine.*
Closed Sun, Bank Hols & wk after Xmas
Lunch not served Sat
♥English & French 85 seats Lunch
£15.50alc Dinner £15.50alc Wine
£5.55 Last dinner 11pm ✦ nc 5yrs
Credit cards ①②③④⑤

✕✕✕**Masako** 6–8 St Christopher Pl
☎01-935 1579
*Authentic Japanese décor with armour, bamboo walls and waitresses in national costume.*
Closed Sun, Xmas, 3 days New Year,
Etr & Aug Bank Hol
♥Japanese 100 seats Last dinner 10pm
✦
Credit cards ①②③⑤

✕✕✕**Princess Garden of Mayfair** 8–10
North Audley St ☎01-493 3223
Closed Xmas & Etr
♥Peking V 150 seats Lunch
£15–£20alc Dinner £25–£30 Wine
£7.50 Last dinner 11.20pm ✦ nc 7yrs
Live music Mon–Sat
Credit cards ①②③⑤

✕✕✕**Tandoori of Mayfair** 37A Curzon
St ☎01-629 0600
*Tropical plants complete the attractive decor of this elegant, modern basement and ground-floor restaurant which offers an interesting menu of Tandoori dishes and curries; smart staff provide friendly service.*
Closed 25 & 26 Dec
♥Indian V 120 seats Lunch £13alc
Dinner £13alc Wine £5.80 Last dinner
mdnt ✦
Credit cards ①②③④⑤

❋✕✕**Au Jardin Des Gourmets** 5 Greek
St ☎01-437 1816
*This long-established French restaurant at the heart of Soho continues to serve impressive meals, professional standards being maintained by the owner, Mr Berkmann, and his young English staff. The gourmet and prix fixée menus are augmented by an à la carte selection which offers such interesting dishes as noisettes d'agneau au vinaigre de framboises, and the extensive, reasonably-priced wine list includes some good vintages.*
Closed Sun, Xmas & Etr
Lunch not served Sat & Bank Hols
♥French 85 seats ✳Lunch
£12.50–£23.50&alc Dinner
£12.50–£23.50&alc Wine £5.25 Last
dinner 11.15pm ✦ ✕
Credit cards ①②③⑤

✕✕**Chambeli** 12 Great Castle St ☎01-
636 0662 Telex no 261927
*The elegantly modern air-conditioned restaurant with well-appointed tables serves curries and Tandoori dishes which are competently prepared from fresh, raw materials. The wine list, though small in size, is well-balanced and reasonably priced, whilst the well-supervised service is efficient.*

Closed Sun
♥Indian V 70 seats S% Lunch
£8.50&alc Dinner £8.50&alc Wine
£4.95 Last dinner mdnt ✦
Credit cards ①②③⑤

✕✕**Chesa** (Swiss Centre) 10 Wardour
St ☎01-734 1291
*Swiss-style restaurant offering authentic classical mostly French cuisine.*
Closed 25 & 26 Dec
♥Swiss V 60 seats ✳Lunch £19.50&alc
Dinner £19.50&alc Wine £6.40 Last
dinner mdnt ✦ ✕
Credit cards ①②③④⑤

✕✕**La Cucaracha** 12 Greek St ☎01-
734 2253
*A maze of small, white, arched rooms that were once the cellars of an 18th-century monastery.*
Closed Xmas
♥Mexican V 65 seats Last dinner
11.15pm ✦ Live music nightly
Credit cards ①②③⑤

✕✕**Gallery Rendezvous** 53 Beak St
☎01-734 0445
*Chinese paintings are permanently exhibited in the restaurant.*
Closed Xmas & New Year's Day
♥Pekinese V 130 seats Lunch £6&alc
Dinner £6&alc Wine £5.50 Last dinner
11pm ✦
Credit cards ①②③⑤

❋✕✕**Gay Hussar** 2 Greek St ☎01-
437 0973
*A small, cosy and popular restaurant, the Gay Hussar has long been established as serving some of London's best, most authentic, Hungarian food. The lengthy menu provides a vast choice of dishes, and service is cheerful, if a little muddled at times.*
Closed Sun
♥Hungarian 35 seats Last dinner
10.30pm ✦

✕✕**Lal Qila** Tottenham Court Rd ☎01-
387 4570
*Good, modern, Indian restaurant.*
Closed 25 & 26 Dec
♥Indian V 75 seats S% Lunch £8–£12
Dinner £10–£15 Wine £5.95 Last
dinner 11.30pm ✦
Credit cards ①②③⑤

✕✕**Langan's Brasserie** Stratton St
☎01-491 8822
*This popular, French-style brasserie features an extensive menu of well-prepared, authentic dishes at reasonable prices. It is well-frequented by London society and by stars of television, stage and films.*
Closed Sun & Public Hols
Lunch not served Sat
♥French 200 seats S% Lunch £16alc
Dinner £16alc Wine £5.60 Last dinner
11.45pm ✦ Live music nightly
Credit cards ①②③⑤

✕✕**Library** 115 Mount St ☎01-
499 1745
*Small charming basement restaurant with a library atmosphere, and lady pianist.*
Closed Sat, Sun, Xmas & New Year
30 seats ✳Lunch £15alc Dinner £15alc
Wine £6.95 Last dinner 11pm ✦ nc
15yrs Live music nightly
Credit cards ①②③⑤

✕✕**Mr Kaj of Mayfair** 65 South Audley
St ☎01-493 8988
*Sophisticated, elegant restaurant serving both classical and regional Chinese dishes.*
Closed Xmas & Bank Hols
♥Pekinese 120 seats ✳Lunch £15alc
Dinner £15alc Wine £6.95 Last dinner
11.15pm ✦ nc 6yrs
Credit cards ①③⑤

❋✕✕**Odin's** 27 Devonshire St ☎01-
935 7296
*Masquerading as an art gallery, this comfortable English restaurant provides consistently good interesting food. Mrs Langham's chocolate pudding is not to be missed!*
Closed Sun & Public Hols
Lunch not served Sat
♥French 60 seats Last dinner
11.30pm ✦
Credit card ②

✕✕**Red Fort** 77 Dean St ☎01-
437 2525
*The exterior of this new Indian restaurant has the air of a pink palace. Inside, exquisite girls in red saris serve cocktails and such regional dishes as spiced and marinated quail baked in a charcoal fire.*
Closed 25–27 Dec
♥Indian V 160 seats S% ✳Lunch
£8–£15&alc Dinner £8–£15&alc Wine
£5.95 Last dinner 11.15pm ✦
nc 5yrs
Credit cards ①②③⑤

❋❋✕✕**Rue St Jacques**
5 Charlotte St ☎01-637 0222
*It seems to us that Gunther Schlender, the chef, cooks far better here than he ever did at Carriers. He seems to have found his feet and is producing deliciously different dishes that absolutely bewitch the palate. He produces a well-composed à la carte menu and a very good value fixed-price luncheon menu. The maitre d'hotel – Vincent Calcerono – has a well-trained brigade who are solicitous for your well-being, and the hierarchy know their food and wine. The wine list of some 170 items is very good and particularly strong on classic Bordeaux and Burgundy. Dishes that have particularly pleased our inspectors were the warm terrine of sole with smoked and fresh salmon in a butter sauce, better than most even at this level, also his lobster and sweetbreads, and melt-in-the-mouth puff pastry with a delicately-flavoured armagnac sauce. Main dishes were a more earthy roast duck with red cabbage, sauerkraut and apple, but pride of place must go to the saddle of hare, superbly flavoured with a mound of*

*pleurettes and morilles, and a game sauce made fruitily piquant with dried black-currants – 'perhaps the best sauce I have had this season' said one inspector. Vegetables are correctly cooked. A classic individual Charlotte Russe was near perfect, sorbets are refreshing and the soufflé of pear with bitter chocolate sauce was a great success. Finish with excellent coffee and petits fours. The restaurant – at ground floor and basement level – is well done so that you will enjoy the total experience.*
Closed Sun, Bank Hols & Xmas
Lunch not served Sat
♥French V 70 seats ✻Lunch £15&alc
Wine £9 Last dinner 11.15pm ⚑
Credit cards ① ② ③ ⑤

✕✕**Sawasde** 26–28 Whitfield St ☎01-6310289
Closed Xmas Day
Lunch not served Sat & Sun
♥Thai V 80 seats Last dinner 11.15pm
⚑✕
Credit cards ① ② ③ ⑤

✕✕**Yumi** 110 George St ☎01-9358320
*Chinese restaurant offering consistently good and well-presented food.*
Closed Sun, Bank Hols & 10 days Aug/Sep
Lunch not served Sat
♥Chinese 70 seats Last dinner 10pm
⚑
Credit cards ① ② ③ ⑤

✕**Alastair Little** 49 Frith St ☎01-7345183
*This little hotel is very popular with an avant garde clientele, providing a friendly and informal atmosphere, a daily menu of imaginative, eclectic dishes freshly-cooked from quality ingredients (notably fresh fish), and carefully chosen and prepared vegetables.*
Closed Sat, Sun, 2 wks Xmas, last 3 wks Aug & Bank Hols
♥French & Japanese 35 seats ✻Lunch £20alc Dinner £20alc Last dinner 11pm ⚑
Credit card ③

✕**Arirang** 31–32 Poland St ☎01-4376633
*There is an authentic atmosphere in this intimate little Korean restaurant, where the interesting menu of delicately-prepared meals is served by friendly, young, national waitresses.*
Closed Sun, Etr Mon & Xmas
♥Korean V 80 seats Last dinner 11pm
⚑
Credit cards ① ② ③ ⑤

✕**Aunties** 126 Cleveland St ☎01-3871548
*English restaurant specialising in home-made pies.*
Closed Sun, 25 & 26 Dec, 1 Jan & Public Hols Lunch not served Sat
30 seats S% Lunch £11–£15 Dinner £15 Wine £6 Last dinner 11pm ⚑
Credit cards ① ② ③ ⑤

✕**D'Artagnan** 19 Blandford St ☎01-9351023
*Small, intimate, friendly French restaurant.*
Closed Sun, Bank Hols
Lunch not served Sat
♥French 34 seats Last dinner 10pm ⚑
Credit cards ① ② ③ ④ ⑤

✕**Desaru** 60–62 Old Compton St ☎01-7344379
*Modern Indonesian restaurant in heart of Soho. Window between restaurant and kitchen shows chefs at work.*
♥Indonesian & Malaysian V 60 seats
✻Lunch £24 (2 persons) Dinner £24 (2 persons) Wine £5.50 Last dinner 11.45pm ⚑ nc 12yrs
Credit cards ① ② ③ ⑤

✕**Frith's** 14 Frith St ☎01-4393370
*Tasteful design in modern style has created a bright and fresh atmosphere in this black-and-white Soho restaurant, which features a table d'hôte lunchtime menu augmented by an à la carte selection in the evening. Wine by the glass is good, though the wine list itself is short, and service is friendly and polite.*
Closed Sun
Lunch not served Sat & Bank Hols
V 60 seats ✻Lunch £14–£16 Dinner £14–£16 Wine £6.50 Last dinner 11.30pm ⚑ Live music Wed, Fri & Sat
Credit cards ① ② ③ ⑤

✕**Fuji Japanese** 36–40 Brewer St ☎01-7340957
Closed 2 wks Xmas
Lunch not served Sat & Sun
♥Japanese 54 seats S% ✻Lunch £14alc
Dinner £25alc Wine £5.90 Last dinner 10.45pm ⚑
Credit cards ① ② ③ ⑤

✕**Gaylord** 79 Mortimer St ☎01-5803615
♥Indian V 75 seats ✻Lunch £7.45–£8.50&alc Dinner £7.45–£8.50&alc Last dinner 11.30pm 25P
Credit cards ① ② ③ ④ ⑤

✕**Ho Ho Chinese** 29 Maddox St ☎01-4931228
*A red-painted, canopied front opens into a restaurant whose simple, modern decor is brightened by old Chinese photographs and prints. The cuisine mainly Pekinese and Szechuan.*
Closed Sun
♥Chinese V 80 seats ✻Lunch fr £8.50&alc Dinner £11–£14&alc Wine £5.50 Last dinner 10.45pm ⚑ nc 6yrs
Credit cards ① ② ③ ⑤

✕**Kerzenstuberl** 9 St Christopher's Place ☎01-4863196
*Here you can relax in a typically Austrian atmosphere to enjoy authentic Austrian food and wine. Personal service is provided by the proprietors, and in the late evenings staff and guests sing along together to the strains of an accordion.*
Closed Sun, Xmas, all Bank Hols & 3

Aug–3 Sep Lunch not served Sat
♥Austrian V 50 seats Lunch £16alc
Dinner £18–£20alc Wine £6.90 Last dinner 11pm ⚑ Live music and dancing Mon–Sat
Credit cards ① ② ③ ⑤

✕**Lee Ho Fook** 15 Gerrard St ☎01-7349578
*Authentic Chinatown atmosphere in this intimate restaurant.*
♥Cantonese V 150 seats Last dinner 5am ⚑
Credit cards ① ② ③ ⑤

✕**Little Akropolis** 10 Charlotte St ☎01-6368198
*Small, intimate, candlelit, Greek restaurant.*
Closed Sun & Public Hols
Lunch not served Sat
♥Greek V 32 seats S% Lunch £9.50alc
Dinner £9.50alc Wine £6.50 Last dinner 10.30pm ⚑
Credit cards ① ② ③ ⑤

✕**Mayflower** 66–70 Shaftesbury Av ☎01-7349027
*Small ground-floor and basement restaurant with small alcoves and good food.*
♥Cantonese 125 seats Last dinner 4am ⚑
Credit cards ① ② ③ ⑤

✕**New World** 1 Gerrard Pl ☎01-7340677
*This large ground-floor and basement restaurant has the authentic Chinatown ambience and atmosphere. Many of the dishes offered are well-flavoured provincial specialities, and service is courteously friendly.*
Closed Xmas Day
♥Chinese V 530 seats S% ✻Lunch fr £4.35 Dinner fr £4.75 Wine £4.50 Last dinner 11.45pm ⚑
Credit cards ① ② ③ ④ ⑤

✕**Regent Tandoori** 10 Denman St ☎01-4341134
*Located in the heart of the West End, this Indian restaurant has been thoughtfully designed to achieve a colourful ambience and an atmosphere of warmth. It tends to offer dishes from all round India, and the competent cuisine is matched by good service.*
♥Tandoori V 44 seats Last dinner 11.30pm

✕**Relais des Amis** 17B Curzon St ☎01-4997595
*Brick walls, tinted mirrors and fresh plants create a cool atmosphere.*
♥International 100 seats Lunch £15alc Dinner £18alc Wine £5.95 Last dinner 11pm ⚑
Credit cards ① ② ③ ⑤

✕**Sav's** 53 Cleveland St ☎01-5807608
*This popular, family restaurant is unpretentious, the decor being plain though attractive. A range of Greek*

specialities is offered on the menu, which is accompanied by a wine list dominated by Greek and Cypriot wines.
Closed Sat, Sun, Xmas Day, Boxing Day & Bank Hols
♀English, Greek & Eastern Mediterranean 44 seats Lunch £2.35–£7.80&alc Dinner £2.35–£7.80&alc Wine £4.95 Last dinner 10.30pm *P*
Credit cards ①②③⑤

❋✕Yung's 23 Wardour St ☎01-4374986
(Rosette awarded for dinner only)
This unusual restaurant, simply-appointed and situated on three floors, is open from afternoon until the early hours of the morning. Its speciality is Cantonese cuisine of a high standard, and the menu includes some interesting dishes.
♀Chinese V 100 seats Last dinner 4.30am *P*
Credit cards ①②③⑤

W2 Bayswater, Paddington
★★★★L Royal Lancaster Lancaster Ter (Rank) ☎01-262 6737 Telex no 24822
A large, modern hotel providing friendly and efficient service, in an impressive situation overlooking Hyde Park, it continues to improve its facilities and offers restaurants in contrasting styles – the elegant, formal La Rosette and a Mediterranean café.
418 ⇄ 🏠 ♨ In 20 bedrooms CTV in all bedrooms T ✕ S%
*sB&B⇄ 🏠 £100.50–£120.50 dB&B⇄ 🏠 £123–£143 Continental breakfast 🍴
Lift ⅅ 100P (£7 per day) CFA xmas
♀International V ♥ ⊻ ✕Lunch fr £10.50&alc Tea fr £5.50 Dinner fr £15.95&alc Wine £9.50 Last dinner 10.45pm
Credit cards ①②③④⑤

★★★Central Park Queensborough Ter ☎01-229 2424 Telex no 27342
Busy, modern, commercial hotel with an à la carte restaurant.
273rm(142⇄131🏠)(15fb) CTV in all bedrooms T ✕ S% sB&B⇄🏠£45–£48 dB&B⇄🏠£60–£66 Continental breakfast 🍴
Lift ⅅ 10P 20▲ (£1.50 per night) gymnasium Cabaret 6 nights wkly xmas
♀Mainly grills ♥ ⊻ ✕Lunch £6–£8&alc Tea 75p–£1.25 Dinner £6–£8&alc Wine £5.50 Last dinner 10pm
Credit cards ①②③④⑤

★★★Hospitality Inn 104/105 Bayswater Rd (Mount Charlotte) ☎01-262 4461 Telex no 22667
This modern hotel provides smart, though small, public areas and well-equipped bedrooms; improvements and refurbishing continue. Breakfast and lunch are served buffet-style.
175 ⇄ (12fb) CTV in all bedrooms ® T sB&B⇄🏠£55 dB&B⇄🏠£73 🍴

Lift ⅅ 🎹 19P 55▲ CFA Live music Mon–Sat xmas
♀English & French ♥ ⊻ Lunch fr £6.75&alc Tea £1alc Dinner fr £8.50&alc Wine £5.75 Last dinner 10.30pm
Credit cards ①②③④⑤

★★★London Embassy 150 Bayswater Rd (Embassy) ☎01-229 2623 Telex no 27727
A busy commercial and tourist hotel with helpful staff, providing some lounge and room service.
193rm(184⇄8🏠) CTV in all bedrooms ® T S% sB&B⇄🏠£55–£66 dB&B⇄🏠£66–£77 Continental breakfast 🍴
Lift ⅅ 40▲ (£2 per 24 hrs) CFA
♀Continental V ♥ ⊻ S% ✕Lunch £8.95–£9.80&alc Tea 95p High Tea £2.50 Dinner £8.95–£9.80&alc Wine £5.20 Last dinner 10.15pm
Credit cards ①②③④⑤

★★★Park Court 75 Lancaster Gate (Mount Charlotte) ☎01-402 4272 Telex no 23922
The well-equipped bedrooms of this large, busy hotel include some executive rooms, and there is an informal, bistro-style restaurant.
412⇄🏠(3fb) CTV in all bedrooms ® T ✕ *sB&B⇄🏠 fr£49.75 dB&B⇄🏠 fr£65.50 🍴
Lift ⅅ *P* CFA ❄ xmas
♀English & French V ♥ ⊻ ✕Lunch £7.50&alc Tea £2 Dinner £8–£8.50&alc Wine £5.95 Last dinner 11pm
Credit cards ①②③④⑤

★★★White's Lancaster Gate (Mount Charlotte) ☎01-262 2711 Telex no 4771
Friendly hotel overlooking Hyde Park.
55 ⇄ 1🏠 CTV in all bedrooms T ✕ S% *sB⇄ fr£99.50 dB⇄fr£120(room only) 🍴
Lift ⅅ 🎹 15P 🚗 ❄ xmas
♀English & French V ♥ ⊻ 3% Lunch £25alc Tea £5.65alc Dinner £25alc Wine £6 Last dinner 10.30pm
Credit cards ①②③④⑤

★★★Bombay Palace 2 Hyde Park Sq ☎01-723 8855
In this comfortable, elegant restaurant, with its own bar, authentic and subtly-spiced Indian dishes are matched by impeccable service from friendly staff. At lunchtime, a popular self-service buffet has been introduced.
♀Indian 150 seats Last dinner 11.30pm *P*
Credit cards ①②③⑤

★★Bali 101 Edgware Rd ☎01-723 3303
Of the two restaurants here, the one on the ground floor is popular at lunchtime for cheaper, à la carte meals, whilst the smarter, more comfortable basement, which serves a set meal, thrives in the evening. Dishes from Indonesia, Malaysia

and Java, ranging from mild and fragrant to fiery hot, are featured.
♀Indonesian & Malaysian 80 seats Last dinner 11pm *P*
Credit cards ①②③④⑤

★★Trat-West 143 Edgware Rd ☎01-723 8203
Sound Italian food can be enjoyed at this bright, noisy restaurant with its bustling waiters.
Closed Etr Sun & Xmas
♀Italian 75 seats Last dinner 11.30pm *P*
Credit cards ①②③④⑤

★Ajimura Japanese 51–53 Shelton St ☎01-240 0178
Closed Bank Hols
Lunch not served Sat & Sun
♀Japanese V 50 seats S% ✕Lunch £5&alc Dinner £9–£19&alc Wine £4.80 Last dinner 11pm *P*
Credit cards ①②③⑤

★Al-Khayam Tandoori 27–29 Westbourne Gv ☎01-727 5154
This large, simply-furnished restaurant has subdued lighting and a good, bistro-style ambience. An interesting menu features curries. Tandoori dishes and house specialities, service by hustling waiters being prompt and friendly.
♀Indian V 70 seats ✕Lunch £10alc Dinner £15alc Wine £4 Last dinner 11.45pm *P* ✕
Credit cards ①②③⑤

✕Ganges 101 Praed St ☎01-723 4096
Modest restaurant serving Bengal and Indian cuisine.
Closed Xmas & Boxing Day
♀Bengali & Indian V 28 seats ✕Lunch £5.50–£6.95&alc Dinner £5.50–£6.95&alc Wine £5.75 Last dinner 11.30pm *P*
Credit cards ①②③④⑤

✕Green Jade 29–31 Portchester Rd ☎01-229 7221
Staff warm to serious eaters in this busy yet cosy restaurant. The range of dishes on offer includes delicious, whole, steamed fish and Peking duck.
Lunch not served Sun
♀Chinese 50 seats Last dinner 11.15pm
Credit cards ①②③⑤

✕Kalamara's 76–78 Inverness Mews ☎01-727 9122
There are two Kalamara's restaurants in Inverness Mews – a smaller, unlicensed one, and this, which provides an all-Greek wine list to complement the authentic Greek cuisine.
Closed Sun & Bank Hols
Lunch not served
♀Greek V 86 seats Last dinner mdnt Live music nightly
Credit cards ①②③⑤

✕Le Mange Tout 34 Sussex Pl ☎01-723 1199
An inexpensive menu is offered by this

small, cosy restaurant on the ground and
lower floors.
Closed Xmas Day & some Public Hols
Lunch not served Sat
♀French V 35 seats Lunch
£15–£20alc Dinner £15–£20alc Wine
£5.50 Last dinner 11.30pm ⌇
Credit cards ① ② ③ ⑤

✕Veronica's Chez Franco 3 Hereford Rd
☎01-229 5079
A pretty restaurant with friendly service
offering French and Italian dishes plus a
British speciality menu.
Closed Sun & Bank Hols
Lunch not served Sat
♀International V 40 seats Last dinner
mdnt
Credit cards ① ② ③ ⑤

**W5 Ealing**
See also **W13 Ealing (Northfields)**
★ ★ ★Carnarvon Ealing Common
(Consort) ☎01-992 5399 Telex no
935114
Modern purpose-built hotel, sited on the
North Circular.
145⇄ CTV in all bedrooms ® T ✕ S%
sB&B⇄£52.50 dB&B⇄£62.50
Continental breakfast ⋒
Lift 〕 150P CFA
♀European ✿ ♨ S% Lunch £13.50alc
Dinner £13.50alc Wine £6.75 Last
dinner 9.30pm
Credit cards ① ② ③ ⑤

**W6 Hammersmith**
★ ★ ★Novotel London 1 Shortlands
(Novotel) ☎01-741 1555 Telex no
934539
This modern hotel stands by the A4/44
which links Heathrow Airport with central
London. It offers spacious public areas, a
choice of two restaurants, bedrooms in the
process of upgrading and a typical English
pub. A large range of facilities for meetings
and exhibitions is available.
640⇄(640fb) ✕ in 20 bedrooms CTV
in all bedrooms T S% sB⇄frf60.50
dB⇄frf74 (room only) ⋒
Lift ⊞ 230▲ (charge) xmas
♀International ✿ ♨ ✕ S% Lunch
£7.25 Tea 70p High Tea £3.50 Dinner
£2.50–£13 Wine £6.75. Last dinner
mdnt
Credit cards ① ② ③ ④ ⑤

✕Anarkali 303 King St ☎01-
748 1760
Serves reasonably-priced authentic Indian
food.
♀Indian 82 seats Last dinner 11.30pm
Credit cards ① ② ③ ⑤

✕Aziz 116 King St ☎01-748 1826
A colour scheme of burgundy and
imitation stone, enhanced by subdued
lighting, creates a warm atmosphere for
the enjoyment of a well-balanced menu of
Tandoori dishes and traditional Indian
curries. Service, under the supervision of
the proprietor, is attentive.
Closed Sun & Xmas
♀Indian V 60 seats Last dinner

11.45pm ⌇
Credit cards ② ③ ⑤

✕Light of Nepal 268 King St ☎01-
748 3586
This friendly, strikingly-decorated
restaurant offers rather different Nepalese
and Indian dishes.
Closed Xmas Day & Boxing Day
♀Indian & Nepalese V 100 seats Lunch
£5–£8alc Dinner £6.50–£9alc Wine
£5 Last dinner 11.45pm ⌇
Credit cards ① ② ③ ④ ⑤

**W8 Kensington**
★ ★ ★ ★Royal Garden Kensington
High St (Rank) ☎01-937 8000 Telex
no 263151
Considerable extension, refurbishment and
upgrading have now taken place at this
Kensington hotel which offers friendly,
attentive service throughout and sound
food in the Royal roof restaurant, where
you can also dance to live music.
395⇄⋒(63fb) CTV in all bedrooms T
✕ (ex guide dogs) S%
✱sB⇄⋒£89–£110
dB⇄⋒£120–£150 (room only) ⋒
Lift 〕 CFA 160▲ (£6.50 per 24 hrs)
♨ Live music and dancing 6 nights
wkly
♀International V ✿ ♨ Lunch
£9.75–£17.50&alc Tea £3.50–£6.25
Dinner £22&alc Wine £9.80 Last
dinner 11.30pm
Credit cards ① ② ③ ④ ⑤

★ ★ ★Kensington Palace Thistle De
Vere Gardens (Thistle) ☎01-937 8121
Telex no 262422
Large, busy hotel with formal restaurant
and a coffee shop, complemented by well-
furnished bedrooms.
298⇄⋒(23fb) ✕ in 32 bedrooms
CTV in all bedrooms ® T ✕
✱sB⇄⋒£54–£85 dB⇄⋒£71–£95
(room only) ⋒
Lift 〕 CFA ⌇ ♨ xmas
♀International ✿ ♨ ✱Lunch fr
£14.75&alc Dinner fr £14.75&alc
Wine £7 Last dinner 10pm
Credit cards ① ② ③ ④ ⑤

★ ★ ★London Tara Scarsdale Pl, off
Wrights Ln (Best Western) ☎01-
937 7211 Telex no 918834
This lively, modern hotel provides
comfortable bedrooms, a formal restaurant
plus brasserie and lounge-service coffee
shop, and a night-spot.
831⇄ CTV in all bedrooms T ✕ (ex
guide dogs) sB&B⇄⋒£57.80–£69.80
dB&B⇄⋒£69.80–£79.80
Continental breakfast ⋒
Lift 〕 30P 70▲ (charge) CFA Disco
Mon–Sat ᕁ
♀French V ✿ ♨ Lunch fr £9&alc
Dinner fr £9&alc Wine £7.50 Last
dinner 11pm
Credit cards ① ② ③ ④ ⑤

★ ★ ★Kensington Close Wrights Ln
(Trusthouse Forte) ☎01-937 8170
Telex no 23914
Large, busy hotel with many modern
facilities.
537⇄ CTV in all bedrooms ® T
sB&B⇄£54.50 dB&B⇄£71.50 ⋒
Lift 〕 100▲ CFA ⌫ (heated) squash
sauna bath solarium gymnasium xmas
♀Mainly grills ✿ ♨ Last dinner 11pm
Credit cards ① ② ③ ④ ⑤

★ ★Hotel Lexham 32–38 Lexham
Gdns ☎01-373 6471
Closed 24 Dec–1 Jan
Quiet, traditional family-type hotel.
63rm(23⇄7⋒)(11fb) ✕ S%
✱sB&Bfr£20 sB&B⇄⋒frf24
dB&Bfr£29.50 dB&B⇄⋒frf36 ⋒
Unlicensed
Lift 〕 CTV ⌇ ⇼ ✿
♀English & Continental ✿ ♨ S%
✱Lunch fr £4&alc Tea fr 90p Dinner fr
£5.85 Last dinner 8pm
Credit cards ① ③

✕✕✕Belvedere Holland House,
Holland Park ☎01-602 1238
This elegantly-situated, aristocratic house
retains its formal English flower garden
and its peaceful, dignified atmosphere. The
chef has a particular flair with white fish,
and many daily specialities appear among
the reliable and enterprising dishes on the
menu. Service is efficient and very
attentive.
Closed Sat Lunch not served Sat
♀French 72 seats ✱Lunch
£20–£25alc Dinner £20–£25 Wine
£6.85 Last dinner 10.30pm 175P
Credit cards ① ② ③ ⑤

✕✕Le Crocodile 38C & D Kensington
Church St ☎01-938 2501
This contemporary, Anglo-French
restaurant is situated in an air-conditioned
and well-furnished basement. Nouvelle
cuisine specialities are enterprising and
beautifully presented, the chef having a
particular flair for classical desserts, and
the menu is sensibly priced at two levels.
Closed Sun Lunch not served Sat
♀French 75 seats ✱Lunch £10.75&alc
Dinner £16.75alc Last dinner 11pm ⌇
Credit cards ① ② ③ ⑤

✕✕Kensington Tandoori 1 Abingdon
Rd ☎01-937 6182
Small, engraved-glass screens afford
privacy to diners at this, one of the best of
London's Indian restaurants. Formal
service and a good wine list complement a
menu of North Indian and Persian dishes,
all making good use of fresh food.
♀Indian 80 seats Last dinner mdnt
Credit cards ① ② ③ ⑤

✿✕✕La Ruelle 14 Wrights Ln ☎01-
937 8525
Set close to Kensington High Street, this
elegant French restaurant features Cuisine
Gourmande. Luxurious decor helps to
create a romantic French atmosphere,
service is attentive, and the chef, Mr D

*Omzet, provides an interesting choice of menus.*
Closed Sat, Sun & Bank Hols
♥French V 70 seats Lunch £12.50–£21&alc Dinner £28alc Wine £10 Last dinner 11.30pm ⚓ nc 12yrs
Credit cards 1 2 3 4 5

✕✕**Sailing Junk** 59 Melrose Rd ☎01-937 2589
*A large mural dominates this basement Chinese restaurant.*
Closed Xmas Day, Boxing Day & Good Fri Lunch not served
♥Chinese 50 seats S% Dinner £13.50 Wine £6 Last dinner 11.15pm ⚓ nc 2yrs
Credit cards 1 2 3 5

✕**Ark** 35 Kensington High St ☎01-937 4294
*Bustling French restaurant serving reasonably-priced food.*
Closed 4 days Xmas & 4 days Etr
Lunch not served Sun
♥French V 95 seats S% Lunch £8–£10alc Dinner £8–£10alc Wine £4.45 Last dinner 11.30pm ⚓
Credit cards 1 3 5

✕**Il Barbino** 32 Kensington Church St ☎01-937 8752
*This tiny, crowded, Italian restaurant is not one for the claustrophobic! Meals are served on ground and first floor level, where an extensive à la carte menu is supplemented by a blackboard of daily specialities including several fresh fish dishes, many of which are temptingly displayed.*
Closed Sun Lunch not served Sat
♥Italian 45 seats S% Lunch £10alc Dinner £10alc Wine £4.90 Last dinner 11.45pm ⚓
Credit cards 1 2 3 4 5

✕**Maggie Jones** 6 Old Court Pl, Church St ☎01-937 6462
*Excellent English food is served at this busy, noisy restaurant, which is decorated on a farmhouse theme.*
Lunch not served Sun
50 seats Last dinner 11.30pm
Credit cards 1 2 3 4 5

✕**Michel** 343 Kensington High St ☎01-603 3613
♥French 40 seats Last dinner 10.45pm
Credit cards 1 2 3 4 5

✕**Siam** 12 St Alban's Grove ☎01-937 8765
*Small restaurant decorated in a traditional style, featuring traditional Thai dance shows nightly.*
Lunch not served Mon & Sat
♥Thai V 85 seats S% ✳Lunch £9alc Dinner £10.75&alc Wine £5.75 Last dinner 11.15pm ⚓ ✗ Cabaret nightly
Credit cards 1 2 3 4 5

**W9 Maida Vale**
✕**Didier** 5 Warwick Pl ☎01-286 7484
*This delightful, small restaurant is to be found in a quiet side street near to Little Venice. In unpretentious surroundings and a concerned atmosphere, you can choose your meal from a short English menu augmented with daily French specialities, everything being fresh and home-baked. Service, though simple in style, is sympathetic.*
Closed Sat & Sun
♥French 35 seats ✳Lunch £13alc Dinner £13alc Wine £5.50 Last dinner 10.30pm ⚓
Credit cards 1 2 3

**W11 Holland Park, Notting Hill**
★★★**Hilton International Kensington** Holland Park Av ☎01-603 3355 Telex no 919763
*Modern hotel with comfortable bedrooms and a Japanese restaurant*
606⇔ CTV in all bedrooms ® T
sB⇔£69–£90 dB⇔£90–£110(room only)
Lift D ⊞ CFA 100 ▲ (charge)
♥International V ♥ ♨ Lunch £9.50–£15.50&alc Tea fr £5.25 Dinner £9.50–£15.50&alc Wine £7.90 Open 24 hours
Credit cards 1 2 3 4 5

✕✕✕**Leith's** 92 Kensington Park Rd ☎01-229 4481
*Popular, well-established restaurant that continues to offer reliable and unusual food, particularly the varied starters. Good fixed-price menu.*
Closed Xmas Day & Boxing Day
Lunch not served
♥International V 100 seats S% Dinner £20.50–£29.50 Wine £8.50 Last dinner 11.30pm ⚓
Credit cards 1 2 3 5

✕✕**Chez Moi** 1 Addison Av ☎01-603 8267
*Tucked away off Holland Park Avenue, this well-established but unostentatious restaurant is patronised by the rich and famous. It offers a cosy, intimate atmosphere, quietly efficient service and a menu that is part traditional and part nouvelle in style.*
Closed Sun, 2 wks Aug, 2 wks Xmas & Bank Hols Lunch not served
♥French 45 seats Dinner fr £16.50&alc Wine £6 Last dinner 11.30pm ⚓ nc 10yrs
Credit cards 1 2 3 5

✕✕**La Pomme d'Amour** 128 Holland Park Av ☎01-229 8532
*Smart French restaurant with attractive patio. Specialising in classical and provincial dishes.*
Closed Sun Lunch not served Sat
♥French 70 seats S% ✳Lunch £9.75&alc Dinner £22alc Wine £5.90 Last dinner 10.45pm ⚓ nc 10yrs
Credit cards 1 2 3 5

✕**Cap's** 64 Pembridge Rd ☎01-229 5177 Telex no 298363
*Small basement restaurant with country style decor providing sensibly-priced French cuisine.*

Closed Sun & Bank Hols
Lunch not served
♥English & French V 60 seats Dinner £10alc Wine £4.85 Last dinner 11.30pm 2P nc 4yrs
Credit cards 1 2 3 4 5

✕**La Residence** 148 Holland Park Av ☎01-221 6090
*Small, pleasantly-decorated restaurant with warm ground-floor atmosphere and cool basement area. Friendly service.*
Closed Mon & Bank Hols
Lunch not served Sat
♥French 70 seats ✳Lunch £8.60–£13.40 Dinner £10.90–£13.40 Wine £5.40 Last dinner 10.30pm ⚓ nc 10yrs Live music Tue, Fri & Sun
Credit cards 1 2 3 5

✕**Restaurant 192** 192 Kensington Park Rd ☎01-229 0482
*The tiny restaurant-cum-wine-bar stands close to the Portobello Road on basement and ground levels. The decor may be simple but it contrasts with a bustling atmosphere as a short menu of interesting English dishes, simply made with quality goods, is served by the lively and cheerful staff.*
Dinner not served Sun
♥English & French 32 seats ✳Dinner £16alc Wine £5.50 Last dinner 11.30pm ⚓
Credit cards 1 2 3

**W12 Shepherds Bush**
✕**Shireen** 270 Uxbridge Rd ☎01-749 5927
*This restaurant offers a short menu of less usual Northern Indian and Tandoori dishes.*
Closed Xmas Day & Boxing Day
♥Indian V 40 seats Lunch £7–£12 Dinner £7–£12 Wine £4.70 Last dinner 11.30pm ⚓
Credit cards 1 2 3 5

**W13 Ealing (Northfields)**
✕**Maxims Chinese** 153–155 Northfield Av ☎01-567 1719
*The enormous Chinese restaurant features an extensive menu which specialises in Peking dishes and includes some interesting set meals for those confused by the breadth of choice. Young oriental staff willingly offer advice on dishes and provide cheerful service.*
Lunch not served Sun
♥Pekinese V 100 seats Last dinner 12.30am ⚓
Credit cards 1 2 3 5

**WC1 Bloomsbury, Holborn**
★★★★**Marlborough Crest** Bloomsbury St (Crest) ☎01-636 5601 Telex no 298274
169⇔(10fb) ✗ in 49 bedrooms CTV in all bedrooms ® T S%
sB&B⇔£85.25–£87.95
dB&B⇔£102.50–£107.90 ▤
Lift D ⚓ xmas
♥French V ♥ ♨ ✗ ✳Lunch £8.50–£10.50&alc Tea £3.25 Dinner £10.50&alc Wine £6.50 Last dinner

11.30pm
Credit cards ① ② ③ ④ ⑤

★ ★ ★ **Hotel Russell** Russell Sq
(Trusthouse Forte) ☎01-837 6470
Telex no 24615
*Large hotel facing Russell Square with
compact modern bedrooms.*
318⇄(1fb) CTV in all bedrooms T
sB&B⇄£63.50 dB&B⇄£85 🅿
Lift ♪ 🎯 CFA xmas
♥ 🍴 Last dinner 10.30pm
Credit cards ① ② ③ ④ ⑤

★ ★ **Bloomsbury Crest** Coram St
(Crest) ☎01-837 1200 Telex no 22113
Closed 23–26 Dec
*Modern hotel with carvery restaurant*
239⇄(1fb) ✗ in 45 bedrooms CTV in
all bedrooms ® T S% sB⇄fr£61.65
dB⇄fr£78.50 (room only) 🅿
Lift ♪ 🎯
V ♥ 🍴 ✗ S% Lunch fr £10.95 Tea fr
£1.25 High Tea fr £4 Dinner fr
£10.95&alc Last dinner 10.45pm
Credit cards ① ② ③ ④ ⑤

★ ★ **London Ryan** Gwynne Pl, Kings
Cross Rd (Mount Charlotte) ☎01-
278 2480 Telex no 27728
*Modern hotel with well-equipped
bedrooms.*
211⇄🈁(19fb) CTV in all bedrooms ®
T ✱sB&B⇄🈁fr£47.25
dB&B⇄🈁fr£57.75 Continental
breakfast 🅿
Lift ♪ 30P 10🅰
♥English & French V ♥ 🍴 ✱Bar Lunch
£4–£7 Tea £1.50 Dinner £8.50&alc
Wine £5.50 Last dinner 9.45pm
Credit cards ① ② ③ ⑤

✗✗**Mr Kai of Russell Square**
50 Woburn Pl ☎01-580 1186
*A modern, well-run restaurant with
friendly and attractive Mandarin
waitresses.*
Closed Xmas Day, Boxing Day, New
Year's Day & Bank Hols
♥Pekinese V 120 seats Lunch
£8–£15&alc Dinner £20alc Wine
£6.50 Last dinner 11.30pm 🎯
Credit cards ① ② ③ ⑤

✗✗**Winstons Eating House** 24 Coptic
St ☎01-580 3422
*The name of the restaurant relates to the
Winston Churchill theme which runs
through it. Tasteful decor and English
cuisine attract a busy lunchtime trade.*
Closed Xmas, New Year & Bank Hols
Lunch not served Sat
Dinner not served Sun
44 seats Last dinner 11.15pm 🎯 Live
music Mon–Sat
Credit cards ① ② ③ ⑤

✗**Les Halles** 57 Theobalds Rd ☎01-
242 6761
*A simple French brasserie with interesting
food and wine.*
Closed Sun & Bank Hols
Lunch not served Sat
♥French V 100 seats S% Lunch

£15–£20alc Dinner £20–£25alc Wine
£6 Last dinner 11.30pm 🎯
Credit cards ① ② ③ ⑤

**WC2 Covent Garden**
*Leicester Square, Strand and Kingsway*
●**Five Red Stars Savoy**
Strand ☎01-836 4343 Telex no 24234
*(Rosette awarded for Savoy Restaurant)*
*For over a hundred years the Savoy has
delighted its discerning clientele with high
standards of food and service. There is the
marble floored lobby to set the tone,
leading to the comfortable and quiet
reading room, and on to the lofty and
superb Thames Foyer with its central
gazebo where there is live piano music.
This is a popular rendezvous for
refreshment and excellent afternoon teas.
Beyond that is the famous, elegantly-
appointed River Room, where Anton
Edelman, the maitre chef, provides fine
food. There are fixed-price menus at
luncheon and dinner as well as the à la
carte menu. There is dancing at night. The
style is basically classical with modern
lighter influences but the cooking of the
best possible ingredients is delicious. This
is the room to which we award the rosette,
but the light-panelled Grill Room also
provides enjoyable food from the à la carte
menu. As you would expect, the service is
courteously dignified and attentive; indeed,
so it is throughout the hotel, with good
valet and room service. There is also the
busy American Bar. The sumptuous suites
have atmospheric views of the river, and
the individually decorated bedrooms are of
a standard that you would expect: huge
bath sheets and real linen bed sheets – like
all the Savoy Group hotels – and special
bathrooms. The rooms are well-equipped
and include in-house movies and video
channels. Under Willie Bauer, general
manager, this grand hotel maintains the
tradition of international hotellerie that so
delights the contemporary discerning
guest.*
200⇄🈁 CTV in all bedrooms T ✘
✱sB⇄🈁£120 dB⇄🈁£145–£195
(room only) 🅿
Lift ♪ CFA 75🅰 (£8.50 per day) 🛗
Live music and dancing nightly xmas
♥English & French V ♥ 🍴 S%✱Lunch
£16.50&alc Tea £7.50 Dinner
£21–£25&alc Wine £6.50 Last dinner
10.30pm
Credit cards ① ② ③ ⑤

★ ★ ★ **Waldorf** Aldwych (Trusthouse
Forte) ☎01-836 2400 Telex no 24574
*Gracious, elegant hotel with a good range
of accommodation.*
312⇄(13fb) CTV in all bedrooms T
sB&B⇄£80.50 dB&B⇄£104.50 🅿
Lift ♪ 🎯 CFA xmas
♥ 🍴 Last dinner 10pm
Credit cards ① ② ③ ④ ⑤

★ ★ ★ **Drury Lane Moat House** 10
Drury Ln (Queens Moat) ☎01-
836 6666 Telex no 8811395
*Hotel with comfortable bedrooms and
Maudies Restaurant.*

129⇄🈁 CTV in all bedrooms T S%
sB⇄🈁fr£70 dB⇄🈁fr£92(room
only) 🅿
Lift ♪ 🈺 11P (£5 per day) 🛗
♥French ♥ 🍴 S% Lunch
£10–£11&alc Dinner £16.50alc Wine
£6.75 Last dinner 10pm
Credit cards ① ② ③ ④ ⑤

★ ★ **Royal Trafalgar Thistle**
Whitcomb St (Thistle) ☎01-930 4477
Telex no 298564
*Modern but cosy, this comfortable hotel
stands just off Trafalgar Square, offering
compact but well-equipped bedrooms and
friendly, helpful service. The new brasserie
offers a French-style menu and mulled
wine.*
108⇄🈁 ✗ in 36 bedrooms CTV in all
bedrooms ® T ✱sB⇄🈁£60–£85
dB⇄🈁£75–£95 (room only) 🅿
Lift ♪ 🎯 🛗
♥International ♥ 🍴✱Lunch fr
£10.50alc Dinner fr £10.50alc Wine
£7 Last dinner 11pm
Credit cards ① ② ③ ④ ⑤

★ ★ ★ **Strand Palace** Strand
(Trusthouse Forte) ☎01-836 8080
Telex no 24208
*Modernised, compact Regency-styled
hotel.*
775⇄ CTV in all bedrooms ® T
sB&B⇄£59.50 dB&B⇄£77.50 🅿
Lift ♪ 🎯 xmas
♥ Last dinner 11.30pm
Credit cards ① ② ③ ④ ⑤

✗✗✗✗✗**Savoy Hotel Grill**
Embankment Gdns, Strand ☎01-
836 4343 Telex no 24234
*Here, creative dishes, based on ingredients
of the highest quality and accompanied by
well-made sauces and seasonally-selected
vegetables, are complemented by
impeccable service from an international
team.*
Closed Sun & Aug Lunch not served Sat
♥English & French V 85 seats S%
Lunch £22.50alc Dinner
£15–£25&alc Wine £8.50 Last dinner
11.30pm 🎯 nc 10yrs Live music
nightly
Credit cards ① ② ③ ④ ⑤

●●✗✗✗✗**Inigo Jones**
14 Garrick St ☎01-836 6456
*This Victorian building was once a stained-
glass workshop in which William Morris
taught. Perhaps it is not stretching the
imagination too much to draw a parallel
between the style of Morris and Paul
Gayler, the talented chef here. Both reacted
against the tired old classic traditions and
tried to break new ground with original
ideas. Certainly Paul Gayler's cooking is
individual, adventurous, often with a
daring combination of ingredients that
nearly always comes off, and is always
attractively presented without looking too
contrived. Despite the flair and skill
evidenced here, one main course of duck
breast disappointed; it was hard and of
little flavour with a passion fruit sauce*

that tasted of overcooked caramel rather than anything else. But first courses of *meuage du mareyeur*, a mixture of various fish, including salmon and mussels in white wine and cream sauce, richly laced with mussel liquor was superb, as was the *farandel* of scallops wrapped in spinach, steamed, and served with strips of beetroot with a delicate Sauternes butter sauce. Delicious main courses tested were fillet of venison topped with a parsley mousse, wrapped in pastry and served with a sapid game sauce; and a tender, succulent fillet of flavoursome beef, enhanced with garlic and accompanied by a zesty shallot sauce. Vegetables are cooked 'al dente', and the puddings were highly-praised: bourbon ice cream with cinnamon flavoured sabayoun, bavarois of lime and lemon with a tangy raspberry cullis and ginger sauce, as well as bavarois of bitter white chocolate with orange segments and armagnac sauce. Good coffee can complete your meal. The long wine list is strong on classics and there is a better than usual list of half bottles. The restaurant is stylish and so is the service, which is reserved but cheerful and friendly. The staff are anxious for you to enjoy yourself and they seem to anticipate your needs. Apart from the à la carte menu, there are fixed-price luncheons and pre-theatre menus which are very good value indeed.
Closed Sun & Bank Hols
Lunch not served Sat
♥French V 75 seats S% *Lunch
£16.95&alc Dinner £16.95&alc Wine
£10.55 Last dinner 11.30pm ⚑
Credit cards ① ② ③ ⑤

✱✕✕✕**Boulestin** 1A Henrietta St, Covent Garden ☎01-836 3819
Gracious and elegant, the Edwardian-style restaurant exudes comfort and affluence. Smartly dressed French staff provide professional and attentive service, whilst the menu offers a balanced and interesting selection of imaginative and attractively presented classical dishes, well-geared to the seasonal availability of food. The extensive wine list is designed to appeal to a discerning clientèle.
Closed Sun, 1 wk Xmas, Bank Hols & last 3 wks Aug Lunch not served Sat
♥French V 70 seats *Lunch
£16.75&alc Dinner £45alc Wine £10
Last dinner 11.15pm ⚑ no babies
Credit cards ① ② ③ ④ ⑤

✕✕✕**P S Hispaniola** Victoria Embankment, River Thames ☎01-839 3011
This restaurant is located on board a paddle steamer.
Closed 1 wk after Xmas
Lunch not served Sat
♥French V 130 seats Lunch £11.50
Dinner £16.50–£18.50 Wine £7.50
Last dinner 11pm ⚑ Live music nightly
Credit cards ① ③ ④ ⑤

✕✕✕**Neal Street** 26 Neal St ☎01-836 8368
Modern restaurant with tasteful basement cocktail bar, serving very original cuisine.

Closed Sat & Sun, 1 wk Xmas & Bank Hols
♥International V 65 seats S% Lunch £27alc Dinner £27alc Wine £7.50 Last dinner 11pm ⚑
Credit cards ① ② ③ ⑤

✕✕✕**L'Opera** 32 Great Queen St ☎01-405 9020
Splendid, plush Edwardian restaurant in gilt and green occupying two floors in the centre of theatreland.
Closed Sun Lunch not served Sat
♥French V 100 seats Lunch
£11.50–£17&alc Dinner
£11.50–£17&alc Wine £5.95 Last dinner mdnt ⚑
Credit cards ① ② ③ ⑤

✕✕✕**Rules** 35 Maiden Ln, Strand ☎01-836 2559
Well-established traditional restaurant with professional, efficient service.
Closed Sun, 24 Dec–2 Jan & Bank Hols
130 seats *Lunch £11&alc Dinner
£11&alc Wine £5.85 Last dinner mdnt
⚑ nc 6yrs
Credit cards ① ② ③ ⑤

✕✕**Chez Solange** 35 Cranbourne St ☎01-836 0542
Good-quality home cuisine in this elegant West End restaurant.
Closed Sun
♥French V 80 seats Lunch £12&alc Dinner £12&alc Wine £7.25 Last dinner 12.15am ⚑ Live music nightly
Credit cards ① ② ③ ④ ⑤

✕✕**Interlude de Tabaillau** 7–8 Bow St ☎01-379 6473
Informal atmosphere, honest French cooking and good value for money.
Closed Sun, Bank Hols, 2 wks Xmas, 10 days Etr, last 2 wks Aug & 1st wk Sep
Lunch not served Sat
♥French 48 seats Last dinner 11.30pm
Credit cards ① ② ③ ⑤

✱✕✕**Poons of Covent Garden** 41 King St ☎01-240 1743
Popular Chinese restaurant with extensive menu and rapid service.
Closed Sun & 24–27 Dec
♥Cantonese V 120 seats Last dinner 11.30pm ⚑

✕✕**Thomas de Quincey's** 36 Tavistock St ☎01-240 3972
Attractive hospitable restaurant serving original, unusual dishes.
Closed Sun, Bank Hols & 3 wks Aug
Lunch not served Sat
♥French 50 seats Lunch £25–£30alc Dinner £25–£30alc Wine £7 Last dinner 11.15pm ⚑
Credit cards ① ② ③ ④ ⑤

✱✕✕**Tourment d'Amour** 19 New Row ☎01-240 5348
Located in Covent Garden, at the heart of theatreland, this small, intimate French restaurant offers a fixed-price menu for

two and three course meals, and helpful staff are delighted to describe any of the dishes to customers.
Closed Sun
Lunch not served Sat
♥French V 43 seats S% *Lunch
£20.25 Dinner £20.25 Wine £9 Last dinner 11.30pm ⚑ nc 10yrs
Credit cards ① ② ③ ⑤

✕**Bates English** 11 Henrietta St ☎01-240 7600 Telex no 922488
This slick, 30s-style restaurant serves an inexpensive British menu to the accompaniment of live music, the quality of its cooking making it deservedly popular.
♥English & Continental 65 seats Last dinner 11.30pm ⚑
Credit cards ① ② ③ ⑤

✕**Le Café des Amis du Vin** 11–14 Hanover Pl ☎01-379 3444
Traditional French street cafe with imaginative menu.
Closed Sun & Xmas
♥French 120 seats Last dinner 11.30pm ⚑
Credit cards ① ② ③ ④ ⑤

✕**Le Café du Jardin** 28 Wellington St ☎01-836 8769
This lively French brasserie offers a limited selection of wholesome dishes, and food is served by aproned French waiters against the background of a suitably Gallic decor.
Closed Sun & Xmas
Lunch not served Sat
♥French 116 seats Last dinner 11.30pm ⚑
Credit cards ① ② ③ ④ ⑤

✕**Café Pelican** 45 St Martins Ln ☎01-379 0309
A large and lively French cafe, the Pelican offers wholesome, provincial-style French dishes in an authentic atmosphere.
♥French V 200 seats *Lunch
£12.95&alc Dinner £12.95&alc Wine £5.50 Last dinner 12.30am ⚑ Live music nightly
Credit cards ① ② ③ ⑤

✕**La Corée Korean** 56 St Giles High St ☎01-836 7235
This small and friendly restaurant offers an interesting gastronomic experience as competent and pleasant staff serve authentic Korean dishes.
Closed Sun, Bank Hols, 3 days Xmas & 2 days New Year
♥Korean V 60 seats Last dinner 11pm ⚑
Credit cards ① ② ③

✕**Happy Wok** 52 Floral St ☎01-836 3696
This cosy, well-run Chinese restaurant stands at the heart of theatreland, offering a good range of well-prepared and authentic dishes served by charming staff.
Closed Sun, Xmas Day & Boxing Day
♥Chinese & Pekinese V 42 seats Lunch £12.50–£19 Dinner £12.50–£19
Wine £5 Last dinner 11.30pm ⚑
Credit cards ① ② ③ ⑤

✕**Last Days of the Raj** 22 Drury Ln
☎01-836 1628
*Bright, popular co-operative featuring
authentic, honest and skilful Indian
cuisine.*
♡Indian V 44 seats S% Last dinner
11.30pm ✔ ✗
Credit cards ① ② ③ ④ ⑤

✕**Il Passetto** 230 Shaftesbury Av ☎01-
836 9391
*Modern Italian restaurant with good
home-made food.*
Closed Sun
♡Italian 42 seats Lunch £19alc
Dinner £20alc Wine £4.75 Last dinner
11.30pm ✔
Credit cards ① ② ③ ⑤

✕**Plummers** 33 King St ☎01-
240 2534
*Busy and lively, this simply-appointed
restaurant offers good value for money in
its selection of American and English food.*
Closed Sun Lunch not served Sat
75 seats ✱Lunch £4–£14alc Dinner
£4–£14alc Wine £4.95 Last dinner
11.30pm ✔
Credit cards ① ② ③ ⑤

●✕**Poon's** 4 Leicester St ☎01-
437 1528
*This restaurant is very popular,
particularly with the Chinese, and its
extensive menu includes a selection of
dishes using wind-dried ingredients.
Service is somewhat rushed, but food is
consistently good, well-prepared and
authentic, and glass panels between dining
rooms and kitchen enable you to see it in
course of preparation.*
Closed Sun & Xmas
♡Cantonese V 100 seats S% ✱Lunch
£6–£20&alc Dinner £6–£20&alc Wine
£4.20 Last dinner 11.30pm ✔

✕**La Provence** 8 Mays Court ☎01-
836 9180
*Small, intimate, informal Italian
restaurant.*
♡French V 50 seats Last dinner 11pm
Credit cards ① ② ③ ⑤

✕**Sheekey's** 29–31 St Martin's Court
☎01-240 2565
*One of the oldest fish restaurants in
London, specialising in oysters.*
Closed Sun Lunch not served Sat
50 seats Last dinner 11.15pm ✔
Credit cards ① ② ③ ⑤

✕**Taste of India** 25 Catherine St ☎01-
836 6591
*This small, elegant Indian restaurant
features some very interesting specialities
and authentic dishes, skilfully prepared
with pungently-spiced sauces and formally
served.*
♡Indian V 140 seats S% Lunch
£10–£12&alc Wine £5.50 Last dinner
mdnt ✔
Credit cards ① ② ③ ④ ⑤

# *GUESTHOUSES*

Places within the London postal area
are listed below in postal district order
commencing East then North, South
and West, with a brief indication of the
area covered.

**E18** (South Woodford)
**Grove Hill Hotel** 38 Grove Hill, South
Woodford ☎01-989 3344
*Comfortably-appointed small hotel offering
good standard of service.*
21hc(5⇌)(2fb) CTV in all bedrooms ⑧
✱B&b£16.10–£21.85
W£112.70–£152.95 M
Lic ⑩ CTV 8P 4🅐 (charge)
Credit cards ① ② ③

**N8** Hornsey
**Aber Hotel** 89 Crouch Hill ☎01-
340 2847
*Converted private house offering simple
accommodation and informal atmosphere.*
8hc(4fb) ✕
⑩ CTV ✔

**NW2** Cricklewood
**Clearview House** 161 Fordwych Rd,
Cricklewood ☎01-452 9773
6hc(1fb) TV in 4 bedrooms ✕ ✱B&b£9
W£59.50 M
⑩ CTV nc 5yrs

**Garth Hotel** 70–76 Hendon Way,
Cricklewood ☎01-455 4742
*Well-appointed hotel with well-furnished
bedrooms.*
54hc(20⇌19⋔)(10fb) CTV in all
bedrooms ⑩ LDO9pm
Lic ⑩ CTV 36P
Credit cards ① ② ③ ④ ⑤

**NW3** Hampstead and Swiss Cottage
**Frognal Lodge Hotel** 14 Frognal Gdns,
off Church Row, Hampstead ☎01-
435 8238 Telex no 8812714
*Comfortable informal hotel.*
17hc(7⇌) CTV in 10 bedrooms
✱B&b£15–£24
Lic Lift ⑩ CTV ✔ 🅐
Credit cards ① ② ③ ⑤

**NW4** Hendon
**Peacehaven Hotel** 94 Audley Rd,
Hendon ☎01-202 9758
*Modern, bright bedrooms, all with colour
TV. Bathroom facilities well above
average.*
12hc(1⇌)(2fb) CTV in all bedrooms ✕
B&bfr£17
⑩ CTV 2P
Credit cards ① ③

**NW11** Golders Green
**Central Hotel** 35 Hoop Ln, Golders
Green ☎01-458 5636 Telex no
922488
*Two modern buildings with well-equipped
bedrooms.*
18⇌ Annexe: 18hc(3fb) CTV in 18

bedrooms ✕ ✱B&b£25–£35
⑩ CTV 10P
Credit cards ① ② ③ ⑤

**Croft Court Hotel** 44–46 Ravenscourt
Av, Golders Green ☎01-458 3331
Telex no 8950511
*Modest but comfortable accommodation.*
15hc(7⇌)(7fb) TV in all bedrooms
LDO6pm
⑩ CTV 4P

**SE3** Blackheath
**Bardon Lodge Hotel** 15 Stratheden Rd,
Blackheath ☎01-853 4051
*Warm, friendly private hotel, tastefully
decorated and offering good standard of
accommodation.*
42hc(26⋔)(5fb) CTV in all bedrooms
✕ ⑧ ✱B&b£25–£44 LDO8.30pm
Lic ⑩ CTV 16P
Credit cards ① ③

**Stonehall House** 35–37 Westcombe
Park Rd, Blackheath ☎01-858 8706
*Old-fashioned and comfortable guesthouse
with pleasant TV lounge and garden.*
23hc(1⋔)(9fb) CTV in all bedrooms
B&b£14–£18 W£84–£108 M
⑩ CTV ✔

**SE9** Eltham
**Yardley Court Private Hotel** 18 Court
Rd, Eltham ☎01-850 1850
Closed Xmas wk
*Small private hotel with very comfortable
and generous accommodation. Extensive
service is available, complementing
friendly intimate atmosphere.*
8hc(1⇌4⋔)(2fb) CTV in all bedrooms
✕ B&b£20–£26 Bdi£24–£30 (inc High
Tea) LDO9pm
⑩ CTV 8P nc 3yrs

**SE19** Norwood
**Crystal Palace Tower Hotel**
114 Church Rd ☎01-653 0176
*Large Victorian house with large,
comfortable bedrooms.*
11hc(2⋔)(5fb) TV in all bedrooms
✱B&b£10.50–£12
⑩ CTV 10P

**SE23** Forest Hill
**Rutz** 16 Vancouver Rd, Forest Hill
☎01-699 3071
Closed Xmas–New Year
6hc(1⇌2⋔)(1fb) CTV in 2 bedrooms
✕ ⑧ B&b£13–£16 Bdi£19–£22
W£129.50–£140 🅛 LDO2pm
⑩ CTV ✔

**SW1** West End–Westminster, St
James's Park, Victoria Station
**Arden House** 12 St Georges Dr ☎01-
834 2988 Telex no 22650
*Simply furnished hotel with easy access to
Victoria Station.*
35hc(10⇌4⋔)(10fb) CTV in all

bedrooms ✠ B&b£12.50–£20
W£75–£95 **M**
**¶** CTV **P**

**Chesham House** 64–66 Ebury St,
Belgravia ☎01-730 8513 Telex no
912881 (ESP)
23hc(3fb) CTV in all bedrooms ✠
*B&b£16–£20
**¶ P** nc 5yrs
Credit cards ② ③ ⑤

**Elizabeth Hotel** 37 Eccleston Sq,
Victoria ☎01-828 6812
*Simply furnished hotel situated near
Victoria Station.*
24hc(1⇄2🅼)(6fb) CTV in
4 bedrooms ✠ *B&b£12.50–£25
W£78.75–£175 **M**
**¶** CTV ✦ (hard)

**GH Hanover Hotel** 30 St George Dr
☎01-834 0134
*An early 19th-century terrace house with
comfortable accommodation.*
34hc(8⇄18🅼)(4fb) CTV in all
bedrooms B&b£19–£25 (W only
Nov–Feb)
**¶** CTV **P**
Credit cards ① ② ③

**Willett Hotel** 32 Sloane Gdns, Sloane Sq
☎01-824 8415
*Terraced house with spacious comfortably-
furnished bedrooms.*
17hc(14⇄)(10fb) CTV in all bedrooms
🅡 *B&b£19.55–£26.45
**¶ P**

**Windermere Hotel** 142 Warwick Way,
Victoria ☎01-834 5163
*Well-maintained, small guesthouse, with
comfortable bedrooms.*
8hc(4🅼)(5fb) CTV in all bedrooms ✠
*B&b£20–£30
**¶ P**

**SW3 Chelsea**
**Eden House Hotel** 111 Old Church St
☎01-352 3403
*Homely Edwardian house with a
comprehensive room service but lacking
any public rooms.*
14hc(4⇄5🅼)(3fb) CTV in all
bedrooms *B&b£16–£25
W£112–£175 **M**
**¶** CTV **P**
Credit cards ① ② ③ ④ ⑤

**Garden House Hotel** 44–46 Egerton
Gdns ☎01-584 2990
Closed Xmas
*Friendly establishment with spacious,
cheerful bedrooms.*
30hc(7⇄7🅼)(4fb) CTV in 14
bedrooms *B&b£10–£34
Lift **¶** P

**Knightsbridge Hotel** 10 Beaufort Gdns
☎01-589 9271
*Comfortable, well-equipped bedrooms,
limited lounge accommodation and small
basement dining room. Ideally located
close to Harrods.*
20rm 7hc(4⇄5🅼)(2fb) CTV in 4
bedrooms ✠ B&b£25.75–£35.75

W£148.05–£204.75 **M** (W only Dec,
Jan & Feb) LDO10.30pm
Lic **¶** CTV **P**
Credit cards ② ③

**SW7 South Kensington**
**Number Eight Hotel** 8 Emperors Gate,
South Kensington ☎01-370 7516
*Small, friendly hotel where bedrooms are
attractively decorated and have many
modern facilities.*
14hc(10⇄2🅼)(2fb) CTV in all
bedrooms ✠ 🅡 *B&b£25–£37.95
**¶ P**
Credit cards ① ② ③ ⑤

**SW19 Wimbledon**
**GH Trochee Hotel** 21 Malcolm Rd,
Wimbledon ☎01-946 1579 & 3924
17hc(2fb) CTV in all bedrooms
*B&bfr£19
**¶** CTV 3P

**Wimbledon Hotel** 78 Worple Rd,
Wimbledon ☎01-946 9265
*This hotel has modernised compact
bedrooms, with limited comfortable lounge
facilities and easy car parking.*
14hc(4⇄4🅼)(4fb) CTV in 2 bedrooms
✠ 🅡 *B&b£21.95–£24.95
**¶** CTV 10P
Credit cards ① ③

**Worcester House** 38 Alwyne Rd ☎01-
946 1300
*This hotel has compact, well-fitted
bedrooms, limited dining facilities and*

breakfast room service.
9 ⋒ (1fb) CTV in all bedrooms ✖ ®
*B&bf21.85–£33.35 LDO11am
⋒ ₣
Credit cards ① ② ③ ⑤

**W1 West End, Piccadilly Circus, St Marylebone and Mayfair**
**Hotel Concorde** 50 Great Cumberland Pl
☎01-402 6169
Tastefully decorated and comfortable accommodation with good lounge. Well situated in the centre of London.
28hc(5⇌23⋒) CTV in all bedrooms ✖
LDO10.30pm
Lic Lift ⋒ CTV ₣
Credit cards ① ② ③ ④ ⑤

**Georgian House Hotel** 87 Gloucester Pl,
Baker St ☎01-935 2211
A terraced house in a busy road just off Marble Arch.
19hc(14⇌5⋒)(3fb) CTV in all bedrooms ✖ B&bf18–£21
W£70–£120 M (W only Nov–Feb)
Lic Lift ⋒ CTV ₣ nc 5yrs
Credit card ③

**Hart House Hotel** 51 Gloucester Pl,
Portman Sq ☎01-935 2288
Imposing, five-storey terrace house with well-appointed bedrooms.
15hc(7⇌5⋒)(4fb) CTV in all bedrooms ✖
® *B&bf15–£25
⋒ CTV
Credit cards ① ② ③

**Montagu House** 3 Montagu Pl ☎01-935 4632
18hc(1⋒)(3fb) CTV in all bedrooms ✖
®
⋒ CTV nc 2yrs

**W2 Bayswater, Paddington**
**Ashley Hotel** 15 Norfolk Sq, Hyde Park
☎01-723 3375
Closed 1 wk Xmas
Situated in a quiet square close to Paddington Station.
16hc(4⋒)(1fb) CTV in all bedrooms ✖
B&bf12
⋒ CTV ₣

**Camelot Hotel** 45 Norfolk Sq ☎01-723 9118
Friendly hotel providing modern facilities

in a range of accommodation.
34hc(13⇌1⋒)(10fb) CTV in all bedrooms ✖ ® *B&bf23
⋒ CTV ₣
Credit cards ① ③

**Dylan Hotel** 14 Devonshire Ter,
Lancaster Gate ☎01-723 3280
Traditional style guesthouse, homely and comfortable.
18hc(2⇌6⋒)(3fb) ✖ ®
*B&bf15–£28 (W only Nov–Feb)
⋒ CTV ₣
Credit cards ② ③ ⑤

**Garden Court Hotel** 30–31 Kensington Gardens Sq ☎01-727 8304
Friendly, family-run, quietly situated hotel.
37hc(8⇌4⋒)(6fb) *B&bf17–£21
Lic ⋒ CTV ₣

**Nayland Hotel** 134 Sussex Gdns ☎01-723 3380
Small, friendly hotel with modern facilities in bedrooms, including videos.
14hc(2fb) CTV in all bedrooms ✖ ®
⋒ CTV 2P
Credit cards ① ② ③ ⑥

**Pembridge Court Hotel** 34 Pembridge Gdns ☎01-229 9977 Telex no 298363
Closed Xmas
Very comfortable bedrooms with modern facilities. Separate restaurant 'Caps'.
29hc(21⇌8⋒)(4fb) CTV in all bedrooms *B&bf25–£40
LDO11.30pm
Lic ⋒ 2▲ (charge)
Credit cards ① ② ③ ⑤

**Slavia Hotel** 2 Pembridge Sq ☎01-727 1316
Hotel offering reasonably-priced simple accommodation.
31⋒(8fb) *B&bf10–£20
LDO10.30pm
Lic Lift ⋒ CTV 2P (charge)
Credit cards ① ② ③ ⑤

**GH Tria Hotel** 35/37 St Stephens Gdns ☎01-221 0450
Imposing five-storey terraced house.
41hc(37⇌4⋒)(6fb) CTV in all bedrooms ✖
Lic lift ⋒ CTV
Credit cards ① ② ③ ⑤

**W4 Chiswick**
**Chiswick Hotel** 73 Chiswick High Rd
☎01-994 1712
Attractive bedrooms and comfortable lounge. The basement houses a sauna and jacuzzi.
30hc(5⇌10⋒)(7fb) CTV in all bedrooms *B&bf19.25–£29.50
Bdif26.75–£34.25
W£168.53–£215.78 ⚡ LDO8.30pm
Lic ⋒ CTV 15P sauna bath solarium
Credit cards ① ② ③ ⑤

**W8 Kensington**
**Apollo Hotel** 18–22 Lexham Gdns,
Kensington ☎01-373 3236 Telex no 264189
Sister to Atlas Hotel, this has many modern facilities and modest prices.
59hc(40⇌10⋒)
*B&bf14.50–£19.50
Bdif20.50–£25.50 LDO7.30pm
Lic Lift ⋒ CTV ₣
Credit cards ① ② ③ ④ ⑤

**Atlas Hotel** 24–30 Lexham Gdns,
Kensington ☎01-373 7873 Telex no 264189
Modestly-priced accommodation with many modern facilities.
70hc(19⇌30⋒)(1fb)
B&bf14.50–£19.50
Bdif20.50–£25.50 LDO7.30pm
Lic Lift ⋒ CTV ₣
Credit cards ① ② ③ ④ ⑤

**W14 West Kensington**
**Avonmore Hotel** 66 Avonmore Rd
☎01-603 4296 Telex no 945922
(Gladdex G)
Very comfortable accommodation offered by friendly proprietors.
9hc(2fb) CTV in all bedrooms
*B&bf17.50–£23 W£80–£150 M (W only Sep–Dec)
Lic ⋒ CTV ₣

**WC1 Bloomsbury, Holborn**
**Mentone Hotel** 54–55 Cartwright Gdns, Bloomsbury ☎01-387 3927
Comfortable family accommodation, with public shower facilities and friendly service.
27hc(4⋒)(10fb) ✖ *B&bf15–£20
W£112–£150 M (W only Dec–Feb)
⋒ CTV ₣ ⤴

# CAMPING & CARAVANNING

Details of sites within the London postal area are listed below.

**SE2 Abbey Wood**
▶▶▶
**Co-operative Woods Caravan Club Site**
Federation Rd Signposted ☎01-310 2233 All year Booking advisable public hols & Jul–Aug Last arrival 22.00 hrs Last departure noon nc 18yrs unaccompanied
*Well-secluded and pleasantly wooded site in quiet residential area on the outskirts of London. Easy access to central London from the British Rail (Southern Region) Station at Abbey Wood.*
10acres 330pitches
330⊕£5.50–£6.25 or
330⊕fr£5.50–£6.25 or
330▲£5–£5.75 awnings
7♣ Individual pitches late arrivals enclosure 46wc lit all night 3cdp ⚇ 38washbasins hc 14⋒ hc 12 ⊖ supervised wash (SD) calor gas camping gaz toilet fluid ☎ ♨ ⊖ ♨ ✓ launderette pub

**E4 Chingford**
▶▶▶
**Sewardstone Caravan Park**
Sewardstone Rd Signposted ☎01-529 5689 Apr–Oct booking advisable Spring Bank Hol, Jul & Aug Last arrival 22.00hrs Last departure noon no single sex groups nc 18yrs unaccompanied
*A new campsite overlooking King George's reservoir.*
12½acres 242pitches 242⊕£6.30 or 242▲£6.30 or 242▲ £6.30 awnings
6♣ Individual pitches late arrivals enclosure 38wc lit all night 3cdp ⚇ 48washbasins hc 28⋒ hc 5⊖ supervised (WM TD) (iron) (cold storage) calor gas camping gaz battery charging ☎ hairdryers facilities for disabled ♨ ⊖ ∪ ♨ ✱ ✓ launderette pub

**N9 Edmonton**
▶▶▶ ♨ ○
**Picketts Lock Centre**
Signposted ☎01-803 4756 Apr–Sep Oct–Mar booking advisable Spring Bank Hol, Jul & Aug Last arrival 22.00hrs Last departure noon nc 18yrs unaccompanied
*Level grass site with trees set in meadowland with direct access to River Lee and main road.*
4acres 200pitches 125⊕£6.35 or 125⊕£6.35. 75▲£6.35 awnings
7♣Individual pitches ⚇ 17wc lit all night 1 cdp ⚇ 28washbasins hc (6⋒ hc) 3⊖ supervised (wash) (TD) (□ heated) (♨) (games room) (cold storage) (licensed club/bar) childrens playground cafe restaurant ☎ ⊞ sports hall sauna solarium roller skating squash courts ♨ facilities for disabled ♨ ⊖ ✓ launderette pub

# STREET INDEX

The map employs an arbitrary system of grid reference. Pages are identified by numbers and divided into six squares. Each square contains a black letter; all references give the page number first, followed by the letter of the square in which a particular street can be found. Reference for Exhibition Road is 19M, meaning that the relevant map is on page 19 and that the street appears in the square designated M.